I'll Smile Tomorrow

Lessons Learned

H. Keith McAdams

I'll Smile Tomorrow

Copyright © 2006
H. Keith McAdams

Cover Design: Greg Martin and Edwine Vilceus

This book was self-published by H. Keith McAdams
ALL RIGHTS RESERVED
No part of this book may be reproduced in any form by any electronic or mechanical means including photocopying, recording, or information storage and retrieval without permission in writing from the author.

ISBN-13: 978-0-9882866-1-0

Book Website: www.illsmiletomorrow.com
Email: info@illsmiletomorrow.com

Published by
ALLKEYz PUBLISHING
PO Box 1498
Fort Lauderdale, FL 33302
(347) 815-KEYZ (5399)
www.ALLKEYzPublishing.com

Library of Congress Control Number: 2013914652

I'll Smile Tomorrow

DEDICATION

To Man, Woman and Child

In Loving Memory of:

Martin Hawkins, Kathryn Dale Winchester,
Holly Hart and Abdun Nur

H. Keith McAdams

I'll Smile Tomorrow

ACKNOWLEDGEMENTS

I would first love to give acknowledgments and gratitude to the Most High Sovereign Creator of All things; who is known around the globe by many names.

To my parents (Mr. and Mrs. McAdams): I love and honor you both so very much. Although I'm sure that many of the gray hairs on your heads come from some of the choices I've made, I express my deepest apologies. My beautiful daughters (Allahia and Kiyanah): you give me the inspiration to write. My big sister (Darnel) and my nieces (Amani and D'airah): thanks Muffin for the Facebook guidance. Larry and the entire Bunce family: hey Ma (MS. Bunce) thanks for rushing me to that hospital as a child. You've been such a blessing to so many individuals. Lynnell, thanks a lot for taking me shopping for clothes once I touched down. Had me feeling like a million bucks. Charlie and his whole family: we lost contact, until our paths meet again. Hey Dee Dee, thanks for opening up your home and taking me in as family, in my time of need. Greg and the whole Martin family: Gee you played a huge part in this project, good looking out for the art work on the cover of this book. Wow!!! To your mom (Aunt Dale) thanks for opening up your home to me when I had nowhere else to turn. Did you ever know that your southern hospitality saved my life? Thanks to my cousins the Sablo and Willams family for all of the love and support you have given and continue to give. Thanks to Dr. Harold Ford as well as Dr. Lisa Smith for taking the time to read my work, give such crucial advice, endorsing and believing in this project. To my lady Edwine "Syncere" Vilceus thanks for all of your many contributions to this ALLKEYz project. I also thank you for acting as the stargate in which my son Atum Ray came into this planet. Atum Ray, you teach me so much each day. Thank You. Long Live the King.

H. Keith McAdams

ENDORSEMENTS

I'll Smile Tomorrow is a motivational story that takes its readers on an emotional journey from pain and anger to hope and pride. It demonstrates the two worlds that many of our youth grow up in; the wide eyed innocence that we have as children and show our parents, and aggression needed to survive in many of our urban environments. H. Keith McAdams is a living example of the power of the human spirit and how one can use the same street smarts needed to survive the streets of New York, to reach any goals we have in life. I recommend his book to many of my students as an example of how in spite of the fact that many of us can come from environments saturated with violence, drugs, depression and lack of opportunity, our faith in ourselves and a higher power can be used to remind us that if we stay strong that we can also smile tomorrow!!
–**Harold A.J. Ford Jr.,** *Ph.D. Professor of Psychology*

In the vein of Iceberg Slim, I'll Smile Tomorrow is a coming of age tale of a young brother trying to survive in this world with the skills he's been taught. Very rarely does a writer come along and make you pause and take it all in. McAdams tells an intricate coming of age tale of growing up in the concrete jungle. Through his eyes you learn about the often harsh lessons one must face when certain paths are chosen. However, what makes this novel much different than others is that there are lessons for all ages found within its pages. Consequences are not glorified but used as a platform to help and grow others. This quick and easy read will introduce you to the life of a boy who became a man and have you cheering for him all the way to its end.
- **Lisa Smith,** *M.A. Psychology*

This book is a must-read for any student of life. "I'll Smile Tomorrow: Lessons Learned" is more than an account of the struggle in the mean streets of pre-gentrified New York. This is an unadulterated, open, honest coming of age autobiography that unfolds as if the central character, Howie (aka Smallz), is speaking directly to you. Incorporating elements of hip-hop, this memoir touches on issues impacting males, their friends and their families in urban or underdeveloped environments: migration, urbanization/suburbanization, foster care, racism, access to labor opportunities, cultural and neighborhood strife, substance abuse & addiction, relationships, fatherhood, violence, incarceration, coping with loss, life post-release, and spirituality…You may cry, you may laugh, but hopefully you will grow as you read through the lessons learned of "I'll Smile Tomorrow".
-**Myrianne Clitus-Bustillo,** *Media Critic*

H. Keith McAdams

> I role with the punches of life.
>
> It ain't nice.
>
> I'm battered and bruised
>
> But still I cant lose.

-Shizzie Raw

H. Keith McAdams

Lesson 1

"Those who are in the know, *over-stand* ... adversities, failures and obstacles in our path are our teachers; learn from them. This is indeed, The Divine School of Hard Knocks."

H. Keith McAdams
The Author

It's July 3, 1995. The sun is high, clouds are few, and the skies are blue. Some may say, "It's a beautiful day." Normally, I would agree, but I'm currently incarcerated and have been for the past twenty-two months.

The time is around 5:00 p.m. and there's approximately seven of us convicts sitting in the day room area, watching *Rap City* on B.E.T. Everyone else is either in the dorm area or out in the yard. Every hour, there's an early go-back-call—you can either stay in the yard or "go back" to your housing unit.

A brother named Church comes busting through the door. He's just coming back from the yard. Church is a light skinned, short, stocky brother, with his hair cut short. I guess I can say he's a cool dude. Well, at least I've never had any altercations with him. Anyway, he enters in the day room ranting and raving.

"Those boys out there are about to kill each other."

So I ask, "Who?"

Still excited he replies, "Those Spanish boys and the brothers. It's about to pop off out there."

I'm looking at him like he's crazy. "Those mothafuckas ain't doing shit. They always barking, ain't nobody bite yet."

He now looks at me like I've lost my damn mind. "Nah, son, this here is the real deal."

We begin to hear this loud roar coming from the direction of the yard, and then the sounds of two gun shots pierce the air. I quickly learn that they were shots from a tear gun. Kent, this tall, kind of slim white guy, begins running around shutting windows, screaming how foul the smell is. He would know; Kent's been in prison for the past 20 years.

We all run to the window but can't see the yard since E-unit is blocking our view. But, we do have a view of the smoke rising from the yard right behind E-unit.

All I can hear is Church in the background yelling, "I told you son. I told you!"

The intercom crackled with the voice of a correctional officer, commanding his colleagues to lock all the doors to all housing units. We notice a flood of prisoners coming from the direction of the yard. The mob appears to be mostly blacks with sprinkles of Latinos. I began wondering where are all the Latinos I know had to be involved with at least half of the drama.

Then, the brothers start attacking the Spanish guys who had nothing to do with it and were just trying to get back to their housing unit. *Damn! I wish they had stayed in the yard with the others.*

From the window of the TV room, I can see this older Latin guy we call Cuba, who is housed in my dorm, walking toward the unit. Behind him are about ten brothers walking angrily in his direction. Cuba turns around and begins waving his hands, as if to say, "No! I had nothing to do with that."

I guess he sees the devil in their eyes, since he turns back around and runs for it. They give chase. Cuba falls to the ground, directly in front of our window. Ice picks and razor blades dig and slash through his flesh. I'm looking on thinking, *Wow!*

At this point, my eyes are jetting side to side and back and forth, watching these Spanish brothers get the shit kicked out of them. To my surprise, the CO's appear to be trying to stop all of the mayhem. I watch as some of the prisoners gain access to F-dorm. I see a brother jump up on a bunk. He appears to be stabbing the guy who was asleep, over and over again.

Now, the brothers outside are trying to break the windows of the dorms and yelling to those of us inside to kill all the Spanish brothers in here with us. So I grab a Spanish buddy of mine named Kenny.

"Let's get them!!!"

Kenny starts shaking his ass off.

I yell, "Kenny, I'm just joking!" I figure he's thinking, *that's a bad fucking joke.* Come to think of it, he's absolutely right. He seems happy it's a joke nonetheless.

We're not going to do anything to the Hispanic guys in C-dorm because we figure, if they had anything to do with the war in the yard, they would be in the yard. So we gave them a pass. Actually, I despise the idea of Blacks and Latinos going to war when we are obviously both in the same boat. The truth is the administration would rather us kill each other. It takes our mind off harming them—you know, those divide and conquer tactics.

Right now I'm thinking, *this shit is serious, so let me grab the two ice picks I have stashed, just in case.*

When I get back to the window my homeboy Max is giving some other guy his family's info. Just in case he gets hurt, they will be notified. See, Max is one of those Puerto Rican cats who is cool with everyone, Blacks and Latinos alike. From the window, I put the word out not to harm Max. I don't know if this will help, but so far Max is the only Latino not attacked and carried off to the infirmary.

The sun is beginning to set and the administration has lost total control of their facility. By now, the guys in the dorm are looting the cubicles of all the Spanish guys in the yard. To my surprise, the Spanish guys in the dorm are robbing them as well. I guess they all feel the administration wouldn't let them back in, once they do gain control again. So everyone's cube was hit.

Guys are outside the window crying, telling us, "Those faggots beat Life with a 45 pound weight and killed him."

Now, Life is well known around the facility for being the best rapper in this joint (But most dudes haven't heard yours truly). The news of his murder was when the looting really got ugly, a little get-back I guess. Now it strikes me, if the drama is in the yard, they killed Life in the yard, and those who did it are still in the yard, why the hell are you up here talking to us? Shouldn't you all be in the yard too? However, I don't have all the facts.

It's around 9:30 p.m., and it seems like the chaos is finally over. Well, maybe not quite. There's a bunch of emergency tactic officers on the scene in full riot gear carrying some big ass sticks. Once you see these fools, you either get on the ground or get your head bashed in. These are your only options.

I'm glad this shit is over. I'm tired and I can't even go to bed 'cause there's glass all over my bed and floor from these fools trying to break the windows, to get at them Spanish guys in my dorm. I go to get a broom to clean up a little, but the closet where they are kept is locked. I tell the cop on duty.

"Can you unlock the closet? I need a broom out of there."

"I can't. I have orders not to give access to any of those items because you guys may use them on each other, or maybe even on me."

Looking at him like he's stupid, I reply, "If we were going to do something, don't you think we'd done it by now. Secondly, you know we don't need a broom or mop for that."

"I understand, but can't you just get a towel and maybe knock the glass off the bed just for the night?"

He's scared to death. It's written all over his face. I can tell he is happy no one slapped his punk ass up, took his fucking keys, opened those doors, and let those wolves in the dorm.

You see, this particular officer was always acting as if he was a tough guy. I mean a real racist cracker. Any other day he would have just said no, looking at me with eyes of hate. You should see him now; *he's like a soft-humbled sissy. Now he wants to explain himself.*

I turn my back to him and head to my cubicle. I'm managing to get up as much glass as possible, make my late night prayer, and then lay it down. We're supposed to have some type of festivities in the yard for the Fourth of July, (tomorrow morning) but you know that's not happening.

It's around 5:30 a.m. and I'm just getting up. I take the two bangers (shanks) I have in my cube, wrap them in paper towels, and toss them in the cop's trash bucket when he wasn't looking. I figure, that's the best place to hide them knowing those emergency tactic police are gonna run up in here tearing the place apart searching for weapons. If they find it, it wouldn't be in my possession. Besides, I could replace them in no time.

Sure enough, here they go, strip searching everyone and wrecking our cubes. I'm standing here in my boxers, watching this pig tear my cube apart, and wondering how long it's gonna take me to put it back together. With no regard, he's riffling through all of my pictures.

Nosey bastard. He won't find a shank in there. *I'm really not feeling this.* He's looking at personal pictures of my wife and children.

"What are you supposed to find in there?" I blurt out.

He responds, "SHUT THE HELL UP. TODAY THIS IS MY JAIL, MY CUBICLE, AND THEREFORE, THESE ARE MY FUCKING PICTURES!"

He then comes across a picture my comrade Mobes sent to me of him standing outside of our project building in Harlem.

Then, the pig speaks again.

"Is this 130th and Amsterdam?"

I don't answer him, but I am impressed that he got all that from a picture without any street signs in it. Not to mention it was eight hours away from where his nosey-ass is at this very moment in time.

He smiles at me as to say, "And you thought I wasn't down."

I give him a smirk as to say, "Fuck you, you fucking lame."

Finished with their assault on our cubicles, they fall into formation and start marching like some soldiers, on some boot camp shit. I guess this was to intimidate us and maybe it is, but they still look like some damned clowns.

Noticing the cop on the unit leaving his post, I kindly take my two ice picks out of his trash can. I put them in my back pocket, let my shirt hang to conceal them better, and go on about my business.

Around twenty minutes after those fools leave the unit, they start sending in all the Latin kings and Nietas who were involved in yesterday's riot. Mind you, these are the same dudes whose belongings were stolen. Now, we're all shocked that they're being let back in the unit—this can get ugly, fast.

They came in peace, but they wanted their shit back. I'm laughing because all these dudes are slowly but surely giving everything back which they took. All but my boy ET. ET isn't a tough guy or nothing, he just wasn't feeling the fact of given anything back that he'd already stolen.

Today we are learning more about the reasons for yesterday's riot. The word is, a brother named Black God snatched a gold chain off some Puerto Rican brother's neck, who wasn't affiliated with any of the Latin organizations. Nevertheless, the Kings and Nietas chose to have his back and retrieve his chain anyway.

So they tell the gods to discipline their brother (this is the agreement all the organizations in the joint had with one another, somewhat of a peace treaty—you discipline yours we discipline ours). However, the guy whose chain was snatched wasn't affiliated with the organizations. The gods said, "No, that dude ain't down with anybody and this here is our brother and we are not harming him."

That being said, they went to war. We also learn that the brother Life wasn't killed. He did however, suffer severe injuries.

The jail is officially locked down, meaning that there is no recreation, library, or work detail, and we have to walk to the Mess hall in single file with only five minutes to eat chow.

On Friday, we are allowed to have rec and to go to work detail. In fact, my work detail is recreation because I work in the gym. My work responsibility is to give out gym equipment like weight belts, basketballs, boxing gloves, etc. Also, when the prisoners come in the gym, they give me their boots and I give them a tag to retrieve their boots before they leave, since boots aren't allowed in the gym area. This has been my job for the last twelve months. It's cool. I earn about sixteen cents per hour, and I get to work out all day every day.

When I'm done with the boots and equipment, I go into the room where we play Ping-Pong. I see one of the heads of the Latin Kings in there. He was in my dorm before the riot. He didn't know this, but I thought he was cool. However, I practiced Islam and never knew if his people and mine would ever clash. Keeping that in mind, I kept my distance because I would never want to hurt someone that I was cool with.

He comes over to me.

"Someone robbed my cube. Do you know who it could be?"

"No."

Then this one cop bursts in the room demanding my ID card.

"What did I do?"

"You know what you did."

"No, I don't."

"Well, you gonna find out, aren't you?"

He seems very pissed off, and I know I won't get any information out of him. I then see a sergeant and ask him.

"Sergeant, what is he writing me up for?"

"You're being charged with assault on a New York State

Corrections Officer and weapon possession."

"That must be a mistake. I was in the dorm during the whole riot."

He just ignores me. I'm then given back my ID and escorted back to my housing unit by three C.O's who seem to be very pissed with me also. Once in the dorm, I tell the cop on duty: "Today is Friday, and I have my Islamic services at 1 p.m., and if I'm not allowed to attend that will be violating my religious rights."

"I'll explain that to the sergeant, but you will have to stay in your cube till he gets back to me concerning this issue."

As I head to my cube, I'm thinking, *what the fuck? Assault on an officer and weapon possession—I wasn't even in that silly ass riot. This is some real live bullshit!* Hopefully I can explain this to one of the other sergeants and all will be well.

It's 1:30 p.m. and the sergeant on duty comes in the dorm. I watch as he begins whispering to the officer on duty who in return points in my direction. The sergeant then smiles at me, very friendly.

"McAdams?"

I nod my head.

"Come here! Let me have a word with you."

As I walk towards him, he looks down at my feet and realizes I don't have any shoes on. "Put some shoes on and bring your ID with you; it'll only take a second."

I'm thinking, *he seems cool, I'll explain myself, and this whole thing will be over.*

He begins walking me to the front door that leads outside of the housing unit. I'm now thinking, *this is unusual, why are we going outside?* He opens the door. I step out first. On the other side, there is the biggest white boy I've ever seen in a corrections uniform with the meanest face in the world, standing there. He then grabs me, throws me against the wall, pats me down for weapons, and handcuffs me immediately.

I'm protesting "What the fuck are you doing? These cuffs are too tight."

The big white boy yells back, "I thought you were a tough guy. You sure seemed tough in the riot the other day."

I yell at him, "I wasn't even out there. I was in my dorm the whole time."

The sergeant says, "We got you on video, jumping around like a little monkey." I respond, "Listen Sarg, I wasn't out there. You can ask the CO, he can explain this to you himself." The big CO responds, "shut up, didn't you hear the Sergeant?" We got you on video, jumping around like a little monkey."

I know where they're taking me—it's what we prisoners call "THE BOX." Some call it solitary confinement, others solitude. However, the authorities refer to it as the Special Housing Unit—"S.H.U."

I'm beginning to calm down slightly hearing them say I'm on some type of video because I know there's no tape of me doing a damn thing.

We approach the S.H.U., and right outside are five eager C.O.s waiting to welcome me. As I pass them to enter the building, I look into each of their faces. All have the deepest of blue eyes, which are staring back at me like I'm a big juicy steak and they haven't eaten in weeks. I'm now led into this little room off to the left. Straight ahead to the right is a small rug in the corner.

"Stand on the rug!"

I do so. He uncuff me and tells me, "Strip all your clothes off, open your mouth, move your tongue around, lift your nuts, turn around, bend over, open your ass cheeks, squat, cough, and show me the bottom of your feet."

Now I'm told to put my hands on top of my head facing the corner, and I'm re-cuffed. The cop who cuffed me says, "So you're one of them niggers who think they're G.O.D, huh?"

"I'm Muslim!"

"So why aren't you in Jumah?"

"The police said I couldn't go."

The pig closest to me punches me in the back of the head, smashing my face into the corner of the wall. I can feel my right eye swelling instantly.

He says, "There are no police here. Where the fuck did you see a police at, nigger?"

Another one, who has this reddish, full, long, bushy beard, then asks me, "So you think I'm a devil, huh?"

Another cop chuckles. The one who asked the question says, "Don't laugh, you're my devil brother."

At this time, the one who laughed punches me in my back twice. I swear it felt like a truck hit me from behind. As I gasp for air, I'm hit again, and fall to my knees. I'm then pulled back up to my feet, I hear the words: "You're not so tough any more. You sure were acting really tough in the yard last week unh? You fucking monkey!"

I cry out, "Fuck you. Take these cuffs off, you fucking bitches!"

From behind, someone kicks me in the balls. I hit the ground again. As they all kick and stomp on my back, ribs, and stomach, I'm thinking, *maybe I shouldn't have said that. THEY'RE GONNA*

KILL ME! Why isn't the sergeant stopping them? Now I'm being pulled up to my feet once again, and I hear the sergeant's voice.

"Come on McAdams, you're one of those "Five Percenters" aren't you? Come on, you could tell me."

His voice sends chills up my back. He sounds like he could really kill me in here today.

"You take these fucking cuffs off, and I'll tell your punk ass!" I don't know why I'm still talking shit, because at this point I'm afraid for my life.

The door opens, and one of the nurses from the infirmary walks in. It's a male nurse, white of course, in his late forties, stringy blonde hair with glasses. He's usually very polite toward me. Every other Thursday, I would see him to take my blood pressure because I suffer from hypertension. Today, he walks in the room with an arrogant vibe. He gives me this nasty look.

"Do you have any complaints on how you've been treated in here?" He says it in a way as if to say *you better say "no" or else.*

I don't want any more trouble, so I say, "NO! I have no complaints."

He walks out of the room, at that time two pigs rush me to a cell down the corridor, un-cuff me, throw me in, throw my clothes in, and slam the gate behind me. Before they walk away, one of them says through a crack in the door,

"That was my friend you attacked. I'll be back tonight to break both of your arms.

Shit I believe him, but I'm not gonna sit there and let him break my arms. I just dismiss it and think to myself, *so this is the Box.*

I've heard of it but never been there. It's a bit smaller than a regular cell, just big enough to hold a bed, a toilet, and a sink. The toilet is filthy, and the floors are nasty. On the walls are all different types of writings, poems, calendars, etc. One of the sayings on the wall read:

I'LL SMILE TOMORROW, IF I DIE TODAY.

As I struggle to understand its meaning, a piece of paper is shoved under my cell's gate. I pick it up, and it's a ticket with my charges and the complaint from the officer. It reads: ON JULY 3, 1995 AT APPROXIMATELY 6:30 PM INMATE MCADAMS SURROUNDED ME WITH ABOUT 20-30 OTHER INMATES. INMATE MCADAMS HAD A LARGE STICK IN HIS HAND SWINGING IT AT ME SCREAMING PROFANITIES, BUT I MANAGED TO AVOID INJURY.

Beneath that, it reads that I was being charged with attempted assault on a Corrections Officer, inciting a riot, and possession of a deadly weapon. I'm like wow. Thoughts of my daughters flash through my mind. Then I sit on the bed, still analyzing the ticket and thinking, *damn, I wasn't even out there.*

Looking back on the wall, I notice another scribble that reads "GODISNOWHERE."

I think to myself, *damn! God is nowhere?* I then think about this little old man I once heard attempting to school who appeared to be his grandson: "Boy, don't you know that every obstacle and every adversity, there is something within that adversity, within that obstacle that will guide you to peace, if you only allow yourself to be taught." I then think, *how did I get into this mess?*

> Count all the fingers and the toes
>
> Now I suppose
>
> You hope the little black boy grows.
>
> (Yea)

-C.L. Smooth

Lesson 2

"An infant's soul is altogether a thing of beauty to see,
Not yet befouled by the body's passions."

Dehuti/Hermes

The way I heard it, it was a pretty chilly day on January 13, 1969. My mom was a twenty-four-year-old employee at NY TEL as a telephone operator. She was sitting in her living room in a 20th floor two-bedroom apartment. She, my Dad, and my sister shared the apartment in Manhattanville Projects in Harlem.

It was almost two-thirty in the afternoon when she began to experience severe lower back pains. She was in her ninth month of pregnancy with yours truly. I figure I was tired of being cooped up in her belly and began to start causing a bit of a ruckus, eager to see what this big beautiful blue planet we call Earth had in store for me.

My moms couldn't take the pain and called her mother, my grandmother, to come over and assist her. They caught a cab to Sydenham Hospital, over on 126th Street where she went into labor. My father, Harold, was contacted at work. He worked as a mail handler for the post office. He and a few other members of the family were sitting in the waiting area of the hospital when it was announced to him that he was the father of a baby boy. He says it was the happiest day of his life.

It was a successful delivery. I was born at 6:30 that evening. I had all my fingers and toes, but I was born with the flu.

Damn, this didn't start off too good did it?

It normally takes two to three days for a new mother and baby to leave the hospital, but it took three weeks for them to let me go because of the flu.

It was early February when the doctors finally released me into the cold, polluted air of New York City. As I type these words out, I wonder what went on in my mind when I first inhaled that cold city air through my nose, into my newly born lungs. How did I feel when I smelled the stench of urine once I was carried onto my building's elevator? Did I notice the graffiti on the elevator's walls and ceilings? I hope my baby ears didn't pop while traveling way up to the 20th floor. Nevertheless, I arrived at home-sweet-home. It would be the first time I'd meet my big sister Darnel. She was three years, eleven months older than me.

She likes to tell me how she just loved her baby brother and wouldn't let me out of her sight. She was a sweetheart. That lasted only four years. Darnel then began to wish she could go back to being the only child.

Oh well, Big Sis, I know you love me.

Considering I don't remember much about those early years, I'll fast forward to when I first began elementary school at P.S. 129 on 130th Street (between Convent and St. Nick Terrace) in Harlem, NY. I wasn't sure about the other children, but I did not like the idea of my mom leaving me in this great big building in the custody of people I didn't know and who looked nothing like me nor any of the other children. So I began crying and begging my mom not to leave me and to take me with her. It didn't work, so I had to stay.

At this time, I thought to myself, they must be nice. *After all, I see them all over the TV. Besides, Jesus looks like them and isn't he G.O.D.'s son?* At any rate, they were really nice and would always smile at me, so I guess I was cool with it.

School was good since all we did was play, eat lunch, take naps, and yeah, we did learn to count and recite our ABCs. Well, in truth, my parents had already taught me those basics. When the teachers, who appeared happy to teach, taught things I didn't know, they made it fun to learn, with little learning games and funny stories.

That was kindergarten. About the time I reached fourth grade, I grew bored of school. Everything just became redundant, and the curriculum just wasn't fun anymore. Each year it seemed like their smiles became less apparent, and they weren't quite as nice anymore. I guess they'd gotten bored also and just stopped caring. Of course, that's if they ever really cared in the beginning.

In the fourth grade, my teacher Miss Irizarry gave me my final report card of the semester. When I opened it, it was like the world just stopped and left me standing there holding this small piece of paper, which felt like it weighed a ton. You might have guessed the situation I found myself in. That paper stated that I was to repeat the fourth grade.

My moms and pops were pissed at me and if my recollection serves me right, my punishment was to stay in my room for the entire summer.

I used to do all type of shit to entertain myself while on restriction. I would take eggs and ice cubes and throw them out of the window at passersby. That was a lot of fun. When someone came out the building wearing his best, G.O.D. forbid he walk down them little yellow step under the J apartments. If so, two eggs would crack him upside his head. No one was spared from being bombed; eight to eighty, blind, cripple, or crazy. If you weren't my family or family of any of my homies, you were a victim if you dared to walk under my window.

Another favorite was to take slices of bread, put hot sauce and some chemicals I found around the house on the bread, mash and ball it up, and then throw it out the window for the birds to eat. That was very interesting because those birds would peck at the bread, shake their heads, and fly off, yet they'd always fly back and repeat the same thing again. I would think *them some stupid birds*.

I would also open up my bedroom window and turn my lights on at night, in order to allow insects to fly in. I would then get a nice thick rubber band and shoot them 'til they were all gone. There were bloody bugs smashed all around the room. I did that for years. I became so good at it that my mom would call me whenever she saw a fly in the house. Sounds crazy, but I had to do something during that summer locked in my room.

When the new school year started in September, I was so ashamed because all my friends had moved on to the fifth grade, and I was left back in the fourth. Every day, I would sit in class feeling like I was among 'lil babies that just left the third grade. The good thing was I knew the work, which would make me think to myself, *how could Miss Irizarry flunk me?* The thought would be dismissed by convincing myself that she never liked me anyway. *So here I sit in the company of youngsters.*

There was this one girl in my class who would just sit there staring at me while sucking her thumb. Her name was Moesha and she lived in the same projects as I, in the next building up from me on Amsterdam. The word was she liked me, but I wouldn't be caught dead with a fourth grader, although I, too, was in the fourth grade.

Go figure.

Every day for the rest of the school year, she would either send me little notes that read, "I like you. If you like me, check a box." There would be a little box for yes and a little box for no.

Or she would send her friends over to talk to me on her behalf. I would just ignore her advances and focus on my schoolwork because I was not repeating the fourth grade again.

That was no easy task because I was always getting into fights with the other children. If it wasn't in the classroom, it was after school. If not then, it was in the street during lunch period. You see, after we ate lunch, they would barricade the street on 130th between Convent and St. Nick Terrace, and allow us to play there if the weather permitted.

One fight I recall was between me and this Mexican guy, Emanuel. Emanuel was the biggest kid in my class. I never thought he was all Mexican because he was so big. Even to this day, I haven't seen a Mexican as huge as him. Somehow or other, we ended up fighting during lunch break.

Emanuel knocked a tooth clean out of my mouth. It was a fake tooth, one of those denture types where you push the denture to the roof of your mouth and the connecting tooth goes into the missing area. William, a friend who lived next door to me had hit me in the mouth with a pink elephant shower brush, after I found him hiding in the shower while playing a game of hide-and-go-seek. That's how I first lost my tooth. So, when Emanuel knocked my tooth out, I ran, picked it up, put it in my pocket and proceeded to put an elementary school beating on him.

Once it was over, someone asked, "What was that you put in

your pocket?"

"Oh, that was my Now & Later candy." After I answered, I thought: *Why would I put a candy back in my mouth after it hit the ground?* No one questioned it, and I was happy 'because I was too tired to fight another round.

I had this buddy named Warren who lived up the hill from me on Convent Avenue. After school, we used to go to City College (which was located right behind our elementary school) to spar with each other on the grass. Warren was a little older than I was and was a bit of a tough guy. We too had a fight when we were in the third grade, when I accidentally spit in his face. We were cool before the fight and we were cool two hours afterward.

Warren and I went to City College every day to sharpen our fighting skills. We set that spot up so we'd have somewhere to take dudes we wanted to fight after school and not get into any trouble.

One guy I took up to City College to fight was Reggie. Reggie wasn't from my neighborhood. He was from Broadway up on 136th Street. Reg wanted to fight me because I struck him in the head with a rock the week before. I'm sure he would have fought me then, but I was with five of my boys from my building.

So, it was Warren, three girls, two other guys, Reggie, and me walking to our little gladiator school to get busy. I couldn't help but notice the confidence Reggie demonstrated as we walked to the location. At one point, he turned around and said to Warren, "I'm not fighting you. I'm fighting Howie, right?" (Howie is a nick-name that I didn't care for but some people called me).

Warren pointed at the two of us, me and Reggie. "Yeah, you two are fighting."

"Okay." Reggie turned back around towards our designated

spot.

The scuffle was on, and I couldn't do anything with the dude. I tried everything, but nothing worked. What made it worse was that he was just playing with me, sticking and moving, and just laughing the whole time. I thought that if I could just grab him I would definitely get him to the ground, but he managed to evade me. That might have been good for us both, 'cause I was so mad I could have killed him. Nevertheless, that was a convincing victory for Reggie.

"Congrats my brother, congrats."

The school year was coming to an end. In fact, the next day I would know my fate. Do I pass, or do I fail? Do I move on to the fifth grade or do I remain in the fourth? I'm telling ya, I knew that, if I didn't get promoted, my parents were going to kill me, especially my pops. You see, Pops was very tough on me. I sometimes felt he enjoyed whenever he disciplined me. Not that he was always whipping me, 'cause that's not the case, but when he did whip me or punish me, he was good at it. Let's just say that maybe when I'd gotten him upset, he was happy to teach me a lesson in consequences.

What made it worse was that it was difficult coming up behind my big sister since everyone thought she was such an angel. Teachers she had previous to me would always tell me how good she was and how bad I was. Yes, there were times I tried to do the right thing, and I noticed how it wasn't even recognized. Those teachers didn't want me to prosper. This one day when I was at home sick, the school called complaining to my mom, "Howard did this and Howard did that!"

She'd tell them, "Howard has been home all day!"

Go figure. So I guess somewhere in my subconscious mind, I thought if everyone would only see the bad in me, why try to show them the good? Aside from that, I knew my sister was no angel.

Knowing my pops would whip my ass didn't stop me from taking seventy-five cents off of his dresser that night. I felt that if I did get promoted to the fifth grade I would celebrate by treating myself to a slice of pizza and soda from the pizza shop up the block on Amsterdam. My exact thought was, *If I pass, I'm gonna have a feast.*

Anxiety kept me up most of the night. All I remember was waking up that next morning. It was a quiet morning. I washed up, got dressed, played with my breakfast, and headed out the door for school. Hiking up the hill from Amsterdam to Convent seemed to take forever.

Finally, I reached my classroom. There were no classes that day since our fate was already written, so we had a half-day. I watched the clock that whole morning and didn't have much to say to anyone. At a quarter to twelve, the teacher began handing out report cards. She would call your name and you knew to go up to her desk and receive your report card.

By that time, I had butterflies in my stomach and those butterflies had butterflies in their stomachs. Then she announced my name. It took every ounce of strength that I could muster to get out of that chair. As I walked to the desk to receive that little piece of cardboard, she looked me in the eyes.

"Congratulations Mr. McAdams, you are going to the fifth grade." Her words echoed in my mind.

Congratulations Mr. McAdams, you are going to the fifth grade. I wanted to tackle her and kiss her a hundred times but thought that might be a bad idea. She might change her mind.

As I walked out of school that day, I thought how proud my parents would be to hear the good news. The feelings of butterflies in my belly were replaced with the feelings of hunger. So it was off to the pizza shop. *I'm gonna have a feast.*

As I figured, my parents were very pleased that I was promoted. It was going to be a great summer, because I would be able to run around with my homies.

My homies lived in my building. We'd known each other since we could remember. One was Martin Hawkins, also known as Marty Rock. Marty was my first friend I remember having besides my female cousin Lynette, who stayed in Paterson projects in the Bronx. Martin stayed on the eighteenth floor. Then there was Michael Hart a.k.a. Mike Ski or Hart Boy. I got cool with Mike right after Marty. Mike was my hip-hop partner; we called ourselves, "The Twice as Nice MCs." All we did was write rhymes and battle rival crews. Mike lived on the first floor. He and Milton Laster were the oldest. Milton also stayed on the first floor. He was the big homie of the crew. Then you had Walter Fox. We called him Walt for short. He stayed on the seventeenth floor. Eddie Diez stayed on the eighth floor. We called him Ed Hood. Kuan Smith—called K-Vee—and his brother Patrick lived on the seventh floor, Brent Crayton from the twentieth and, of course, there was Joey Cruz from the fourteenth floor.

Sometime in 1978, my parents moved down to the twelfth floor. In early January '79, while I was gazing out of my bedroom window, I noticed these two brothers who had just moved into my building playing in the snow. They were in the yard of my soon-to- be Junior High School 43 (J.H.S 43) which was located right in my housing project. They were making snow angels. That's when you lie on your back in the snow and open and close your legs repeatedly and wave your arms, creating the impression of an angel in the snow.

Their names were Larry and Billy Bunce. Larry was my age and Billy was three years younger. I was celebrating my tenth born day that month, and my parents were throwing me a party that upcoming weekend. So, later that day, I ran up to the eighteenth floor to invite Larry to my party.

His mom answered the door. I explained to her the situation, handed her an invitation, and ran back down the hall to the steps.

She hollered down the hall to me. "The little one, too?"

Initially I thought, isn't he a baby? 'Cause when you're ten and someone's six or seven; they're just a baby to you. Regardless, I screamed back down the hall to her, "Yes!"

Billy was cool; he actually fit right in. I also invited a couple of other younger dudes from the building, Conrad and Joey, and we all had a good time at the party. Of course, every little girl in the building was there as well. It was the place to be.

I'll Smile Tomorrow

" The ghetto has a way of

Manipulating the children

Tricking them into believing

That life has no meaning

Down here. "

-Lyfe Jennings

Lesson 3

"It takes a village to raise a child"

African proverb

The name of our squad was "The Wonder Boys" (T.W.B); I came up with the name because I wondered what our parents would think if they knew what their boys were outside doing. We were all basically "good kids," but as the saying goes, "Boys will be boys." I say "good kids" 'cause I could recall the good old days of us all playing tag together or a game we called "Tap Tap."

The rules were simple. We would use the top of a pole, around four feet tall, connected to a fence in front of our building for the base. So, whoever was "It" would bow his head into his arm on top of the base so he couldn't see. After counting to 20, he would go looking for the other players who were hiding. For instance, if I noticed Kuan hiding in the building and he knew I saw him. We would both run to the base; him to touch the base to scream "safe" and me to holler "Tap Tap Kuan 123 in the lobby 123" as fast as I could. I never knew the rationale for the Tap 123 part and never bothered to ask. But it was fun. We played a lot of games like that for years.

I say "boys will be boys" since we used to run around killing birds, squirrels, cats, and rats. Shit, Marty and I used to go to Riverside and hunt rats. We chipped in for a rat trap, and we would steal hotdogs out of our refrigerators, chop them up, put them on the trap, and watch rats get clobbered while we sat in a nearby tree laughing. We all used to arm ourselves with rocks and hunt those creatures down.

Once, I killed a bird and hung him by the neck outside of the window of my classroom. That next morning everyone started screaming. It was hilarious.

This was the summer when Reggie was trying to get down with us. We wouldn't let him because he wasn't from Manhattanville, even though he was in our projects every day. Reg used to live across the street and was cool with all the number men in our hood. They treated him like their son.

In the beginning, I didn't want Reggie down with us and kind of liked the fact that no one else did either. Well, you know why I didn't? It was because he beat me in a fight just the year before. Yet, I knew deep inside he was a good dude and great candidate. We used to let him play Tap Tap and other games with us even though he wasn't a Wonder Boy. That was until Mike got into a fight with some guy named Miguel who bit him. Reggie then took Mike's place and just started to knuckle the guy up. Just like my fight with Reggie, Miguel "couldn't do anything with the dude." From that day on, Reg was family, and I was actually happy that he was.

That was also the summer we started to smoke weed. We were so young. We used to have to beg older people to buy for us and of course they always wanted some for themselves. I would also sneak weed from out of my father's dresser drawer. Pops had a big butter bowl full of the shit, rolling paper and all.

We would ask the older fellas in the building to roll-up for us up until we got the hang of it. The very first time I ever smoked was with some of my older cousins at a family reunion cookout. What's crazy was we didn't have any matches to light-up with, so my cousin Bob asked my pops for matches and Pops gave them to him. I was so nervous as we walked away; thinking that my pops would call me back and ask me what we were up to. I looked back, and he was standing there watching me walk away, never saying a word.

I couldn't keep hitting my pops for his stash, so we came up with a system. It was 75-75-75-75. That meant if four of us got seventy-five cents each we could afford a tray bag from Yellow Man off Amsterdam on 125th street. That was our spot at the time. After scoring, we would go back to our building's staircase and do the damn thing. Often times, we would have three spliffs (fat joints) going at once. We called that a Chicago. Why we called it that beats me. I was just happy to be in Chicago.

One day, I came home smelling like weed, and my pops stood over me sniffing me.

"Were you just smoking pot?"

"No."

"So why you smell like it?"

"When I was running down the staircase coming here, some of the older guys made me rap for them. They were smoking, not me."

He gave me two more sniffs and walked away.

That was close. That was fast thinking on my behalf 'cause it was well known that I could rap, and someone was always smoking in them stairs. Why couldn't it have happened that way?

At the time, you couldn't tell us anything. Life was a great big game, and we were just having fun. Harlem had so many things going on that could have a great impression on a young, black child's mind. There were many great positive influences despite the fact that they seemed to be overshadowed by all the negative influences. For instance, you could walk down 125th on any given day and hear the brothers and sisters preaching brotherly love through knowledge of self and of G.O.D. But they were just a handful compared to the pimps, hoes, drug dealers, stick-up kids, pickpockets, and all the various types of con artists who infested the streets of Harlem from the West to the East. So that peace and love blabber went in one ear and out the other. Besides, who did I know personally who was capable of introducing me to this knowledge of self and G.O.D? *Whatever that means.*

Don't get me wrong—my parents taught me right from wrong to the best of their knowledge, as with all my homies' parents. However, when we walked out our parents' apartments alone, we were bombarded with the knowledge of *our village*. And this particular village was a motherfucker.

We were still too young then to get into any heavy shit. These days are much different. Besides killing animals and smoking pot, we used to steal from the stores in our 'hood. We got the money to smoke from packing bags and helping people home from Fair Way supermarket behind our building on Amsterdam.

I loved packing bags. Making money made me feel like the man. I would remember the big tippers and watch for which cashier was working the fastest. Then I would wave the big tippers to the fastest cashier because that meant more money for me. A big tip was one dollar. For a nine or ten year old and where I'm from, that was doing big business. I would also watch for the old ladies and ask them if they needed help home with their groceries. On a good day, that could land a five-dollar bill. Usually it wasn't less than a buck, but that was all good too.

Eventually, summer was over, and I was about to start the new school year in the fifth grade. I basically had the same classmates from the year before. You remember, the "little babies" from last year. At any rate, they were now my peers, and a lot of them I now call my friends.

The girl Moesha who had a crush on me in the fourth grade was in my class as well, though in the fifth grade she didn't have any words for me. The sad thing was that I now had a crush on her. Maybe it was the fact that she no longer paid me any mind. Nevertheless, she was definitely looking cute.

By the middle of the school year, I broke her out of that silent treatment shit she was giving me and not long after, she became my girlfriend. You may be thinking that's so sweet, puppy love at ten years old. The fact is Moesha was the first girl I was with sexually, and that was when I was ten years old.

On every floor in every building in the projects, the maintenance guys had a room to keep stuff for cleaning the floors. All that was in there was this big ass sink with mops and brooms. This room was also where the box to hook up the cable TV was located. This room's door was painted blue, so that's why it was called the Blue Room. That is where Moesha and I would go to screw.

I remember the very first time we ever did it, like it was yesterday. I sat her on the sink in front of me, and we began kissing and touching.

She asked, "Do you want to do it?"

I gave her a kiss and nodded my head as I replied, "Yeah."

She pulled down her pants, and I noticed her panties had some writing on them that, at first, I couldn't read. With a closer look,

I noticed it read "MAYBE" in big red letters on some pretty pink panties. So I pulled down my pants and her panties, stood up in front of her, and began to hump her, but I wasn't even inside of her. I didn't know any better, until she pushed my shaft to the side, and I felt myself slide right inside of her. I guess it felt good; still we were just big babies, playing adults.

I remember thinking, *where did she get some pretty panties that had "Maybe" written on them?* Mind you, I was ten and she was a year younger than I, but I never thought about it again. I knew she was already sexually active, 'cause I overheard her earlier that year telling another girl in our class she was wearing a blouse that zipped down the back 'cause, after school, she was going to see her boyfriend Bobby. That shirt was "easy access."

My whole crew wanted to hit that, and tried too. Still, she never let them. I think I was the first out the crew to actually have sex. Yeah, we would have kissing contests with some girls in the building, but that was as far as it would go. Knowing Moesha was giving it up meant she had to fight off a bunch of horny little boys.

Many of the guys in her building hated me in those days which I believe was due the fact she was my girl. By then, Bobby was out of the picture. So I used to be in her house just chilling. Her mom liked me, and I liked her too.

Moesha had two older cousins who had a little name in our 'hood. They didn't know about us until someone started to call her house at one and two in the morning saying they were me. Her cousins started running around the projects looking for me, and someone told them who I hung with. The bigger cousin, Cal, told Larry that when he found me he'd kick my ass for calling his aunt's house so early in the morning. The word got back to me, and I must admit I was a bit shook, because Cal was four years older than me, much bigger, and was a well-known knucklehead in the streets.

Later on that day, Larry, Mike, and I walked up Amsterdam where Cal usually hung out, not to see Cal, but to go to the store. Sure enough, he came walking down the hill straight towards us shouting.

"Word is bond, when you see Howie, you let him know I'm looking for him. Word, you let him know."

Very hesitant, I said to him, "I'm Howie."

I figured it would be best to tell him before he found out later and really thought I was afraid of him. I was a bit jittery, yet, on the other hand, it was best if he didn't know that. Aside from that, we all walking toward his building could be interpreted as meaning we were going to see him to straighten shit out. Not that he would've taken that like I was some tough guy, but he couldn't take it like I was some coward. On the other hand, he may have known exactly who I was and was testing me. However, where I'm from, you didn't admit to being scared, and you definitely didn't show it.

Cal walked towards me. "Why you be calling Moesha so early in the morning?" Then he grabbed me and gave me a hug. "Stop calling so early man! My aunt is asleep."

I told him, "Cal, that's someone else calling."

He was cool, though, which he very well had better been, because I was just about to whoop that ass! (Laughs) But, on a more serious note, Cal was murdered some years later.

R.I.P Big Bro. Rest in Peace.

Moesha and I went on like that well into the sixth grade. At this time, all my partners graduated to junior high school and left me up the hill in elementary. It was what it was, but it had its advantages, like, most times after school, my homies would walk up the hill to pick me up, and the children in my school would think that was so cool.

When it was time for me to graduate, it was a great day. I was clothed in a blue three-piece, pinstriped suit, some nice black shoes, and a good-looking haircut. I was most definitely sharp. We sang that Whitney Houston classic, "The Greatest Love of All" that day, and I remember we sang that song with all of our hearts. That was also the day our music teacher died, and it was she who had picked, trained, and rehearsed the song with us over and over again. Earlier that morning we received the heartbreaking news. Please have no doubt; we let it be known that all of her hard work had paid off.

Once the ceremony was over, we all went crazy with joy, throwing our caps in the air, hugging each other, and taking pictures. Like I said, some of them became my friends. They were like my second crew; these guys lived up on Convent Avenue. Back then, if I wasn't down in the projects I was up the hill with them. As a matter of fact, that was the name of the area from Convent to St. Nick Terrace where they all lived—The Hill.

Some of you may recall the hip-hop legend Kool Moe Dee, formerly from the group The Treacherous Three. Moe Dee had gone solo and dropped a single entitled "The Wild Wild West" to represent for Harlem's West Side.

I really looked up to Kool Moe Dee. That brother stayed fly and was always cool like his name. He was my favorite out of his crew with Special K and LA Sunshine, yet those guys were hot as well. Special K was my fifth grade teacher's (Mrs. Keaton) son, and boy did she love talking about his career. She would play some of their songs for us during break.

There was another big rap group that came out of my hood in the late 70s, early 80s—The Fearless Four. It consisted of DLB, Tito, Mike C, and Peso. Mike C and Peso came from my projects. Tito was from our neighboring Grant Projects, and DLB was from The Hill. They all used to throw block parties in the hood, and many times they would let Mike and I bless the microphone.

I wasn't satisfied with just rocking block parties. I figured the Twice as Nice MCs needed to step their game up and try their hand at the world-famous Apollo Theater. I don't mean the "ShowTime at the Apollo" you've been witnessing these last few years. Instead, the Apollo, which the greats like Little Stevie Wonder, Richard Pryor, Smokey Robinson and the Miracles, Diana Ross, you name them, they graced that stage. I wanted to do the same.

The idea came to me in the early 80s, while sitting in the audience watching my father's friend's son and his crews come up short in their performance. Afterwards, I went back to the 'hood and told my partners "Hart boy" and Jazzy-Bo Jeff what I believed should be our next move.

Jeff was one of our older homies who lived up on the eighteenth floor. He always had our back. Some say he was the best human beat box in Harlem and that he taught the world-famous Doug E Fresh the basics.

We went to audition, and not too long later, they gave us a call-back to be on the show. Our families and our whole hood were ecstatic. However, on the day of the show, everything went wrong. First, they had us performing under the name of B-bop, when it should have been Twice as Nice, with Jazzy-Bo Jeff. Secondly, we were told that they had to cancel us and that they would certainly schedule us for the next week. This was terrible news. If that wasn't enough, all of our family and friends had already purchased their tickets at the door at $10.00-a-pop and were patiently sitting in the audience.

Most of my family was there except my grandfather. Although he really wanted to be there, he was home sick. I really wanted him to be there as he himself won at the Apollo three times straight singing ballads. He was also a member of a very famous group in the 40s—Day, Dawn, and Dusk. My grandfather was Dusk because he was the darkest member in the group and actually replaced the original Dusk. They put out many records and did many tours. My grandfather has since passed on, but I will always remember him for his exceptional knowledge of music.

Despite being sick my grandfather did eventually show up that night to see us perform. Once he heard I wasn't going to touch the stage that night, he stepped right to Ralph Cooper, the host at the time. I don't know what he said to him, but I do know that we were allowed to grace that stage, that night.

When they called us to the stage, we didn't rub the tree bark but were told to go back and do so, and we did. We didn't know the significance of rubbing the tree bark back then, but that was the tree that once stood where the Apollo stands today. Rubbing it was said to bring about good luck.

It was the moment of truth. I don't recall any nervousness once on stage. I do remember not being able to see the audience with the spot lights shining directly in our faces. Man, you could hear a pin drop. Suddenly, Jeff set it off with that music from his mouth, and it sounded crystal clear.

Mike and I then jumped in on cue with an original piece on nuclear war, how it was coming and what we as a people would do when it happened. Keep in mind, we were twelve and thirteen years of age, and we chose to speak on the violence that we recognized sweeping across the globe. I remembered hearing someone boo. Sandman, who was sitting right behind the curtains, tried to intimidate us by speaking just loud enough for me to hear.

"You better hurry up! You better hurry up!"

In case you been living under a rock for the last few decades, Sandman is an Apollo legend who comes out to toss the performer off the stage in the most hilarious way he can, once he hears the boos of the audience.

I remember thinking, *why is he trying to scare me?* It didn't work. After that one boo, there weren't any others. Mike and I burst into quick solos, with a more traditional hip-hop; it was all about us-type flavor. We then walked off the stage, and the audience exploded with cheers.

They called all the contestants that didn't meet Sandman back to the stage. In those days, they waved an envelope with money over your heads, and there were four places. When they waved that envelope over our heads, the crowd went crazy. I could recall seeing Larry in the audience cheering. I also noticed LA Sunshine from the Treacherous Three and Mike C from the Fearless Four acting a fool for us as well. Among the crowd was a lady from my floor in our building, who was not clapping for us at all. I felt like she was hating on us. In spite of her, we came in third place and won one hundred dollars. Our group became the first rappers ever in the history of the Apollo to win.

After the show they took pictures of the winners and told us these pictures would be seen all over the world. The fourth place winners were four girls about our age. They were pissed off, though they shouldn't have been, since many went home without anything.

The Mighty Mike Cee and L.A. Sunshine came up to us while we were still on stage reaching out to shake our hands. As we bent down from the stage to accommodate them, they pretended to had lost their voices. In the raspiest voice they could muster, they told us, "Ya have to buy us a soda. We lost our voices yelling for ya to win." I asked them, "How did we do?"

Still with a big smile Mike Cee replies,

"Yo you did good man."

When I got home, I was so excited. My parents quickly doused that flame when they insisted that they had heard our material on the radio before. I don't know if they underestimated our talent, or said that to see if I would admit that it wasn't original work.

I was hurt, after all the writing, rehearsing, and just plain hard work. How could they say they heard it on the radio? That's when I hollered for my sister, like the house was on fire.

"Darnel! Nel! Yo Nel. Come here!"

In a flash, she ran into the room where we were having this heart-breaking discussion.

"Moms and Pops are telling me that they had heard what we performed tonight on the radio before. Do you agree with that?"

My big sis looked over at my parents and insisted, "No that was their materiel for real." She was always one of my biggest fans.

In any event, we made the paper. "WBLS and WLIB present amateur night.

The one hundred dollar third place winners were the Twice as Nice MCs with Jazzy-Bo Jeff, Howard McAdams, Michael Harden, and Jeffery Williams."

We were all so very happy. The only negative was the paper

spelled Mike's name wrong. His name is Michael Hart, not Michael Harden. However, when life gives you lemons, make lemonade. We just started calling him Mike Harden. Even to this day.

> Broken glass in the hallways,
> Blood stained floors
> Neighbors, look at every bag
> That you bring through your door
> Lock the top lock
> Momma should have cuffed me
> To the radiator,
> Why not
> It might have saved me later,
> From my block.

-Nas

Lesson 4

"Do not let yourself be overwhelmed! If you are wise, strong enough to survive the threatening atmosphere of the streets then channel that same energy into thriving in that same atmosphere at your school."

Bill Cosby

T.W.B. didn't last long. We then started a new squad with some Dominican brothers we were cool with. We called ourselves the Crazy Lunatics, but that didn't last long either. There was a squad emerging out of my hood those days, called the Stick up Mob or "SUM." It consisted of many projects in the area, Manhattanville, Grant, and St. Nicholas. There were even members from Lincoln projects and areas in between. You couldn't walk in the hood those days with anything of value without getting stuck-up, hence the Stick up Mob.

We wanted to be down with them bad, especially Larry and me. We used to hang with them when we could, like when they met up in the pizza shop before they rolled on some other crew. They were all older than we were and often told us we were too young to rock with them. Mind you, at the time I was still in elementary school. Larry was in junior high school. Most of them were seniors in junior high school or freshmen in high school. You see, my elementary school went up to six grades, and junior high was seventh to ninth grade.

The year I started junior high school, it was on. Like I said in an earlier lesson, Adam Clayton Powell JHS 43 was right in the heart of my project, right in front of my building. My whole crew was in there, and all we had was us.

In junior high, you were allowed to leave the school for lunch, which was for an hour. Both my parents worked, so, as the saying goes, when the cat's away the mice shall play. With no one home to tell me what I could or could not do, and my sister way downtown in high school, I was able to bring girls over during that hour break from school. Not that we were always fucking, but it was cool to have females over without having to sit in front of my parents on the couch. No girls were usually allowed in my room, even with my door wide open, and my room was the first bedroom in the apartment, between the living room and my parent's room. But it was all good. My parents' schedule gave me my Plan B.

One thing I wouldn't do even with my parents at work was smoke weed in our apartment. Marty's apartment was where we did that, and that was almost every single day. The crazy thing was that we would get high and go right back to school, eyes red and stinking of the smell.

Some teachers knew but didn't care. Hell, they were working in the heart of Harlem, inside of a housing project, where the children were fighting every day and carrying weapons. The educational system in inner cities was a deadly joke, we weren't laughing.

Fighting and carrying weapons was for real. Every year, we would have a few days fight with the Fully Down Boys, a Dominican gang. They were from 135th between Broadway and Amsterdam and up to maybe 142nd Street. They were an offshoot of the Ball Busters, who were like their big brothers and well known in the area in those days.

I remember my sister's Sweet Sixteen birthday party. My older cousin Freddie and I were walking to the Center in my projects where her party was being held. Fred was yelling and talking a bunch of shit as we walked toward 133rd Street.

"Freddie, chill! The Ball Busters are up here. They gonna hear you."

He yelled out, "The Ball Busters? Who the fuck are the Ball Busters? Fuck they gonna do, bust my balls?" Being from the Bronx, he had never heard of them.

He then stared at me and appeared agitated.

"You scared of the Ball Busters? Fuck the Ball Busters. Wish they would say something to us."

A bit shaken, I thought, *Okay Freddie, I am impressed, but please just shut the fuck up.*

I said all of that because these Fully Down Boys were younger Ball Busters. Every year, we had drama with those dudes. We all would meet up after school to do battle. All but Marty, that is, He would just go home. Martin wasn't a fighter, but he played his part. He would always give us his mom's .38 caliber snub nose, just in case.

One year the Fully Down Boys came to fight without warning, and we had no gun. My God brother Rufus (R.I.P) from the hill went to set it off (start the confrontation) with one of them, and the dude pulled out a knife. Darwin, who was also in our clique and lived in the building behind ours, pulled out this big ass machete. That dude quickly turned and ran up Amsterdam. As I watched him run, I noticed Larry up the hill whooping one of the Fully Down Boys' ass. While he ran with the knife still in his hand, he headed in Larry's direction. I gave chase, yelling Larry's name at the top of my lungs.

"Larry! Larry!"

Like all of the many sounds of the city, it faded amidst all the objects that stood in place. All that existed in my mind at that moment in time was Larry, me, and the knife traveling between us.

I must have yelled his name ten times as I ran trying to catch that guy, but Larry couldn't hear me. In fact, his back was turned toward him, as he was bending down beating the other dude.

Then it happened. He struck Larry twice in his back and kept running.

Once I reached Larry, I grabbed and shook him to get his attention because he looked to be lost in the moment and our eyes connected. Trying to catch my breath I yelled at him, "You got stabbed! That mothafucka just stabbed you!"

He didn't know because of the adrenaline rush.

"Take your jacket off. Let me see how bad it is."

Larry began pulling his coat and jacket up trying to look to see his back.

He shouted, "Did he stab me? Did he stab me?" By this time the guy he was beating, got up and jetted up Amsterdam. Larry's well-being being my only concern, I didn't bother to give chase.

Taking a closer look at Larry's back, I saw that he was stabbed once.

"Yes, he did hit you, although it doesn't look as bad as I thought!"

I guess the other poke didn't penetrate. Happy that it wasn't too serious, I knew my Dog would live to fight another day. Thank G.O.D.

Larry received a few stitches and was sent home the same day.

That evening, the whole crew was on the terrace of the eighteenth floor when he and his moms returned home from the hospital. His mom was talking to, I believe, his aunt.

"I don't know where his friends were."

She sounded so pissed off. I felt like the statement was directed towards me. I wanted to plead. "Miss Bunce, I tried to stop him, but I couldn't. I couldn't catch him. He was way too fast for me. Please believe me, I really did try." Larry's mom is like my second mom. In fact, she had saved my life just the year before.

That story goes as so. It was a scorching hot summer day, and we were all throwing water balloons at each other to beat the heat. We would fill the balloons with the water from an open water hydrant using empty beer bottles.

Reggie had hit this Spanish man who owned a little Bodega (grocery store) on our block with a balloon. Pissed that he was all wet, he gave chase, and we all took off running. I imagine he focused his chase on me since I was the smallest. Once he got close enough, behind me he swept my feet from under me causing me to fall with the bottle still in my hand. I did a pushup, and then stood. Blood gushed out of my hand. I never knew that much blood could come out of a person's hand.

As we all ran off to the building, I yelled to the man, "Wait 'til I tell my father. He's gonna fuck you up. You just watch he's gonna fuck you up."

When we got on the elevator, Mike took his shirt off and wrapped it around my hand. Before the elevator doors closed, you could see Mike's white tee turning red from the blood. The elevator stopped on the tenth floor, and Mike got off and ran up the steps to the twelfth floor to prepare my parents before I got off the elevator.

Once we got off the elevator, I looked down the hall, and Mike was banging down our door. He looked at me and shook his head, as to say no one's home as he continues to bang. Not knowing what else to do, I spazzed out. Yelling at the top of my lungs, I started swinging my hands around and kicking the hallway walls.

Then Larry said, "Come on" and we ran to his house to get his mom.

She took one look at my hand and, with a very worried yet comforting voice, she understood, "Let's go." She rushed me to the emergency room at St. Luke's Hospital where I received one hundred and forty stitches and stayed in the hospital for about a week. People in the neighborhood thought I was shot because of all the blood.

When I did return home, there was still blood on the hallway floors, walls and ceiling of the twelfth floor where I freaked out after learning my parents weren't home. So, I will be forever grateful to Miss Bunce for her help. Now, here she was wondering where his friends were to prevent her son from being stabbed.

My hand had just been taken out of the cast the week before, and it was very hard to ball a fist. Still, that night, I vowed I would find one of those Fully Down Boys and kick his ass for the stabbing of my Main Dog.

Later, we all headed to a well-known hamburger place called Jimbos which was down the block on Amsterdam. I saw a guy from my class named Flaco. Flaco was a friend of mine, but he was also a member of the Fully Down Boys. Even though we were cool, I had to flip on him.

He didn't want to knuckle up 'cause he had on a suit, tie, and shoes, so he asked if we could do it the following day. In consideration that we were cool, I agreed. Flaco wasn't any punk. I had witnessed him in fights in school. He was a tall guy and in this one fight with a dude his height, he kicked at the guy's face and just missed him. So I knew that would be something I would have to watch for the next day, being much shorter and all.

The following day, we all were walking down to Jimbos again when I spotted Flaco walking straight toward us. He was definitely dressed for the occasion, sweat suit and sneakers tied tight.

Once he got closer, he asked, "What's up, you ready?"

I had no words. I just started swinging. I caught him a couple of times, grabbed him and brought him to the ground in fear that he might kick me. We were tussling on the ground when the police came to break it up.

The short chubby officer states: "What the hell is you guy's problem; out here fighting in the middle of the street like fucking idiots?"

Then the taller officer points at me and says:

"You take your little ass and walk down the block"

He then commanded Flaco: "and you take your silly ass up the block"

So that's what we did until the police left. We walked down the hill and turned at the corner of 125th Street and Amsterdam headed west. Then this older guy pulled me to the side and told me to follow him because there was a bunch of Fully Down Boys running behind us. My people stopped in the middle of the block to confront them. But this tall, slender, older black dude kept telling me to follow him to his job at the McDonalds down the block on Broadway, because he "got something for those Dominican mothafuckas."

I looked back down the block and noticed there were a lot more of them, and they had their leaders, twin brothers Frankie and Juan, with them, and those two hated Larry. Then I thought to myself, *this is my fight. Why am I walking with this asshole?* I ran back toward my team and all the drama. Once I got there, they pointed at Flaco.

"He wants to fight again."

I looked at Flaco. "I just fucked you up. You still want to fight?"

I was hoping he said no because I couldn't make a tight fist and the palm of my hand was starting to hurt.

"Yeah, come on."

We put our hands up. I swung and connected. He hit the gate of the store and began to slide down it. I put him in a headlock and punched him twice more, and his buddies broke it up. I was surprised we didn't have to fight them all off. However, Mike was there and he was cool with both Frankie and Juan.

As we walked back to the projects, we all were feeling good, then Gilbert, an O.G. (original gangster), from our 'hood confronted me.

"You did well, but you should have finished him off."

I didn't reply, but I will always remember his words. There was extreme wisdom in them.

The fight was on the weekend. Monday through Thursday, all was well. However, things changed. That Friday, Friday the 13th, in fact, fell on my 15th birthday. There were Fully Down Boys and Ball Busters outside our school at the end of the day, and they were in the company of another gang who called themselves Another Bad Creation (ABC). They didn't attend our school; they were only there to scrap.

We were out of our league; the older guys from our building and a couple from other buildings in our projects came to our aid. It seemed like the whole school was out there. I remember running and pushing through the crowd to get to the happenings. As I pushed people out of my way, they would turn around to beef and see it was me. Then, they got out of my way. They knew who the players were and were happy to see me running toward the field to my team.

Once I got up the hill, there was no fighting but a whole lot of arguing. Some dude was beefing about one of us having taken his leather coat when he took it off to fight with us the prior week. He said it was me who took his coat.

Not knowing what the fuck he was talking about, I told him, "Nah, I didn't take shit, homeboy." He's telling me. "One of you punk mother fuckers did and I want it back now!"

Larry's sister Lynnell shouted, "Punch him in his face, Howie."

Hearing Lynnell say this meant something. Shit, if she had been a guy, she would have set it off. So I'm like *word, I should punch him in his face 'cause it's a lot of talking and ain't no one thrown a punch yet, why shouldn't it be me?* As I waited for the perfect opportunity, an O.G. from the building, Brent's uncle Juanie, pulled me to the side and told me to chill because he and a few of his boys had those hammers on them. I figured Juanie didn't want to have to pop that thing off in broad day light. I honored his request. I chilled out and nothing popped off that day; that may have been a good thing.

I mean, of course, we should have been channeling our energies away from these streets and focusing on our academics. No, I won't insult your intelligence explaining this is how we grew up or blame it totally on where we are from. The simple fact is that many of our school mates managed to overcome the odds, right here in the 'hood. As for us, we may need to learn the hard way.

It went back and forth like that during the school year, but during the summer, I can't think of any drama with The Fully Down Boys. That may be on account of my parents sending me to summer camp on a couple of occasions. One of the spots was a go-away camp. They would send me away for two to three weeks thinking I was in good hands, but I wasn't. On my first visit to camp, I was twelve. We were somewhere in upstate New York, and they didn't have room for me with the younger boys, so they sent me to the older part of the camp (which was for age thirteen and up) and I loved it.

This camp was a party camp. Every weekend they allowed us to party with our female counterparts who stayed on the other side of the camp. I used to tell them I was thirteen. They'd say I looked younger, but they knew the age requirements for the guys in my group.

Some nights we would sneak over to their part of the camp to try to fuck, and the crazy part was that our counselor would encourage it. One day he sat us down to talk about an upcoming festival.

"During this festival, you have to hook up with a willing girl to visit her cabin at night. We won't have much time once we're there, so we have to go in, do the plumbing, and split."

At the time, I thought he was the coolest dude on the face of this planet Earth. All I could do was smile. I did what he advised and hooked up with this chick, and we all sneaked out that night to "do the plumbing."

I didn't score, but I was definitely outside of her cabin. Her counselor was up walking around and talking. My hot date noticed me outside and, from the window, signaled to me that it was a dead deal. Since I wasn't sure of the way back to the cabin, I had to wait for the rest of the guys to come out of their dates' cabins to head back.

I was actually afraid to try that again, knowing that at any moment the counselor could wake up and catch me. *What will my parents think of me?* In addition, the cool counselor transferred somewhere else in the facility, and the new one was a straight up cornball.

There was this one pretty girl who I met at one of those parties named Robin. After some time, we made arrangements to meet at her cabin. Yes, I know—I said I was afraid to sneak out to the girl's side again. However, I allowed temptation to lead me astray. Some of the guys in my cabin already had plans to see their girls, so I rolled out with them. Once the counselor was asleep, I had to come up with a plan to prevent us from being caught. I advised everyone to put their duffel bags in their beds, cover their sneakers with socks, and allow some sneaker to peek from beneath the blanket. It was four of us, and out the door we went.

It started to rain on our way there, but that didn't stop us at all. We didn't plan on being outside very long, but we did plan on getting wet if you know what I mean. Then, all hell broke loose; there were counselors everywhere. These assholes had to go and disturb my plans. They gave chase, and we all took off running through the woods. It was funny because I had three of them on me, and they were just slipping and falling, getting up and falling again due to the slippery mud.

All four of us made it back to the cabin. We immediately got undressed and hopped in our beds. A short while after, two counselors entered the cabin, with flashlights shining. I watched them as I played sleep. They checked everybody's sneakers and walked out.

That next morning the four of us were called to talk to the head counselor. He explained how it started raining at 11:45 p.m. and wanted to know how our sneakers were found muddy and wet at 1:00 a.m. over an hour later when bedtime was at 10:00 p.m. He then threatened to call our parents and to send us home. Instead, he let us go with a warning, which was cool because I didn't want my parents to hear about it.

Camp was a lot of fun. They had a couple of fraternities that used to march, stomp, and sing around the facility. The most popular were the Feather Men. I wanted to be down with them bad, except they were all older. However, I did pledge for this one fraternity since they allowed younger members and they spoke highly of brotherly love. My whole cabin was being initiated, all except one guy named Cornell. Cornell considered us idiots for calling these guys "sir," and allowing them to spank us on our asses with wooden paddles, while we holler, "Thank you, sir, may I have another?"

That didn't bother me, but what bothered me was one day we were throwing rocks in the woods, and someone hit one of the other cabins. The counselor of the cabin ran out, grabbed me, slammed me to the ground, and started to strangle me. He was so angry. His eyes were full of evil. He was most definitely trying to kill me. I lay there gasping for air as his hands wrapped tighter around my throat. I actually watched him snap back to his senses. Briefly, he seemed not to know where he was at that very moment. He most definitely lost control. I'm sure he's either dead or locked-up in somebody's prison today.

I never told any of his supervisors on him though maybe I should have, but where I'm from you just don't tell. That was the last day of me trying to join that fraternity, because not one of them tried to stop him, and no one was down to help me get him back, even though we would always state to one another in a firm and believable tone "I am my brothers' keeper." Man, that dude choked me so bad I couldn't talk for days.

My parents came up that weekend to the camp for a big family picnic. I was so happy to see them. I didn't tell them about the counselor attacking me, although maybe I should have. G.O.D forbid he killed a child he was employed to protect.

Aside from all that, camp was fun, yet I don't think it was the type of place my parents would have sent me away to had they known all the facts.

It was then, though, that I first noticed I was taller than my mom.

> On a one way trip to prison,
> selling drugs
> We all wrapped up in this living,
> life as Thugs.

-The Late, Great, Tupac Shakur

Lesson 5

"If the blind leads the blind, both will fall into a ditch."
Matthew 15:14
The Anointed Savior, Jesus the Christ

When I was about twelve, Reggie introduced us to this older guy who just came home from prison and lived across the street from the projects with his girl. His name was Richie Blacker, and he was about twenty-two years old. Rich took a liking to us and took us under his wing. He was definitely an original gangster in our eyes, a straight-up hustler so, yes, we also took a liking to him.

To this day, you can find hints of him in most of our personalities. When Rich spoke, we listened. When you were in a conversation with him, you'd learn fast he was gonna give you dap (give you five) hundreds of times, so you would never get to put your hands in your pockets. We didn't mind because he was the coolest, he stayed in the latest gear, and spoke with the newest slang. To us, he was what Master P calls "Bout it."

Rich used to sell weed, dust, and heroin in Harlem and appeared to be making some change. I used to help him bag up the shit, and he taught me a few tricks of the trade. One day, we got out of a taxi and this guy from our projects came up to me.

"What type of weed ya holding?"

"Tye Stick mixed with a little regular."

Rich heard that and yelled at me. "Fuck is wrong with you?

You don't tell anyone we mix shit!"

"No! Rich, he lives in my building its ok he'll still buy." Rich looks down at me with disgust. "It's ok he'll still buy?" "Well it's not ok! What if he tells four people and each of them told four people? Would that be ok would they all still buy?"

That never happened twice. Yeah, Rich would school us on shit like that all the time.

I was always nice with my hands, and Rich took notice of that, so he would love to play fight with me. On any given day, you could catch us slap boxing or wrestling in the grass in the projects. After a while, he couldn't do anything with me. Some of the older guys in the building would bully me and get mad when I started throwing them around, and they realized them days were over. But not Richie Blacker, he loved it. He used to have us in his house smoking weed and lifting weights. Plus when he spoke it was always some gangster shit. Seems like, he was molding us all.

Once, Larry, Reggie and I were walking up Amsterdam towards our block. Rich waved to us to meet him across the street on 130th. I noticed two guys cross the street with him. I figured those were his people.

Once we approached him, he started slap boxing with me. I remember thinking that it was strange to just start playing out of nowhere, but of course, I obliged. We then walked into the projects and sat on the orange benches, our usual hang out in those days. The two guys also came and sat on the benches with us and engaged with Richie Blacker in conversation. One was a short, stocky, light-skinned brother and the other was a tall, dark-skinned brother, with some fucked-up cornrows in his head. The dark-skinned one actually never said a word. He just wore this cold expression and had something rolled up in a newspaper in his hand. The light-skinned one did all the talking, asking Rich questions about blocks he knew him from hustling on. He kept a smile on his face, so it appeared like he came in peace.

Eventually, Rich looked at us and said, "Come on," and we all walked up the hill which we affectionately called "Snake Hill" because of its shape. We left the two guys behind. As we walked up the hill, Rich told us those guys were there to hurt him.

I started to bust his balls by telling him, "Them niggas ain't thinking about you."

"I know what the fuck I'm talking about; just come on!"

Once we got up the hill and made that right toward our building out of their sight, Rich motioned to us to hold up, and we backtracked. We looked back down the hill and spotted them running up the hill behind us. We took off running toward the back steps of our building. Rich took that time to scream at us for doubting him.

"I told you stupid niggas what was up. Ya need to fucking listen and stop being so damned hard headed."

I was thinking, *nigga, shut the hell up! Let's just get the fuck out of here.* We ran up the steps straight to the 18th floor and hid out at Larry's crib. About an hour or so later, we went back outside hoping the coast was clear. Once we walked down the yellow steps, there they were right there near the orange benches. Rich put his right hand under his tee shirt and pulled down the hem with his left hand. He did this to give them the illusion that he had a gun on him, and he was very convincing. It didn't seem to faze them though. They remained cool as a fan. The light-skinned one did have a little base in his voice, as he explained to Rich that he wasn't welcome on a certain Harlem block anymore, where heroin was being sold. Dude then looked at us.

"You little mothafuckas better walk away from him right now." When we didn't budge, he continued, "Get the fuck out of here before you get sprayed from a car with him."

I remember thinking, *"Damn, sprayed from a car with him, now that sounds scary,* yet we still didn't move. Whatever was going to happen to Rich was going to happen to us as well. When Rich was finished going back and forth with them, we all walked away the same way we came—together. Oh yeah, we were willing to blindly follow Rich's blind ass to his grave.

They were under the impression that Rich lived in our building in the projects, although he lived across the street from the projects. Later on that night, as I watched out of my window, I observed them return to the block. First, they walked into Rich's building, then into the bar inside. I guess they got the answers they were looking for, because I noticed them standing right under Rich's apartment looking up at his window.

Rich had to get low for a while, so Larry's moms Miss Bunce allowed him to stay with them until the smoke cleared. If memory serves me correctly, Larry had an uncle or something, who also ran the streets and even advised us to stay low until things were straightened out. We didn't listen. You could find us right in front of our building playing in the grass with Richie Blacker's German shepherd pup Mecca. Rich went and got him a handgun and used to take us up in Knickerbockers (the name of the closed hospital up the block from us, called "Killa Blocka") for target practice, and he kept that pistol from that point on.

A few days later, the Fearless Four and Treacherous Three

threw a block party in the swimming pool on 129th. It was a big success and of course, Mike Hart "Hart-boy" and I were scheming for the microphone. When Rich walked in the party area, you would have thought he was carrying a bag of groceries, when in actuality, that was a decoy for the next bag he had. Inside the bag with the groceries, he had his finger on the trigger of a gun. I'm thinking, *Damn he's the smartest.* He didn't stay for long. He only stopped to check on us, and then kept it moving.

I swear right after he left, two cars pulled up, and a bunch of guys came into the spot looking for someone. I recognized the one guy with the fucked-up braids. They weren't bouncing their head to the music, looking at no chicks or nothing. They were looking for Richie Blacker, and he had just left.

That beef eventually died down, and we just had to move operations to another block in Harlem where that dust was on the menu. I use that word "we" loosely. I wasn't on the blocks. I helped bag up shit in our hood, but Reggie was really the one hitting the blocks with Richie.

When Reggie was around thirteen, he had gotten himself locked up for pushing that heroin for Rich. I recall feeling afraid for him when I heard the news. He stayed there for about five days.

During the time Rich was still in hiding from them guys, Larry and I started summer jobs. I got a job as a youth counselor, which I was actually too young for, but I had that accident with my hand and couldn't do any labor jobs.

Being a summer youth counselor was fun. The only catch was cashing your check on payday. Not that there was a problem with the checks, the problem was getting past every stick-up kid in Harlem on check day. To counter that, we had our boy Kuan's oldest brother Eric Smith (everyone called him Smitty) take us to pick up and cash our checks.

Then one day Larry and I figured, fuck that; we were going shopping on 125th Street. Once we hit the strip, the wolves were out. Our first time out alone, Larry and I were only fourteen, and there were all these niggas out there in their late teens and early twenties. Once we reached Dr. Jay's clothing store, a bunch of dudes out front looked at us like they were stranded on a hot dessert and we were two ice cold glasses of lemonade. That's when we pulled out our little Louisville Slugger baseball bats 'cause we weren't giving up our money. We went into Dr. Jay's clothing store and this well-known bad ass named Sean followed us in to see what we were looking to purchase. The thing is, he knew just who we were, so he didn't even look at us. He just pretended to be looking at the same shit we were and went back outside. We didn't like the vibe and decided to keep it moving. When we walked out of that store we had a small mob around us.

"Yo Shorty, who you gonna hit with them fucking bats?"

Larry responds something like, "Whoever!"

I just repeated it, "Word, whoever!"

We then noticed we knew one of them. His name was Dave, from out of Grant projects. These dudes were older then we were, but they were amateurs or something 'cause they kept trying to talk us out of our money saying shit like "Did you get paid today? How much money do you have on you?" We didn't answer them punk ass questions.

"Who are you out here with?"

I answered, "Rasheed."

That was one of the most gully dudes I had ever come across

and he was from our 'hood, so I figured what better name to give? Did it work? I don't know. However, as we continued to walk west on 125th street, eventually they were gone. We headed back to the hood and went up to Larry's apartment to inform Richie Blacker that we had a problem with some older dudes, and we knew where we could find one of them.

"You know I gotta stay low. I got niggas out there looking to kill me."

I remember looking at him as he said those words feeling disappointed thinking, *this nigga's scared.* I would have bet my whole check that he would have run out that house looking for them fools.

I guess he was right—dudes were definitely looking for that ass. However, our building was full of brothers that would ride for us. Me and Larry went outside and told our big homie Todd the story, and he took us right to Grant projects looking for Dave.

Todd asked everybody in his hood, "Yo, you seen Dave? Ay, Yo, you know where Dave at?"

We never did find Dave that day. The word was another dude named Pap got there first and let his gun off, 'cause them same niggas tried to rob his little brother Stan. Stan was one of my homies in my class. Pap was another bad ass from our projects that always had his nose in something.

When I was about eleven, Pap and I had a little fight 'cause he tried to rob me for the money I made from packing bags all day at the supermarket. It was a quick scuffle, which I walked away from with every dime. We never had a problem after that, which I was cool with 'cause he was a bugged-out dude.

There was a time when Reggie had beef with him years later,

and Rich grabbed Pap up, and it almost got ugly. I wasn't out there that day, but I heard that, when it was over, Larry told Rich, "You better go get your totes (pistol) 'cause Shorty is definitely coming back with his."

Rich replies to Larry's suggestion, nigga, "You should know I got my shit on me homie." Minutes later, Pap came walking right up to the building where Larry and Rich were standing. He took one last puff of his cigarette and flung it in the grass with one hand. In his other hand, he was carrying a small .25 caliber handgun. Richie Blacker then pulled his piece out, and they both stood there with their guns aimed at each other's face, beefing back and forth. No one popped off, and Pap walked off toward Amsterdam.

So, as far as those summer jobs, we all came up with a plan that would prevent the older dudes from trying to get us for our gwap (money). The plan was that the whole squad would hit 125th Street together and shop, since there is always strength in numbers. Shit, that's how all those old-ass, stick-up kids used to roll. The plan then changed a little: we figured why couldn't we rob some dudes while we were out there ourselves?

There was this one day Reg had just purchased a pair of Timberland boots, which he gave to me to hold as they all ran off to rob a couple of guys we saw. I couldn't go because my hand was back in a cast from me busting some stitches. It would be too easy to ID me with it on. So here I was on the corner of Lenox Avenue and 125th Street, a little fifteen year-old, with a bum hand, by myself on payday, holding a bag with a pair of fresh Timberlands inside. The inevitable happened: about seven guys walked up and surrounded me, yapping off about the Timberland bag I was carrying.

All I was thinking was, they are not taking these shoes from me. One of them demanded, "Hand those shoes to me."

I looked at him like he was retarded. "No."

"Open the box. Let me see what kind of Timbs those are."

I stared at him. "No they don't belong to me." Now I was thinking, why didn't any one of these assholes try to take them from me? Not that I wanted them to, but that's just what I would have done. They started asking me stupid shit.

"What size are they?"

"Don't know they not mine."

Someone then ordered me to look on the box. "I'm not looking on the box, and I'm not letting you have them either."

Then one of them, who was short and powerfully built, with a nappy head and beard, walked up to me, looked me dead in my eyes and said, "I'll put your head out."

Now, that was the first time I had ever heard that term for knocking someone out, and thought that sounded a bit painful. Still, somebody was gonna have to "put my head out," to take my Dog's shoes from me.

As they all stood around me, I thought of one of my favorite movies, *The Warriors* when Swan was down in the subway with that silly chick where that one gang was scheming on him. When Swan looked up the steps, he noticed his team walking down. I was just hoping my team would come and see me in that situation, so like the Warriors we could whip these punk ass old niggas' asses. I snapped out of my pleasant daydream when some even older dude they knew walked up.

"Let me show you how to do this."

The older dude bent down and reached his hands out toward

me. I'm thinking *he's going for the bag* and was just about to hit him with an uppercut with my cast. Then I felt him patting my pockets. He stood back up and stated, "he ain't got shit" and walked away. The crazy shit was I did have money since I had just got paid. I guess he wanted them to leave me alone, seeing how I wasn't having it. It worked though since they all just bounced.

I was happy I didn't get hurt. I then turned around and looked at this older guy from my projects named Bernie, who was right there sitting on a mailbox watching the whole thing and never tried to stop it. I gave him a little smirk as if to say, *I knew you were there, but I didn't need you nor did I ask for your help.* I then walked off looking for my boys. Later that evening, back in my hood, I saw Bernie.

"I wasn't gonna let them get you, Howie. I just wanted to see if you break under pressure. You did well."

I'll Smile Tomorrow

> If life goes passing you by
> Don't cry
> If you're breaking the rules
> Making your moves
> Paying your dues
> CHASING THE COOL

-Lupe Fiasco

Lesson 6

"If you don't know where you are going, any road will take you there."

Lewis Carroll

My junior high school went as far as the ninth grade and all during the eighth grade, my parents were telling me and my sister that we were moving to the Bronx and that's where I would be attending the ninth grade. I told all my friends that I was moving soon. Months went by; I don't think they believed me. I hoped my homies were right, because I didn't want to go anywhere. However, I knew it was true 'cause I heard my parents speaking about it all the time.

In August of '85, I was informed by my parents that they had found a house in the Bronx, and my pops and I were going to move up there first. The reason being was for me to start school in the beginning of September, and for my pops to start getting the house ready for my mom and sister to move in later.

I guess you might call it a nice house. It was a duplex with eleven rooms: including four bedrooms, two full bathrooms, indoor porch, computer room, two dining rooms, living room, front yard, back yard with a two-car garage, and a big basement. Beats the projects huh? Well, in those days I would have disagreed. I'd rather had stayed in those projects in Harlem.

Pops and I moved in September for school. What I did like was hanging with my pops alone. He always seemed cool when it was just the two of us. Not that Pops wasn't cool other times, but when it was just him and his boy, it was felt. We slept in sleeping bags on the living room floor. There was nothing in the house but those sleeping bags. My pop's Uncle Joe stayed close by and was a real handyman around the house. He helped my pops out a lot.

Even though I didn't want to move, that soon changed when my pops begin to talk about getting a dog. I asked if we could get a pit bull. He was cool with that because he wanted a watchdog for the house. My mom and sister did not want a dog, let alone a pit bull in the house. So they started plotting to convince Pops not to get one, and told him how afraid they were of pit bulls. Now I was afraid my mom and sister were going to succeed, but when they saw Pops wasn't budging, they started threatening to kill the dog whenever it was brought into the house.

One day, while I was in our apartment in Harlem, I received a phone call from my boy Larry.

"Yo, you know Raymond and Junior's sister Jay? They're selling pit bulls. Yo, they got a bunch of them, come up stairs now." Maaan, I was knocking on the door before he hung up the phone. The Torres' were a Puerto Rican family who also lived up on the eighteenth floor. The two sons were a couple of our older homies that we looked up to when growing up. Their big sister Jay came down from Boston with a litter of pit bull pups, which came from their pit, Star.

Star was a big, mean red-nosed bitch who we had to pass to get to the back room to see her litter. Good thing she was chained up to the kitchens radiator; she made sure she gave us the mean look when she saw us. It was like she knew we were there to take one of her pups. When we got to the back room and the door was opened, there were about six pups playfully running all around jumping up on us. But there was one particular pup that really caught my eye—a red-nosed male that looked just like the mother. I couldn't tell you how any of the others pups looked; all I saw was him.

"Jay, I want this one," pointing at the red one. "How much are you charging for him?"

She wanted $150.00, so I asked her to hold him and that I'd be back after I told my pops.

Pops was up in the house in the Bronx with my mom, so Larry and I jumped on the 2 train to tell him the good news. I explained the whole situation to him. He told me to tell them to hold him until he got there in two hours to check him out. Larry and I rode back down to Harlem to tell Jay that we were going to purchase the red-nose. However, Jay was now trying to talk me out of the red-nose. She said she has someone had offered her $300 for him. She offered me two female pups for $100 even, but I wouldn't take no for an answer.

"Okay Howie, since I've known you all your life, you can get him."

"Thank you, Jay."

I went downstairs and sat on the mailbox right in front of my building on Amsterdam and 130th Street. One hour passed, two hours passed, three hours passed, still no sign of my father. I spotted Jay and her husband leave the building with Star, get in their van, and drive off. I was hurt because they had no pups with them, and I thought they might have sold them all. My pops said he'd be there in two hours, but he and my moms came strolling in an hour and a half late. They parked the car and I met them at the yellow steps and as we walked up. I asked Pops, "So, you still getting the pup right?"

My mom responded, "Your father ain't got any money for no dog."

Her words were like a stake through my heart. I didn't know what to say after that.

My pops then said, "Come, let's check him out."

When we got upstairs, my pup was still there, he and one of his sisters. My Pops started to pet him.

"So what do you want for him?"

I thought, *Come on Pops, I told you what their price was. What you gonna do?* Mrs. Torres, Jay's mom told him, "One hundred and fifty dollars."

Pops went in his pocket and pulls out a small wad of money, which he began to count and all I saw were singles. I'm thinking, *Come on Pops, you're killing me here.* Then, I started to see hundreds, and I was relieved. I walked out of there with my little brother. He was a pit bull, and his name was Slugger.

My father said he wanted to do the honors and name him. That was cool with me. Shit! He purchased him. But, at first, he was going to name him Swifty because he ran around so fast. Now, you know I hated that name. If it was up to me his name would have become Trouble, because when he got older and you saw him, you would say, "Here comes Trouble."

Okay, I've gotten ahead of myself. So, when we walked out with him that day, he wanted nothing to do with me. I tried to walk him around the projects. I had to practically drag him with me. My feelings were hurt for sure. Then my pops took him home, and I stayed in Harlem that night.

That next day I was supposed to meet up with some chicks, and they were late so I thought, *why am I down here? I got a pit bull pup up in the Bronx.* So I jumped on the train and went to see my baby bruh. When I got in the house, he must have heard me and started to whine at the door of the basement. Once I opened that door, he ran out jumping all over me and ran around so fast, he was so happy to see me. I was the first person he had seen since he was put in the basement the night before. I fed him some Puppy Chow and took him for a walk. From that day on, he was not only my little brother; he was my best friend.

The high school I was to attend was called Evander Childs, which was located on Gunhill Road, four train stops from my house. Since we hadn't officially moved from Harlem yet, every day after school, I would take the Number 2 train back to the 'hood and my pops, and I would go back to the Bronx together that night.

Evander Childs. The name alone sounded soft, so me being from Harlem and seeing all those houses, I thought the students would be too. To my surprise, they were just as wild as we were. They were on some territorial shit up there though. You had all these neighborhoods fighting each other for I don't know what. You had Eastchester projects, Gun hill projects, Edenwald Projects, Boston Road, White Planes Road, and Valley Park. After school was like a violent movie. There were one-on-one fistfights, ten-on-one beatings, and stabbings. It was a relief to now be an observer and not participant in the drama.

At first glance, it appeared that Boston Road was running shit because they were the main clique, getting it popping in the school and out. That was until I met my boy Don from Eastchester. Don eventually became my Dog, although I used to see him walking around the school like he was the shit before we got cool. One day he was in the lunchroom, posted up in his b-boy stance, when this dude from Boston Road accidentally stepped on his shoe. Donnell looked at homie and pointed to his foot.

"A, yo money, you just marked me."

Dude replied, "Oh," then bent down, brushed his foot twice, and walked away.

I thought, *Okay, so this dude must have some strength in this place.*

I had gotten a little reputation in the school for my hip-hop skills. In homeroom, I would rap with the other rappers in that class, and my homeboy Cee would do the human beat box. Cee and I are cool to this day. He lived on White Plains Road. Then there was my boy Dwayne from the Paterson projects in the South Bronx. He, too, did the beat box and rapped a little. So, one morning, we would be in the back of our classroom giving our fellow classmates a show before the bell rang for first period.

I also met another one of my Dogs through hip-hop. Andy was a Last Stop Bastard because he and his team resided at the last stop of the 2 train. Andy was one of those real hip-hop heads, and he loved my lyrics. He was good at banging tunes on desks, walls, anywhere. One day, he was banging a beat for this senior whose name was Magic Cee, and the word around the school was Magic Cee had the hip-hop belt since his freshman year. So I walked in the staircase where they were performing, before the 7th period class begins and Andy bigged (made me seem bigger than life to the others) me up.

"Howie, come on, kick a rhyme."

I didn't feel like it because Magic seemed so comfortable up there in front of his fans. "Nah, ya do ya thing, I'm chilling." Magic starts yapping about battling me:

"So you're a rapper home-boy? There's only one way to find out, let's do it, me and you what's up? We have plenty of time before next period"

I still refused. "Nah, I'm okay," knowing I would crush him.

A pretty little dark-skinned chick that I had a little crush on asked, "What's wrong, you scared?"

Without a second thought, I hit him with my second best rhyme:

How ski is the name/ rap is the game/

Ask any mc and he'll tell you the same/

That I… rock on the spot/ known for hip-hop/

So if you battle me prepare to stopped/ bruh.

You couldn't win/ if you had a twin/

And he was better than most/ I'll just strangle you both. /

Cause if I had a dime/ for every mother fucker that I dissed wit a rhyme/

This world would be mine/.

Wow! Please forgive I can't recall the rest.

As I thought, *I crushed him.* After each bar of my lyric I noticed a look on Magic's face that said, "Ah shit, what did I just get my silly ass into?"

Once I was finished, I turned around to walk out of the staircase to go to my seventh period class. Behind me were about twenty students staring at me with their mouths wide open, like I was some hip-hop god. They all just moved out of my way as I walked through the crowd. That feeling was almost as good as when I won at the legendary Apollo Theater. Nonetheless, Now I was that nigga.

One day, we were all in homeroom jamming as usual, and we found out that this new dude in class was a rapper also. Cee called him out for a battle. The new dude was Ron Derrick. He turned around in his chair and looked directly at Cee.

"You don't want to battle me." He turned back around, as cool as he did the first time.

Dwayne hollered to him, "I'll battle you."

Dude repeated the same extra cool routine with him. "You don't want to battle me."

Both Cee and Dwayne then hollered, "Howie will battle you. Howie will battle you."

He turned around. "Do you want to battle me?"

I was intimidated by his confidence, yet I did appreciate the fact that he felt I was worthy of his time. I replied, "Yeah, what's up?"

He came to the back where we all were sitting and grabbed the seat in front of me. I did the honors and went first. When it was time for him to shine, that's exactly what he did. He had so much energy, projected his voice well, and was full of total confidence. My style was more laid back. All I could do was slap him five and sincerely tell him, "You're the man." Guess there's a first time for everything.

Afterwards, the class told me that I had won, but they were just holding me down 'cause I was their peoples. I knew the truth, which was that I lost. Yet I learned a lot that day, which enabled me to never lose again. That was to always rap from my heart, and act like I wanted that victory.

qq, my math teacher was absent, so a few of us were in class banging on the table rapping. Ron Derrick, who wasn't in that class, came in and joined our little hip-hop cipher. Without the pressure of a battle, that was my chance to prove what I was capable of and to redeem myself. When it was my turn, I just went at it. The look on Ron Derrick's face was a look of amazement, and my every turn was better than the one before. Mission accomplished.

That day he asked me to call him J.V.D. I never asked him what the initials stood for, but hell, it sounded good to me. So, from that day on, J.V.D. started to introduce me as his new rap partner. The thing is, I was still affiliated with my partner Mike "Hart boy" in Harlem, but I still got down with Dee; the kid was nice. Besides, I thought it was a great show of respect towards me to consider me his partner after we battled. My only loss soon became my partner. How real is that?

Yeah, I was really starting to like Evander. I met a lot of good friends there. My second quarter homeroom class was where I met that brother Don from Eastchester. Remember the brother who made the guy wipe off his shoe? Even though Don was hard when it came to other cliques, I noticed he was really a cool dude. He introduced me to some of the guys he ran with like Cirol who was from the Valley. They liked the fact that I was from Harlem and wasn't down with any of that territory shit.

One day Dee (Don) said he was hungry for a patty and cocoa bread. I asked, "What's a patty and cocoa bread?"

"You never had a patty and cocoa bread?"

"Nah, what's that?"

He started laughing and yelled to Cirol while pointing at me. "Yo, Cirol, he never had a patty and cocoa bread."

Cirol looked at me. "I'm gonna buy you a patty and cocoa bread after school."

Still intrigued, "What's a patty and cocoa bread?"

Don explains: "A Jamaican beef patty inside some type of delicious cocoa bread. You eat it like a sandwich, don't worry Howie you're gonna love it."

I can truly tell you this, I love patties and cocoa bread to this day.

It didn't take long to be cool with damn near everybody. I had homies from Gun Hill Road, Edenwald, White Plains Road, Valley Park, Boston Road, Eastchester, etc. I never claimed any clique because I figured the beef those guys had was going on for years, so I stayed neutral, if you want to call it that. Still, I really got cool with some of them Valley and Eastchester dudes. Although they were few, they were strong and didn't run around starting trouble.

Like my boy Corn from the Valley—he was a really cool dude and humble brother, yet he carried two guns to school every day. One day he came to me and showed me a shotgun he had up the sleeve of his coat. He explained to me how the bag this chick had for him was too small and asked if he could use my bag to carry it. I had one of them big green Benetton bags with the drawstring on the top, so I put it in the bag and told him I'd carry it. Today I think, "What a stupid thing to do." But guess what? I knew it was stupid then. I carried that thing almost every day. I guess I just liked the feeling that I could kill anyone that I wanted to, if they asked for it. The crazy thing is, today Evander Childs has metal detectors, and from what I understand, they were the first school in New York City to receive them. Go figure.

One day, while I was snooping through my pops' belongings I found a small handgun. It was a tear gas six-shooter, but you couldn't tell the difference at first glance. I had a lot of fun with that thing, but we won't get into that. However, there was this one time I had a problem in school with this big muscle-bound dude, so the next day I took it with me. I usually saw him on the third floor right before lunch so, when lunch period came, I pulled it out of my black army coat pocket. With gun in hand, I walked through the hall toward the area where I usually saw him. The plan was if he stepped to me on some drama shit, I was gonna shoot him in his face, knock him out, and get away in the stampede before the guards knew what happened. Thank G.O.D, it was all peace and I didn't have to use it.

Yet during the eighth period, I was sitting in class when there was a knock at the door, and it opened. I noticed the sleeve of a school security officer uniform motion to the teacher. Something told me that they were there for me. Once the teacher reached the door, she must have been asked if I was in class, 'cause she looked at me looked back at the officer, and nodded. As this was going on, I had taken the gun out of my pocket, sat on it, and motioned to a classmate to come and get it.

Two security officers bust in and one of them yelled to me, "Mr. McAdams, grab your stuff, and come here right now! Do it right now!"

I grabbed my bag and walked out the door. There were eight of them standing out in the hallway once I got out there, and damn did they look shook. They asked for my bag, searched it, and walked me down to the principal's office. There, the officers patted me down and searched my bag again.

They came across my umbrella and asked me, "Were you walking through the halls with this in your hands today?"

I told them, "I probably did. Why? What's going on?"

One of them walked out of the room I was in and went into

another. When he came back, he said to the rest of them, "She said this is too big. It was a lot smaller."

Now I knew it was a chick, but I still acted like I had no idea why I was even there. They frisked me again.

"Where did you put the gun you had earlier?"

I put my poker face on and started beefing. "What fucking gun? You not pinning no gun on me. I don't have any fucking gun."

They ended up letting me go once school was dismissed. They had nothing to keep me. Outside the school, I met up with my boy I gave the gun to. He handed it to me, and I noticed it was scratched up. I asked him what happened to it.

"I had to throw it out of the window and got it after class. Don't you ever put me in that kind of situation again! I was scared as fuck."

He was dead serious too, and I respected that, so, after that day, I never carried a gun in school again. I put the gun back in my pops' drawer, and he never asked about the scratches on it. Thank G.O.D. A few months later, one of the school security guards informed me that he himself witnessed me take the gun, sit on it, and call for one of my friends to retrieve it. He said he was standing at the back door and saw the whole shit.

I asked him, "Why are you telling me this now? Why didn't you just do your job?"

"I owed you one for not letting you get your shit off that day in the lunch room."

He was talking about the time when this one dude from the school and I were dealing with the same chick. In the beginning, I never knew she was dealing with anyone, because shit, it didn't matter. It came to my attention while she was at my house one day sporting a nice gold chain with a nice sized letter K medallion hanging from it. Keith being my middle name, so I asked her to let me rock it for a little while. She agreed but right away warned me, "Do not get it wet."

Long story short, I lost it. She then told me that it belonged to her boyfriend Desmond. So to make matters right, I told him that I would replace it for him.

He asked, "Can you get me the letter D?" and I agreed.

I went to 125th Street to get some fake shit from the Koreans and gave him that. You see, I remembered that she told me not to get it wet. I asked her later, "Did he tell you not to get it wet?" and she said "Yep." That spelled fake to me, so that's what I gave him—fake. Then, one afternoon, while I was in the kitchen area of the school cafeteria getting lunch, someone slammed a yellow envelope with the word "fake" written all over it down on the counter beside me. I looked up to see who threw the envelope on the counter, and there stood Desmond.

"This shit is fake man."

I simply told him, "So was that shit I lost."

"No it wasn't, my shit was real," he barked.

I barked back, "Get the fuck outta here. That shit turned green in the shower."

We were just beefing back and forth, and the cooks asked us to take it out to the dining area, and we did. We continued to go back and forth. I knew he wasn't about to get what he came for, which was some real jewelry, so I offered him all I had.

"What's up, you wanna fight?"

His silly ass told me, "No."

My boy Dee saw us beefing there and told me, "Punch him in

his fucking face."

"Nah, he doesn't wanna fight." I asked him again, "Do you want to fight?" In a humble whisper, he stated, "Nah, but my brother gonna get mad."

"Fuck your brother. I don't give a fuck about him."

He was extremely nervous. "Ay Yo, just chill. I'm just trying to talk to you about this."

A security guard grabbed me. Once I was subdued, faggot ass Desmond punched me in the face. I stood still in shock for a moment. It was like the whole cafeteria stampeded up to the scene. A few guards rushed him out of the cafeteria and down the steps and made me wait. Calmly, I turned around and told my boy Corn to get my book bag (which I kept that shotgun in). Turning full circle, I jetted down the stairs after the dude.

The lunchroom was on the third floor and the principal's office, where I knew they were taking him, was on the first. Two officers were standing between the second and third floors to stop me. At least, that's what they thought. When I saw them, I stopped, and jumped completely over them both; tumbling at the bottom of the steps like I was competing in the Olympics. At that point, I noticed my gold bracelet had popped and landed in the corner. Once off, the bracelet was left behind. The pursuit was more important. All I could think about was getting to the office and beating the snot out of that fool.

Upon reaching the first floor, there were about six officers running toward me. They grabbed me, but I was wrestling them off me when the others from upstairs caught up. Even with at least ten officers, they still could do nothing with me. Suddenly, one of them picked me up off of my feet and threw me to the ground. At this point, they dragged me into an empty room and blocked the door. Knowing my mission for revenge was over, I started crying and yelling.

"Leave me the fuck alone. Why you fucking with me, you saw that nigga hit me? Why can't you mind your business?" I turned my attention to the first officer who grabbed me in the lunchroom.

"This is your fault. Why you grab me? You let him hit me, you fucking punk. Why you ain't grab him? You wanted him to hit me."

Of course, suspension was automatic. Actually, the principal had witnessed the whole episode on the first floor. No doubt my parents were pissed with me, but because I told that security guard off that day, it made him feel guilty enough to let me slide with that gun issue on a later incident. Praise G.O.D. It didn't matter what road my parents took. Harlem, Bronx, where ever—their little boy was going to act like a fool.

> And let's start it like this son,
> rolling with this one
> And that one, pulling out Gats for fun
> But it was just a dream for the teen,
> who was a fiend
> Started smoking woolies at sixteen.

-Raekwon The Chef

Lesson 7

"There is no darkness but ignorance."
William Shakespeare

Growing up in Harlem, there were so many ways to obtain drugs and alcohol in our hoods that the majority of the inhabitants would dabble in some sort of intoxicant to ease the pain of everyday living.

As you know, my team and I was very much into smoking weed. Then we got turned on to mescaline. We called them tabs. They were little pills that we would pop while sharing a couple of forties. Then, in an hour or so, we would be laughing at everything. Sometimes we would get on the elevator when it was crowded, and Marty would make the funniest faces in the world and have us die laughing. People would look at us like we were stupid. More than likely, if we could have seen ourselves, we would have thought the same.

I remember a time when the whole squad was on the train going to the Bronx, and we were all laughing at who knows what. I mean, we were looking and acting real silly. So I took notice of our behavior and stopped laughing. But then, this old white guy, who was sitting right next to me, turned and looked me dead in my face, with his funny-looking self.

"Do you have the time?"

Why did he do that? I just burst out laughing and couldn't stop. Yeah, that mescaline would usually have me feeling real happy.

However, once in a blue moon, you might get a reverse reaction, and instead of feeling happy, you might experience feelings of depression and violence. Those days were something else. Also, there were many nights when I would just lie in bed watching the sun rise because the drug would give me insomnia. When I did get some sleep, once I was awake, strange things became obvious: my shoes would be scuffed up and my clothes dirty or torn, with no memory of what happened. It felt like an episode of *The Twilight Zone*.

Those days we had our ears and eyes to the street. We noticed most of the people we looked up to getting involved with sniffing cocaine, so we, being the little nosey, ignorant followers that we were, got involved as well. I personally didn't like doing it. It made my nose feel so strange and wide open. Then, we learned that we could put it into cigarettes. When I tried this, the smell of the cocaine mixture blew the whistle on a few influential people of my community. I remember smelling that same odor coming from many cigarettes during my young life.

Back then, cocaine in cigarettes was called coolies. This was odd because there wasn't anything cool about them. Coolies were made by squeezing some of the tobacco out of the cigarette, putting some cocaine into the tip, twisting it up, and giving it a shake. Next, you took the filter out and put some cocaine in the back, put some of the filter back, then shake it again. Some even ran pass their lighter a couple of times before actually lighting it.

We were pretty young doing this. It was three days after we moved to the Bronx when Larry spent the night, and we hit this club on 241st and White Plains Road called the Galaxy. We were at a table in the club building coolies, and we were only about fifteen years old at the time. We didn't mess with coolies too much because cocaine was very expensive. We just stuck with burning our trees, until one day, this guy from Reggie's building named Pumpkin introduced us to a new drug that was on the scene called crack. Standing on Amsterdam at 129th Street, I was mystified.

"Crack? What the hell?"

Reggie replied, "Yeah, it's nothing but coke that is made into a rock. What you do is crush it up and roll it up with some weed. It's cool come on."

All of us left to pick up the brand new drug.

Crack would change the lives of many people, who, if they had known better, would have run as far away from it as possible. So here we go walking through the threshold of complete ignorance. I remember standing in the staircase of the building, taking my first puff of the mixture of rock cocaine and weed, which somehow got the name of woolas, woolies, or woos. Pumpkin coached me through that first time.

"When you take a puff you have to hold it in."

Sixteen years old and we were passing that joint around to each other. I don't know what the high was, but it had a taste that attracted me more or less. I guess we liked it better than those coolies we had experimented with just the year before. It quickly became very popular, and most people my age who were smoking weed started mixing it with rock cocaine. Well, it wasn't an everyday thing; we did it every once in a while, and even then, we would smoke one spliff, and we'd be cool, until whenever we decided to do it again.

Even up in my high school in the Bronx, the smoking of woolas really caught on. You could walk in the school's staircase and smell the aroma of someone smoking cocaine. I always wondered how it was so easy to get high in school. Children were smoking weed, crack, dust, or drinking alcohol; you name it, it was going on in my high school. If the smell of drugs was strong all day, the teachers and security had to smell it. Plus, if students could tell if a child was under the influence of illegal drugs, why couldn't they? Go figure.

So ask yourself, why didn't they put an end to the drug dealing and using in the schools? It should have been a major issue to be dealt with immediately. How are you going to teach children when they're high on drugs? Maybe they couldn't care less about us. You know, "Fuck you. Pay me." Maybe that's why it's called "high school".

During that time, I started to work for a Pathmark supermarket, located off Central Park Avenue in Yonkers, New York. I was hired to work in the produce department. It was very educational, so, yes, I liked my job. Plus, I met a whole lot of good people at Pathmark including a bunch of fine female co-workers, which made it a pleasure to go to work. I even got my boy Cee a job there, right in the produce department with me. I told you about Cee from my homeroom class. We really started to hang out after he and Dwayne came to my house to see my pit bull that they didn't believe I owned.

We would go to work after school and come home afterwards. Cee soon became a very good friend of mine, along with my homeboy Shane. I met Shane in school while I watched some guys playing *Monkey in the Middle* with Shane's sheep skin hat. When his hat was tossed to me, I gave it back to him.

Shane didn't work in Pathmark with us. He worked in the Alexander's department store, which was located right in front of Pathmark. The three of us were always together, even though Cee and Shane didn't get along to well those days. It was like they both were my homies and would be hanging with me and just put up with each other.

One day, I arrived for work and learned that Cee had just been fired for stealing money from a Spanish lady's purse who worked with us in the produce department. The assistant manager on duty was out for my head because I had recommended Cee for the position. That entire night he kept pushing my button, beefing about nothing, trying to make me snap so he could fire me. The next day when I got to work I was called to the office where the main manager was waiting for me. He told me some bullshit about how he was forced to fire me because of whatever his underling told him. I could tell he honestly didn't want to fire me. I told him I didn't do anything and was being unfairly singled out for the behavior of someone else.

"I understand but my hands are tied, yet I will give you this advice. Call your union and tell them your situation. They should be able to help you in some way."

His advice worked. In two weeks, the union called back and told me to go back to work Monday. When I got to work there were two checks waiting for me for the two weeks I was out of work. That's when I learned that joining a union was a great move. Before that, I became distraught when they took money from my check every week for union dues.

Despite the very good news, Pathmark had a trick for me. You see, this was a part-time gig, with a work schedule subject to change. They stopped giving me the hours they were giving me before my termination. Also, we were paid double-time, not time-and-a-half for Sundays, but Sundays were never again part of my schedule. As if that wasn't enough, they removed me from the produce department and put me on carts, and gave me the title of cart boy. Yet, that job had its good and bad attributes, like when the store wasn't busy, and it was a nice day I could just chill out and take it easy, but when the store was busy there were lots of carts to retrieve and put in its proper place. And I won't get into those cold, snowy winter days.

I figured they were trying to get me to quit by punishing me, but I wasn't going to give them the satisfaction. The good thing was that there were other guys out there working with me. There was one dude named Joc. He and I got cool fast. He was thugged out and I liked that. He had a brother who worked there as a stock boy who was just as cool. We used to burn a lot of weed together. Since they also smoked woos, there were a few times we would drive all the way to Harlem from Yonkers to cop.

By this time, I had already turned Cee and Shane onto this drug shit. Sometimes, we all would hang out and get high. It was cool. We had it all "under control." On Saturdays, the #25 bus stopped running at a certain time and we needed to catch the #20 to Woodlawn Avenue. Once we're off the #20 line, we would have to walk from Woodlawn Avenue all the way down to 233rd and White Plains Road. Now when I say all the way down from Woodlawn to 233rd and White Plains Road, there was a distance of at least twenty blocks between the two. So, one Saturday, Shane, Joc and I worked late and had to walk down this long (block-infested) hill on the side of creepy Woodlawn Cemetery in the Bronx (in the dark) at about two in the morning.

To pass time, we started a little rap session with me rapping and

Joc on the human beats. Little did we know that we were about to pass a block with about twenty or more drunken white guys in the cut, out of our sight. They appeared on our left once we reached the end of the block, and one of them started laughing at me. He was standing behind some chick, affectionately holding her with one hand and pointing at me with the other. Soon the others joined in with the laughter. I laughed back at them as we kept it moving down 233rd Street. We didn't get but half a block when I heard a bottle bust and a loud roar. We looked back and saw three of them running towards us with broken bottles in their hands.

Joc hollers, "Come on, let's run."

"No, I'm not running," I responded. Joc talked enough gangster shit every day. He should have been eager to stay and fight. I knew my partner Shane was gonna fight, even though a year prior he couldn't fight and wouldn't hurt a fly, but he had been snapped out of that soft shit. He was ready and willing now. Plus, only three of them were pursuing us, so I thought the rest of them weren't getting involved and, shit, there were three of us. Fuck are we running for? I had already stopped when I first heard the bottles break. The main one laughing was a short extremely muscular white guy who walked up to me. As he rolled up his sleeves, I noticed his arms were ripped.

"What's up?" I asked.

"You were laughing at me?"

"What?" *I'm laughing at you? Your bitch ass was laughing at me.*

He must have thought I threw a punch because his punk ass went to block a punch that was never thrown. It was time to throw some real punches, so I hit him with two stiff ones. We went at it, and before we realized it, a bunch of Europeans had me surrounded. I should have known the rest of them would end up coming down the hill eventually. To my surprise, they were allowing the two of us to fight, and I was getting the best of him. I even noticed the girl he had been holding looking on with a very worried look on her face.

At the time, I thought the look was for him, but, later on, I wondered if she was worried about me, because she had to see what they had planned for me next. While I glanced at her, someone else pushed me, and I went tumbling down. They caught me with the oldest trick in the book—you know when someone gets down behind you and someone else pushes you over them and you go tumbling down. Yeah, they did that faggot shit to me. Then they put a little beating on me. I managed to get back to my feet, and they allowed us to fight again.

At some point, I threw a sloppy right punch due to fatigue. He rushed me, and my initial ring flew off my finger from the impact. As I fell to the ground, my mind was on that ring because my parents had purchased it for me for my Born-Day.

While on the ground, he kicked me dead in my head with his boot. I felt myself blacking out, but out of fear of what they might do to me, I struggled to get up as they continued to whip my ass. That's when I heard them conversing with one another.

"Let's kill this nigger! Come on, let's kill this nigger."

But there was another voice that kept yelling, "No! No!"

I knew I had to get to my feet if I wanted to get out of there alive. Using the clothes on the one I was fighting, I pulled myself up with all of my might until I could stand. Totally surrounded, I looked in my pockets for my razor that I used to cut open boxes at work, but I couldn't find it. One of them stretched his arms out like he was on a cross and started yelling.

"Shoot me! Go ahead shoot me!"

I'm looking at him *thinking if I had that thing on me I would have blasted once I saw ya with bottles in ya hands.* Not knowing what else to do, I tried to intimidate them on that note. While still digging in my pocket looking for my blade, I started yelling.

"Yo Joc, blast that shit, blast these mother fuckers. Or give it to me, give it to me Joc!"

That didn't work because they continued to talk among themselves.

"Let's kill this nigger."

I'd had enough of that shit. I ran right into the street, not thinking of getting hit by a car. As I ran, I noticed a smaller crowd off to the side, looking like shit was happening over there as well. A figure ran from that group and punched me dead in my face which caused me to drop to the earth in the middle of the street. It actually didn't hurt a bit, but I grabbed my face and looked up at them as if to say ya got it, man, you won.

One of them then helped me up. "Aright then, get the fuck out of here." He kicked me in the ass and yelled, "Hurry up, go!"

As they all ran off and I staggered across the street, I realized that was the voice that kept arguing on my behalf not to kill me. I collapsed on the other side of the street about a yard away from the cemetery. Shane and Joc ran up to me, and all I said was "I lost my ring." That was all I cared about. Joc went to look for it.

While he was gone, Shane informed me, "Joc didn't help. He didn't do shit, man. He was watching it all with the fireman over there."

There was a fire station right there on 233rd Street, and Shane told me that's where Joc was standing watching the whole time. As I pulled myself up to sit on a large rock, I watched Joc in disbelief as he was across the street looking for my ring. I thought to myself, this can't be true. Joc's always talking 'bout fighting or slapping someone around. If what Shane says is true, Joc was a fucking phony, and if a phony, he might try to pocket my ring. He picked something up off the ground and walked back towards us.

Ambulance sirens screamed in the background as Joc passed my ring to me. "I'm sorry my brothers, let's go get my dogs and my pop's gun. I'll make it up to you."

In shock, "it came to me like a rhyme I wrote:"

"Shame on you/ having this lame wit you/

If his thug claim is true/ why is he acting like he ain't wit you?"

The ambulance arrived and the EMT team got out, and a female paramedic asked Joc, "What happened here?"

"Some white boys beat him up."

She got really snotty like she was offended at his answer. "Excuse me?"

Joc's scary ass stated, "I'm sorry, some guys just beat him up."

"Some white boys just beat the shit out of me," I blurted out.

She didn't get angry at all. They just rushed me to our Lady of Mercy down the block on 233rd Street. Shane called my parents and then he was checked for a cut on his arm that he received from a bottle while he scuffled in the brawl. My parents got there and were worried about me, but I felt fine. I was ready to go home. The hospital felt they had to do a bunch of tests to detect any brain injuries, but after approximately three hours, I was released. I told my parents that I lost my I.D. during the tussle, and my father's eyes lit up.

"Come on, we gonna find your I.D." He just wanted to return to the scene of the crime, hoping they were still out there. But it was quiet. Not a soul in sight.

That night I thanked G.O.D for letting us get out of there with no major damage. I also recalled Joc's words telling us to run. I should have known that he wasn't helping if we decided to stay. It reminded me of my neighbor's dog. He would bark and growl all day, yet if you reached out to pet him, he'd welcome you with a wagging tail. That's now a metaphor for life: "Every dog that bark doesn't bite."

That next day I told my girl what happened, and she came to see me at my house. She was happy I wasn't hurt bad, just some bumps and bruises.

"If anyone asks tomorrow where I was, you tell them I was with you." I went back out there with a double-barrel shotgun I borrowed, but I never saw anyone out there ever again. Trust me, I looked whenever I had the chance.

> When I'm alone in my room
> Sometimes I stare at the wall
> And in the back of my mind
> I hear my conscience call.
> Telling me I need a girl
> Who's as sweet as a dove
> For the first time in my life,
> I see I need love.

-LL Cool J

Lesson 8

"Choose your life's mate carefully. From this one decision will come ninety percent of all your happiness or misery."

H. Jackson Brown, Jr.

I got that Pathmark gig just before I turned sixteen. When the incident with them white boys happened, I was seventeen and that is when I fell in love. It was a nice winter day on January 13, 1986, when Shane and I were cutting our eighth period class. We walked into the number two train subway station of Gunhill Road and got on the escalator to get upstairs, to catch the train headed uptown. I noticed two girls were at the top of the escalator looking down at us whispering.

"Yo, peep it, those chicks up there checking us out."

When we reached them, the light-skinned one asked me, "Aren't you in my eighth period class? Why aren't you in class?"

"Nah, I'm not in your class."

"Yes you are. You sit in the back of my English class."

If this fine little thing thinks I'm in her class, fuck it, I am in her class. "Oh yeah, you are in my English class. What's up?"

We had just started talking, and before I knew it, we all were on the Uptown 2 train headed to my house. Shit, my parents weren't home. I had two good-looking females coming over, and it was my seventeenth Born-Day. Their names were Thelma and Helen. Helen was the one whose classes just received my name on the roll. On the train, Helen reiterates, "So why aren't you in class? I told her some shit like,

"A little bird told me that my future wife was waiting to meet me."

Waiting to meet you?" "Boy, I just got here so it's not me honey" I respond with a bit of a chuckle.

"Helen you crazy." We both burst out laughing.

It was that moment when I realize that I'd met Helen on an earlier date. It was actually the end of Cee's eighth period class when I notice him and Helen in a very heated argument. As I watched from the side line at Helen pointing her finger at Cee yelling at the top of her lungs in a rage.

"Fuck you, you not going to do anything to me mother fucker! Are you serious? Fuck you!" Followed by Cee:

"You doubt me? I will fuck you up bitch. Keep fucking with me Helen I will fuck you up!" I notice then how cute she was and now she sits beside me on a train to my house.

Next she asked to listen to the walkman I was carrying, and I obliged. When my stop was up next, we all stood by the doors waiting for them to open. Shane and I stepped off, however, the doors began to close with the girls still on the train. Shane and I hustled to stop the doors from closing. I immediately took my walkman out of Helen's hands.

"Fuck is you doing? Trying to steal from me?" As they got off the train, Helen said, "Nah, we just playing, come on."

We laughed it off and were off to our original destination, yet I couldn't help but think briefly, she wasn't playing; they wanted them doors to close. Little did she know I had seen her before. She would have seen me much sooner than she thought she would have. But I wasn't mad; shit, everything was still going according to plan.

We entered my place and started to talk. She was really talkative and very open. That was one thing that I really liked about her. Well, that and her pretty army green eyes. As she talked, I learned that she was a foster child and lived not too far from me. Then I asked if she lived there all her life, and she explained to me that she wasn't there that long, maybe two years, but she'd been in and out of many different homes. I instantly felt so sad for her.

Then I learned that her father lived down the block from me, and how her mom one day went to the store while she was still a baby in her carriage and never returned. Not too long after that, her pops put her and her older sister up for adoption and didn't want anything to do with either of them.

At that moment I thought, I would always be there for her and will do all I can do to never cause her pain. But, being a teenager alone with a girl, I snapped right into the original idea and that was to try to "hit that." No matter what I tried, she was not going for it at all, but we did a lot of kissing and touching. When she left my house, she had at least five hickeys on her neck. Since it was starting to get dark, I walked her home. We promised to stay in touch. I kissed her good night and walked back home thinking of her. Yes, I definitely had a happy born-day.

The next day in school, I saw her on the second floor between classes, and we spoke for a while and decided to cut class and hook up at my house the following day. On my way to my next class, I started fantasizing on what I was going to do to her that next day. That next day seemed to take forever to come. Once it did, it felt like forever as I waited for her.

Then there was a ring at my door, I looked through the window and there she stood, in her red and black lumberjack jacket. I remember thinking, *that's one ugly jacket but her beauty compensated for that.* That's when I opened the door and let her in. She entered with her jolly self, which I liked so much about her. She gave me a hug as she said hello and helped herself to a seat.

It didn't take long before I was all over her, trying to get in her pants. Still, she wouldn't give in. no matter what I tried or said, the answer was always no. She explained how she was a virgin and was afraid to have sex. We ended up sitting down watching TV and doing a lot of talking. Helen and I would meet at my house almost every day, and it was always the same routine, her not letting and me trying to get some, followed by us sitting down watching TV and talking. This is how I really started to develop feelings for her, and her not having sex took her out of the category of the other chicks I knew, which made me even more attracted to her.

It was eight months later when she finally gave in. We were upstairs in my room kissing and caressing each other. Somehow, I got her to take off her clothes and there she lay, buck-naked on my full-sized bed. Still, she was being very resistant lying there stiff as a board on her stomach.

She turned over and said in a very tense voice, "Okay, come on." She was so nervous. She began to tremble and squeezed her eyes shut tightly.

I don't know what happened, but I couldn't get an erection for the life of me. I don't know if her nervousness was contagious, but it didn't pop off that day at all.

As fate would have it, she soon moved to a group home in downtown Washington Heights and attended school there. I would go down there to see her, but it was very hard for us to be alone at my house again because our schedules conflicted. Soon after, one of the female security guards at her new school learned her situation and saw money signs and took her in as a foster child. This made it harder for us to see each other. We promised to link up when we can but we didn't miss a beat with our phone conversations.

It was actually two weeks later when I learned there was a Waldbaums Supermarket opening up on East Gun hill Road. I put an application in for a job there because it was in the Bronx, not far from my school. When Waldbaums called me for the job, I was more than happy to quit Pathmark. Besides, they wanted me to leave anyway, fucking with my hours and all. I told everyone in Pathmark that Waldbaums was hiring before I left, hoping everyone would leave that punk ass Pathmark.

I was hired to work in the frozen foods department, and I hated it. I mean I was going in and out of a huge freezer all day long and I seemed to always have a cold. Stocking pricing frozen foods all day would have my hands so numb that I could hardly feel the food packages that I was stocking. My supervisor began to complain that I was slowing down more every day and moved me from frozen foods to carts. Yes, back to cart boy and in Waldbaums we had to retrieve carts from way out in the parking lot, and they had one huge parking lot. By this time, my people from Pathmark were being hired at Waldbaums. Ashamed to be back on carts, I quit. Yes, I quit a job without having another job and that was indeed a no no. Without a job, the only thing to do after school was go home, do my homework, study my academics, write raps, and look at the walls of that house. Now you know that sitting in the house thing was not what's up, so I either ran the streets with Cee and Shane or went and hung with my peoples in Harlem or both.

Getting left back in the tenth grade was the result of running the streets. Soon after, I was thrown out of school for a couple more fights I got myself into. One of them I felt I could not avoid. You see, it was with this dude named Von who lived up on Nereid Avenue, in my same neighborhood. Can't recall what caused the dispute yet I do know once he wrapped his hands around my neck and squeezed. I figured I should be throwing punches, so I did.

Before Helen moved away she advised me.

"Howard you need to stop getting into trouble, before these people kick you out of school." Man do I miss her.

I'll Smile Tomorrow

> "It's like a jungle
> Sometimes it makes me wonder
> How I keep from going under"
> -Melly Mel

Lesson 9

"I think it's demons in the weed I'm smoking; G.O.D keeps me going."

Gregory "Gee Ali" Martin

My parents were pissed off over my unemployment and indefinite expulsion from school. I was actually pissed off at myself. How the fuck do you get kicked out of school? I had one other alternative and that was to go for my G.E.D. I signed-up to take my GED and was placed in an elementary school on Hoe Avenue in the South Bronx. The GED part was located on the top floor.

A school like that was the last chance for teenagers like me who couldn't cut it in high school. It seemed like every knucklehead child in the Bronx attended that school. Shit, you even had childcare in the basement for the teenage moms. While standing outside the school on my first day, I saw that dude I had a beef with over that punk-ass chain in Evander walk toward the entrance to the school. He noticed me from across the street and we made eye contact. We exchanged mean looks with one another, yet we both understood this school was our last straw for some type of education, so we let it ride.

While we were in school, it was like a real circus. Most of my schoolmates were wild and just didn't give a fuck about learning anything. Man, they would curse the teachers out and just be outright rude. The deal with the G.E.D. was that, if you passed the test, you would be issued what they called a High School Equivalency Diploma. When a test was scheduled and you felt you were ready, you could take the test. A lot of people in my class had taken the test and failed many times. One girl was in that school for four years and just couldn't pass the test. So when they would make fun of the teacher and just be clowning around, I would participate slightly. I say slightly, because I first made sure I knew what the topic was the teacher was trying to get across to us.

On my second day, I went to the bookstore and bought me a big fat GED book. Each day after school, I went home and studied what the teacher had covered in class. When the next test came up, I wasn't playing. I knew I had to finish this school shit. I was already eighteen. After the test, I didn't have to attend school while I waited for my results. Meanwhile, I found a job at a spot called Cahill Gordon as a messenger, down in the Wall Street area.

My job duty was basically delivering packages by foot or subway to different companies in the city. It was cool because I would take my time, and I got to know a lot about getting around the Big Apple. During the summer, the job was even cooler because you really could just chill in the street and take your time. Don't get me wrong, you had to make your deliveries but at your own pace. Between deliveries you could be up in the waiting area with all the other messengers and relax. I would usually take that time to sharpen my hip-hop craft, often in the back of the waiting area scribing lyrics. Another guy did the same whenever he had a chance. He and I never spoke until this Spanish girl said something mean to me in Spanish and I asked him what it meant.

"I don't know."

"Aren't you Puerto Rican?"

"No."

"Then what are you?"

He raised his hands up from his sides as to say what you mean? "I'm black."

It turned out that his mom was white and pops was black. That's why he appeared to me to be Latin. His name was Gee. When we met, he lived in Brooklyn's Park Slope section. He later informed me he was from the Fort Green area of Brooklyn. Through our mutual love for hip-hop, we became good friends. Gee and I would have friendly debates about who was the best rapper in the game.

"Yo Gee who do you believe is the best MC in the game?"

"Come on bruh you know I got to stand strong with Rakim Allah." Though I too think the god Rakim was a force to be reckoned with but there was one guy from out of the Bronx who had the city buzzing as well.

"Yeah ok Ra is most definitely a hot MC but that title must go to KRS One of the Boggie Down Production posse."

Later, we met another brother at the job named Eli who also loved hip-hop. Eli wasn't a rapper. He was a music producer from out of Brooklyn's Bed-Stuy section.

Eventually, it came to our attention that Eli had a small production studio in his home, which he recorded on reel-to-reel. At first Gee would go every Saturday and always asked me to come along. I finally agreed and went with Gee to Eli's house. It took me a while to agree because I lived way up in the Bronx and Eli lived in Brooklyn, on Gates and Nostrand. That meant riding three trains to Nostrand, then walking what seemed like ten blocks to Gates. After the first trip, I don't believe I missed another Saturday at Eli's.

Eli provided the first experience to record my songs, and I loved it. Watching Eli work was very interesting. He made beats from scratch and just made the whole thing come to life.

I recorded many songs there, and then I would go home and listen to them over and over fantasizing about making it big someday.

One day, through a connection Gee had with Rock Candy Records/B-Boy Records, we had a meeting with an executive there to listen to our music to see if they would like to sign us to a deal. I was very excited because this was the record label that launched my favorite rapper's career, Mr. South Bronx himself, KRS-One of the B.D.P posse.

The meeting appeared to be going great. I recall the guy bouncing his head a little to one of my joints. Yet, he didn't sign us. He told us he liked us but gave us advice on what to do to make it better and afterward come back. We left a little disappointed although I was happy to be at the same label, around the same people, in the same office, and to travel the same blocks which my idol traveled. It was just back to the drawing board for us.

It was shortly after that meeting when, one day on the job, I received a page from my moms. She had some news that I'd been waiting for weeks now—the results of my G.E.D test. In order to pass, I had to receive a score of 225. My mom told me that I had earned 228. I jumped up in the air in complete joy and felt like I won the championship. After hearing how excited I was my mom expresses.

You only passed by three little points, I thought. Shit, I could have gotten 225 and still been the man considering all the people at the school who were still trying to pass. I told my moms goodbye, hung the phone up, took a deep breath, and popped my collar. If my moms only knew what I had accomplished, considering a great majority of the youth in that school would never learn, because somewhere in their hearts they had learned not to care. Trust, the school was like a mad house, like one of those terrible schools you see in motion pictures. Man, it should have been a motion picture. It was like I was sent into a lion's den and managed to escape with the plate. Of course, I wish I'd finished regular high school. However, I sure did study for that Plan B and was out of that school in a month.

Not too long later, my pops hooked me up with a job with Goodyear tires. Goodyear had a contract with New York City Transit, repairing and maintaining the tires for the buses. My job was very important, keeping New York City safe while its people commuted on a day-to-day basis. My pops got his transit job the same year I was born, so, when I was eighteen, he was able to politic for me to skip the long waiting list. They were going to pay me $12 an hour, although minimum wage was only $3.65 an hour in those days. So, of course, I gave that messenger job the boot and started rolling with Goodyear tires.

I began working at the East Tremont bus depot in the Bronx. It wasn't hard work. The only down thing was I had to punch a clock at 6:00 a.m.; so it was hard to get there on time. Well, it wouldn't be hard if I wasn't out all night getting high. Sometimes I would just go straight in to work after a night of partying. More money meant being able to afford to mix more cocaine with my weed.

Slowly slipping into addiction like so many others, at eighteen, I was in denial. Anyway, I still was rocking solid gold rings on every fingers, fresh kicks and wears. I remember one night, after getting high, telling myself to not spend any more money. I had to hang out the next night with my girl, who at the time that lived in Canarsie, Brooklyn. There was a voice in my head telling me, "To hell with her! You don't need her! All you need is me." That scared the shit out of me. It seemed like someone was really speaking that shit to me. I took my ass straight to the crib, asking myself some obvious shit: *"Damn, do I have a problem?"*

The next day I made it to her house. You know I really liked her if I took the #2 train to 14th Street, transferred to the L train, took that to the last stop, and then transferred to a bus that took me to the last stop which was in front of her project building; traveling two hours. She would do the same thing to see me in the Bronx. My mom didn't like us seeing each other. It wasn't that she didn't like her; she did. It's just that she was my cousin's wife's sister. We met at my grandmother's Born-Day party. She wasn't family, so I saw no problem dealing with her and neither did she.

There was one time we went to the movies at King's Plaza in Brooklyn and afterwards went to a fancy Chinese restaurant. The prices were high, and she was ready to order. If it had not been for overindulging the night before, paying for it would have been no problem. I began to become nervous.

Like magic, she says, "Let's just get a bunch of chicken wings and take it back to the house."

Now that's what I'm talking 'bout. She didn't know how close I was to telling her something in the same ballpark. We eventually started to drift apart, and she eventually cut me off over the phone one night. It was all good though. She was cool, and I was happy to have met her in my travels. Besides, I sure had a lot of fun with her.

Things really started to go downhill from then on. Goodyear gave me twelve sick days in the course of a year, so I started to call in sick often. My mentality was that, if I received twelve days in a year, what's the problem? Well, there was most definitely a problem after my fifth sick day. My workday ended with the main supervisor and his assistant coming in to terminate me for my absences. I asked for another chance and was denied. I emptied my locker and went home.

When I walked through the door of our house, my pops was right there.

"Why do you have all your stuff with you?"

"They doing some spraying for roaches over the weekend, so I had to bring them home."

He bought it until Monday came around; then I had to tell the truth about my termination.

Weeks later Reggie was starting to make a move by flooding our 'hood in Harlem with crack. Not that it wasn't in our hood already, but no one was on 129th to 130th on Amsterdam. Soon we all were out there hustling. Cee and I soon found an area in the Bronx that was popping and wasn't far from where we lived. The negative was we would work for someone else earning crumbs, while competing with the other dealers for the same paper and keeping an eye out for the police. There were no positives.

That drug shit had beaten me because I'd begun to get high every day. There was a time when I could roll up smoke and then just chill with a pocket full of money and not think about using more. Three years later, that wasn't the case. The plan became to smoke for most of the day. I often times wished someone—anyone—had strongly advised us all to stay clear of those demons that we were smoking with our weed.

Cee and I were the only so-called "Americans" on the block.

Everybody else was so-called "Jamaicans." Today, I use the word "so-called" because we both were taken as slaves and placed in these geographical areas. There were also many Africans in the Americas long before Christopher Columbus "so called" discovered it. However, only a few people were allowed to sell their own product, yet there was one guy who supplied the whole block.

One late night, I was out there with Cee working for this Dread. He was a cool dude until that particular night. This guy named Paul came on the block to get money, and usually the block would stop and allow him to get it. Paul was a bald, dark-skinned brawny brother of Jamaican descent. He'd come on the block for roughly twenty minutes and bounce. Everyone else would then get back to business. I always thought that was some bullshit, but that was how it was long before I got there.

While Paul was trying to make a sell that night, the Dread I worked for gave me orders in his Jamaican accent.

"Brethren, get that sell Star. (Homeboy) Go now."

I hesitated and looked at Dread as if to say "for real?"

"Fuck him, we got to get money."

That's what the fuck I'm talking 'bout. Fuck this nigga. Let's start the revolution. I stepped up and tried to cut his throat for that paper, trying to snatch that customer from him. Paying Paul no mind, I began showing the customer my rocks and told him, "Look at this here, I got that, come back. You fuck with this, and you will be coming back to see me partner."

Paul told me something like "Get the fuck outta here, I got this!"

Ignoring him, I told the customer to walk with me. Unexpectedly,

I felt a punch in my face. He had given me the best he had, but I didn't drop nor was I hurt. I jogged over to give Dread his rocks back. He was sitting only twenty feet away. It was time to take Paul's head off, and in case the police popped up while we were scrapping, I wouldn't have any drugs on me. I wasn't mad or embarrassed. I looked at it as a chance to display my hand skills on the strip.

Once I reached Dread, I noticed he was on the edge of his seat. He had a knife out which he tried to hide from my sight. It made me think why he was trying to hide it from me, unless it was to be used on me.

"Rude boy, just cool. Paul, him my cousin, hear? Just cool."

That's when it struck me. That mothafucka set me up to get hit and was gonna stab me if I retaliated. I should have known better than to think it was time to start a revolution. Cee and I had already recognized that we were the only so-called Americans on the block; why would they let me get mine off?

Three days later, I was back on the block. Paul was in the store and spotted me. After making his purchases, he got on the phone and ran out of the store straight into his car and drove away. I didn't think he was afraid at all. He had no need to be. The whole strip was with him. Minutes later, the police pulled up right in front of me. I tossed the last two capsules of rocks in my mouth. They threw me against the wall, so I started to swallow them. As I choked and gagged on them, I realized I wasn't being searched for drugs, this was a pistol search. Go figure.

I let that shit ride. I was way outnumbered and didn't want to involve my people. Yeah, I thought about some gunplay, but it was too close to home, and Cee lived even closer. Besides, I really don't remember seeing Paul out there again. But I did see Dread elsewhere years later.

I'll Smile Tomorrow

> At this point in my life,
> Done so many things wrong,
> I don't know if I can do right.

-Tracy Chapman

Lesson 10

"Never think of yourself as so low that you are lost forever; nor so high that you have no greater goals to gain."

Rev. Dr. Malachi Z. York

If it wasn't one thing, it was another on that strip. Cee and I began working for this really nice, short, bright skinned older Jamaican lady named Diana. Whenever Cee would get arrested, she would send a lawyer to court for him, and he would get right out. She was a loyal lady since it wasn't like we made her that much cash, so I respected that.

Cee, on the other hand, didn't respect anything. One day, we were both high, and he talked me into running off with $150.00 worth of coke that belonged to Diana. He told me he would give it back the following day, and I believed him. It wasn't completely his fault because I knew I shouldn't have done it. Cee knew that he could tell me anything when I was high, and I'd listen. He had nothing but excuses the next day. Diana was hunting me for her money and calling my phone three times a day. I had my own phone line in my room, so I would just answer my phone with "Sam's Deli" in a phony accent. If it was her, I would repeat "Sam's Deli" and wait to see what she said next, and then hang up. If it wasn't her, I'd holla at my people. In those days, there wasn't any Caller ID, so that was how I screened my calls.

One afternoon, I heard the house phone ring. My moms called me into her room and handed me the phone. When I answered, it was Diana.

"Don't you hang this phone up? I will call back and tell your mom everything."

I was in a crazy situation. My mother was lying in the bed one foot away from where I was talking on the phone. My best acting was needed.

"Hey, how are you? Call me back on my phone."

Diana was very angry. "You better pick it up, or I'll tell her I swear."

"Yeah, you got my number; call me now."

Damn, she had me by the balls. With her goons on the street, I knew I would have to deal with this one day. I would have preferred the goons rather than chance getting my moms involved. As I entered my room, the phone began to ring. I quickly answered. Diana explained she wanted her money by the next day or she would tell my mother. Even though I had no clue where I would get the money, I agreed to her terms. Before we hung up, she told me that she got my house number from Cee.

I quickly called Cee. "Yo! Did you give Diana the number to my moms' house?"

"Yeah, man, I was mad at you. She said that you told her that you got fired from Pathmark because of me."

"I did get fired from Pathmark because of you, but why would I share that with her?" Still, that's what she told him, and she got what she wanted. It didn't matter what he told her about me. I would never have done him like that.

Any money I made came from the strip. Since I had been avoiding it, there was no way to work there to get her money, so I went to my pops and told him the whole story. Pops wanted to meet with the lady and give her the money in person. I wouldn't allow that. He gave me $75 and a message for her.

"If she wants the rest, she has to meet with me." I would never set up such a meeting; though I did call Diana to ask her if I could repay her loss of drugs with drugs.

"Oh fuck no! Listen me want back me money, hear?"

"I don't have it, but I have some shit here that's bigger than that shit you have and way more potent."

"So whose shit is it?"

"It belongs to you, this is all I have and it's a good deal"

"Ok then, ok we'll see how this works you're usually trustworthy."

I took that money down to 129th and Lenox to a place in Harlem we called Castle Greyskull to pick up fifteen nickels. She'd have her money back once she sold them for dimes.

I decided to stop going back on that strip and to look for a legal gig, so I landed a job as a security guard and was assigned to work at the Fashion Institute of Technology. There were so many fine females on that campus. Black girls, Spanish girls, Asian girls, whatever your cup of tea was, they had it at F.I.T.

One quiet night, a fellow employee and I were standing under a little bridge that connected one building to another. A voice came over the loud speaker informing us that a robbery suspect had just run out of the building and to catch him. We saw the guy and quickly gave chase down 10th Ave. The guy ran down into a nearby subway with me after him with my partner behind me. When I was nearly twelve feet from him, he put his hand in his coat, then motioned like he had a pistol.

He looked me dead in the eye, "Get the fuck out of here. You better get the fuck out of here."

"Shit!" I stopped dead in my tracks and did as I was told. I wasn't about to get killed for that bullshit-paying job. My partner felt the same. We walked back up the steps to the street. All the top security bosses were running our way. They gave us lip because we didn't catch him. We tried to explain that he motioned like he had a firearm and there wasn't anything we could do. All we had were punk ass walkie-talkies.

The top supervisor yelled, "You two go get your shit and get the fuck out of here. You are fired."

Pissed off, I screamed at them. "Fuck you, who the fuck you think you are? I'm not dying for you. Where the hell were you when I was down in the subway with him? All of you mothafuckas can go the fuck to hell."

I was so surprised to witness my partner pleading to keep his job. Normally, I would not have knocked that; on the other hand, every day he talked "Fuck this job, I'm gonna quit. They can kiss my ass. I don't need these mothafuckas," and on and on. He kissed all over their asses and didn't miss a spot. He proved to be just another of the many barkers that I'd come across in my life.

When would I learn? All that begging didn't help him a bit. He had to get his shit and leave just like me. In fact, we were on the same train to the Bronx.

Soon after, I received another job as a security guard, this time at the ABC building, you know, the TV channel. Sometimes I would be on the set of daytime soap operas like All My Children, Ryan's Hope, and Loving. A female actor on one of those shows lost a necklace and was running around frantically looking for it. Everybody was shook, and all along I thought the props were all costume jewelry. Watching her run around the set I couldn't help but wonder if it could be an act since she was an actress. I thought to myself, she probably got that shit in a stash somewhere.

When Christmas came around, I didn't have a dime to buy gifts for anyone. I took one of my pops' favorite herringbone chains from out of his dresser drawer. Larry took me to this pawn shop that he knew of and that's what I did—pawned it. The guy at the shop asked me what I wanted for it once he weighed it and checked to make sure it was authentic. I told him I'd take $80; I spent $20 on my mom, $20 on my dad and $20 on my sister. We got high with the $20 left.

About one week later, my pops woke me from my sleep and asked if I had seen his chain. I looked at him with the sleepy face and told him no. My plan was to get it back that week, but, since he never spoke about it again, I just didn't worry about it again.

There was another issue that was going on in my household. When I had gotten paid, I would let my mom hold my money for me. For the reason that I knew where she would put the money, I would go and take money out at will, and my pops didn't like that. He would tell me I was stealing.

"But that is my money. I can't steal from myself."

Eventually he told me I couldn't live there anymore and wanted me to leave. He didn't just kick me out, though; he put a security deposit on a little basement studio apartment we found off Gun Hill in the Bronx. Even though he wanted me gone, he didn't like the fact that I was so gung ho to move out, even before we found that apartment. Man, I couldn't wait.

Two days before I moved into my new place, Helen and I had an argument over the phone. Yeah, we were always going back and forth with our relationship, but this time I thought it was genuinely over. She was in a foster home in Queens somewhere. That same afternoon we broke up, I bumped into an old female friend I used to work with at Pathmark who had a little crush on me. I used to go to her house sometimes when her mom wasn't home, and we would fool around but never sexed. Nicole was a beautiful sister. Though we hadn't seen each other for a little while, we bonded like no time had lapsed. It was destined for us to meet, especially after breaking up with Helen that same day. Nicole was right there with me when I moved into my new apartment.

Although you already know that I started having sex at an early age, it was always what I call nervous sex. We were always doing it in places like the blue room, staircase, at a friend's house etc. It was different with Nicole. We would go at it all night long, with no worries at all. In the morning, we would take the train together, me going to work and her to school.

Nicole damn near lived there with me. She said her mom didn't care what she did, which was cool with me. I liked having a lady's touch around my apartment and sleep-in pussy. She would always make things look nice, over and above; she looked damn good running around the house buck-naked. One day while we were home, Nicole was in the bed nude, and I was in the kitchen cooking dinner, in the nude. There was a knock at the door, so I threw on a pair of sweats and Nicole pulled the covers way up to her neck. When I answered the door, it was my pops. He dropped by to show my Uncle Gene my new place (RIP Uncle). When they came in, I introduced them to Nicole, even though Pops had met her at his home on a previous occasion. It was funny because she was acting all shy, and my pops had this look like "That's my boy." On the other hand, the real funny part was my uncle; he had a bit of a speech impediment and was trying to hold a small conversation with Nicole.

"So you are my nephews' girlfriend. He's a good guy so you make sure you take care of him."

She had no idea what he was talking 'bout. She would just lie there smiling and nodding her head; it was hilarious.

I didn't have that apartment long after fucking up my money and not paying rent. I didn't want to explain anything to my landlord, so I packed a bag and left everything else behind. No, I didn't return to my parents' home. I was addicted to cocaine, and I knew it was just a matter of time before they figured it out. Besides, although I was fucked up dwelling at my personal rock bottom, I faithfully felt deep within that "This drug shit is temporary." It was just a feeling I had that would tell me, "Don't worry, you will get out of this one." Therefore, I understood that I wasn't too low to raise myself back up. I just couldn't put my finger on how.

My whole crew was now paying for that great mistake of experimenting with cocaine, and we all regretted it. I would sit up nights cursing that nigga Pumpkin for introducing that shit to us. I would get so angry, I wanted to kill him. Today, I know it wasn't his fault; he was in the same boat we were in.

I ended up staying with Gee out in the Park Slope area of Brooklyn. He lived with Mary, an old friend of his mother's. Mary was an older white lady who took me into her home with open arms. Before meeting Mary, I never knew any white people. Growing up in Harlem, the only white people I came across were the school teachers. Up in the Bronx, there were some white people in the neighborhood, but I never dealt with any of them. Anyhow, once blacks moved in they all began to slowly move out. So Mary was my first real experience with a white person, let alone living with one under the same roof.

It was cool hanging out and living with Gee—he didn't use any drugs or alcohol, and wasn't running the streets selling drugs. Don't get it twisted, Gee was far from a punk, he was just smarter than the rest of us. All he wanted to do was play ball, holla at females, and pursue his career in the music industry. I had no objections with that, so he in actuality became family.

We used to share the biggest bedroom I had ever seen. It had one big ass bed that looked homemade. It seemed to have two queen-size mattresses put together, which we shared. It was Mary's son's room before he moved, and he didn't leave without leaving a piece of his mind behind. There were drawings all over the walls, floors and ceilings. At the head of the bed was a drawing of an angel with a halo around his head and under it was the word, WHY? I would sometimes lie there pondering the significance of this particular drawing. Even today, it sometimes crosses my mind.

One night, Larry spent the night there, and he too pondered the same piece of art. Today he has it tattooed on his arm. Helen called me one afternoon and I told her where I was staying and Mary even let Helen stay there with us. So we all shared that monster bed together. I now had my chance to redeem myself from that time at my parents' house when I couldn't perform. Whenever Gee went out to play ball or whatever, we would be humping like rabbits.

Helen used to tell me that Mary would ask her why she dealt with me, and that I would have a bunch of girls coming in and out of the house when she wasn't around. I don't know why Mary told her that because she was supposed to be my people. She didn't know what Helen was doing when she was out of my sight. I just took that as a white lady looking out for a girl who could have passed for white if she had worn her hair in a certain style and wore a certain wardrobe. Mary knew Helen's father was black and that she grew up as a black girl. At the time, I believed if she'd been all black, Mary wouldn't have bothered to mention anything to her. Today I believe she would have probably done it regardless if Helen was an African pygmy.

Helen stayed for maybe over a month. She was still in high school and had to go back to her foster home. Nevertheless, Mary was cool; I had even given her the title of my "White Mother," but she could go crazy on occasion. Gee and I could be in the back chilling and she would burst into the room and tell us that we had to leave, that she didn't want us there anymore. We'd find ourselves riding the subway trains at night, then go to our jobs in the morning.

I would take it as a big joke; I don't know why. Perhaps it was a character I had to make up to survive at that stage. It felt as if it wasn't really happening to me, but that I was witnessing it like a film, knowing it would only last for a short time. It was like G.O.D was right there with me, allowing it to happen but also guiding me through the whole ordeal and assuring me I would get through it, although I had not one clue on how.

My boy Gee was another story. That shit wasn't for him, although it wasn't for anyone. He had caught the flu out there on the subways; soon after, he went to Florida where his mom lived. He informed me years later that he was sleeping on the subways to keep me company. Gee had no problem with drugs. That's one of the things I thought was cool about him. Shit, when I bought a beer, he would pick him up a strawberry Yoo-hoo. I managed to keep my use of cocaine from him. He knew I was a big pot-head though. I wouldn't allow anyone to know I was using who weren't. When I got high, I would almost always have someone with me who would cop. I didn't want it to get out, because I hoped to someday be a big hip-hop star. Anyone who could say they knew for a fact that I used coke, were probably right there with me, mixing that shit with that weed themselves.

There is one story I must share with you about my days on the subways. It was sad at the time it happened, but I do find it funny today. I guess that saying, "I'll laugh about this tomorrow" fits in this case.

I was riding the subways one night, and if memory serves me correctly, I was riding the "A" line downtown. Keep in mind I rode trains back and forth, timing them in order to make it to work on time. At the last stop, one of the subway workers woke me up with a big smile.

"Hey brother, you missed your stop. This train is now out of service." He continued in his very polite tone. "What you want to do is take the uptown and catch your stop."

"Thanks."

He acted like he had done me a great service. Still smiling, he said, "No problem brother. I know how it is. You just got to pay more attention."

You see, I didn't look like the average homeless person; that's how I managed to fool a lot of people. I made sure my hair was cut and my sneakers were clean, so at first glance, it was hard to tell. I ran off to catch the train going uptown. The next thing I know, I was being awakened by the same transit worker at the last station in Brooklyn but this time he's looking at me with a very sorry face like, "Damn homeboy, what the hell is your problem?" No words were exchanged. I just got off and caught the train going back uptown.

My bad, what the hell was I talking about? That was not a funny story, neither then or now.

By now, I had left the gig at ABC for another security gig at Effective Security. My mom's youngest brother was like the top dispatcher, and he would get me the good sites to work. He eventually got me something for the phone company at a site located on 129th between Convent and Amsterdam. My hours were from midnight to 8 a.m., the graveyard shift. It was near where we used to live on Amsterdam and 130th. My Harlem crew was still slinging their loose cracks on 129th and Amsterdam. I would hang with them and at midnight walk up the block to work.

During the graveyard shift, I would be the only one on the premises, which allowed time to sleep. Anyone who wanted to enter had to ring the bell to get my attention. There were even showers there, so I had a chance to wash my ass, plus I kept a bag of clothes in the security area. After work, I would go get something to eat and walk around until around 11 a.m. when Reggie or Larry would come out to hustle. Hanging on the street with them would have to do until I got myself together. Now there's a downside to that: what I would do on my days off. I would go to Mary's house during my off days. When she opened the door, I would just tell her that I was there to pick up some clothes. She would be so lonely, we would get to talking, and she would eventually ask me to stay.

> "Looking for the Remedy
> But you don't know what's
> Hurting you
> The revolution is here,
> The revolution is personal."

-Talib Kweli

I'll Smile Tomorrow

Lesson 11

"Instead of wallowing in my misery, I just made some changes."
Stephanie Mills

It was the beginning of '88 when Reggie first established 129th with cracks. It wasn't hard to do. You just let mothafuckas know you had it and where you'd be. That shit would sell itself. Reg was working for someone at the time, but it didn't take long for us to get our own product from the Dominicans up the block, for cheap. The block started to bubble a little, and we all were trying to get money it wasn't a problem. We were family so it was all good.

Larry started using the name Mobes. He took that as his street name from another Harlem soldier that he knew who got himself locked up for blaming (shooting) some dudes with an Uzi in the 80s. Mobes' little brother and his crew started getting money on the block too; so everybody was eating. The difference was these little niggas weren't getting high off coke. They saw its effects and knew not to deal with it. We, on the other hand, came up when we didn't see anyone fall off from the drug. There was no prototype for us to take heed from. Actually, what we saw were people who were hustlers and ballers in the hood doing it and didn't notice the change until years later, once it had spun way out of control. A lot of these young guys were lucky that they weren't born in our era, running the streets and smoking weed.

Around that time Gee came back to New York from Florida.

Eventually, we both were staying at the phone company. The little area where I kept my bag of clothes became cluttered with both of our belongings. Our good thing was soon to come to an end, because there was one telephone guy who would come in some late nights and would notice Gee there sleeping in the security area one too many times. I got a phone call telling me they were relocating me to another site because they were getting calls that I had someone staying there every night who wasn't an employee, and that there are bags all over the place. I didn't want to be relocated, so I finally took Helen up on her offer to come stay with her in Florida.

She had gone to Florida to visit her sister for a week and decided to stay. She would always ask me to come out there to stay too. I didn't want to go since she told me she was an Exotic dancer. She claimed it was in a bathing suit, but I just wasn't feeling it. When Gee was out there, I had given them each other's math (phone number) so they could link up. Gee met up with her and watched her and her sister dance in some spot in Ft. Lauderdale.

The main reason I decided to go was that I didn't know what else to do to beat my addiction. There was a choice to make: should I leave and try to change my life for the better or stay and watch my life change for the worse? A voice within told me, "this is your door, walk through it". An advantage was that Helen's sister Alley had relocated to Florida from the Big Apple, so I had a place to lay my head. That Friday, when I got paid, Gee and I made arrangements to jet down to the Sunshine State. He would stay with his family, and I would stay with Helen and her sister Alley.

There were these chicks that I knew from out of Queens who offered to drive us around picking up my belongings from

Brooklyn, Harlem, and the Bronx. They first took us to Queens' Astoria projects. They were acting like they couldn't wait to get there. Their body language suggested they were going to cop some drugs. I really can't describe what I detected in their body language. Put it like this: this is just one of those cases of "it takes one to know one." Trust me. By looking at these chicks, you would never think such a thing.

We were two cars deep, and the Brooklyn stop went well. The problem came when I stopped in Harlem and managed to ditch Gee. I linked up with Mobes and wanted to smoke one for the final time. The thing was once we copped and burned that blunt, I wanted to cop again. Mobes was trying to talk me out of it.

"Nah Smallz, don't spend no more money; you about to go to Florida. You need that money, don't fuck it up."

"Man, I'm not gonna fuck it up; it's just that this is my last time. I just want to get one more!"

We left to cop again, and when that was finished, I wanted to cop again, but my boy wasn't having it.

Pissed off he told me, "No, I'm not getting it. Go to Florida, Smallz. Shit, I wish I could go to Florida. This is your shot, man; you have to go." He then looked me in my eyes and, with a very serious face, said once more, "Smallz, you have to go."

That's why Mobes is my brother. If you ever hear me introduce him as such, it's because of love like that. I mean, he could have said okay and gotten high, except he didn't. I knew sober mothafuckas who claimed friendship who would have taken advantage of me, especially if I allowed them.

My drug-addicted silly ass told Mobes, "You ain't got to go. I'll get it myself." Mobes replied disappointedly, "Hold up, let me see something first.

We walked through the back of the building to the front where I saw Gee. Knowing there would be no way to ditch him twice, I miraculously snapped out of my high and ran up to him. "Yo, where you been, you ready?"

Now we had to wait for them chicks to come back from whatever they were doing. When they returned, we headed to Cee's crib in the Bronx. I ran up in his house, grabbed my stuff, and jumped back into the car. Next we headed somewhere deep in Westchester to one of the girl's house up there. Once there, one of the chicks met up with her man, and they decided to go back down to Harlem.

After counting my money, it was short for tickets for Gee and I to catch the bus to Florida. The girl gave us permission to drive her car around and, when we were finished, wanted us to park it in front of her house. At that moment, all I could think about was stealing her car, since she wouldn't be around to know it was gone. Guess she trusted us because we were friends with her girlfriends. Bad move.

The truth was it wasn't even her car; it was a rental. I knew she was still responsible for it, but I couldn't care less. I had to talk Gee into taking her shit. Gee could drive and I couldn't, so I really needed him. Just before she got into the car with her man, Gee called her over to her car and asked her if we could take the car to Florida.

She laughed and said, "We'll talk about that." She then got into her boyfriend's car and drove away.

I was thinking, *she thinks it's a fucking joke.*

Gee had to be worked on because he didn't really want to

steal it. I honestly didn't blame him a bit. Our situation wasn't that serious to him, yet it was do or die for me. If only I could drive, I would have been gone; he could have gotten a ride with the chicks. He eventually agreed, and before we jumped on the I-95 Gee thought it would be smart to rip some information from the corner of the rental agreement. He also signed his name to said document, after which we jumped on the I-95 south headed for that sun. Shit, he was totally with it now, and all was going well. That's until we were somewhere in Jersey and noticed flashing lights behind us. Yeah, you're right, the fucking police. My heart didn't even skip a beat.

As I put my sneakers on, I thought to myself, if I can't go to Florida; fuck it just go to jail in Jersey. It didn't matter where I went; I just had to get away from the 'hood for a while. I did feel bad that Gee had to go through this shit, because he was basically in the dark when it came to my true motives.

The cop was a short, pudgy black man. He reminded me of the father on the sitcom Family Matters. He approached the car and explained why he stopped us. He said we were doing 80 in a 65mph zone. Immediately a fact from a TV show that said most criminals are apprehended for traffic stops came to mind. Gee explained that we were on our way to Florida and how his aunt rented this car for us to make the trip down there.

The officer then asked for his license, took the rental agreement, and walked back to his squad car. He returned and explained that he wished we hadn't ripped the paper and asked us to step out of the car. In the middle of searching the car, he stopped.

"I see what seems to be cocaine residue. Do either of you use drugs?"

We both answered him with a nice strong, "No!" I knew those bitches were coping coke.

The officer then asked, "Is there anything you want to tell me?"

Again, we answered, "No."

Another officer arrived on the scene that appeared to be of Latin descent. The two officers spoke a little, and then the black one walked back towards our direction.

As he walked in our direction, we were shook.

Then Gee says, "I'm telling him the truth, I'm telling him." Gee thought he could tell that cop the truth and, in some way, spit some game that would get us out of our current situation.

"No, don't tell him shit."

"I'm gonna tell him the truth."

He cleared his throat, took a deep breath, but, just before he could get the words out, the black cop spoke to us.

"This is what I'm going to do for you guys." He pointed down the road. "There's a Howard Johnson's hotel and a bus depot over there. I'll drive you guys over, but I am going to have to take this car. Your aunt will have to come and get it; there shouldn't be a problem."

The officer allowed us to grab two bags apiece, out of the many bags that we had stuffed in that car. He then searched the bags we picked, which was very smart. If we were trafficking drugs or weapons, those might have been the bags we would have selected to take with us.

While in the squad car, Gee sat in the back, and I was in the passenger seat. The cop looked at me and nodded his head.

"You know we black people have to stick together."

I looked into his eyes, and it appeared he knew the car was

stolen. I quickly dismissed that thought since I'd encountered many cops, and none of them would let us slide with something like that. Could I have just met one?

He dropped us off at the Howard Johnson's where we used the bathroom. We had to dash across a busy highway in order to get to the bus depot. Cars sped towards us, but we made it safely.

In the depot, we saw another officer coming towards us. When he got to us, he didn't say a thing. He walked around us trying to get some reaction out of us. He then broke his silence.

"Why were you guys running across a busy highway?"

I thought to myself, why did the chicken cross the road? To get to the other side. Asshole.

We happily answered him. He then asked for ID which we handed to him. Not having anything to pin on us, he allowed us to keep it moving.

Jersey had no buses to Florida, which I probably couldn't afford anyway. But they did have buses going back to New York's Port Authority, and that took more money out of my pocket. We found ourselves back in New York, with little if any money. I had a leather jacket that I was ready to sell, in order to "Escape from New York."

When that failed, Gee called his mom and explained the whole situation. She sent the remainder of the money we needed by Western Union to get a bus down there to her.

When our bus was just about to board, I called my mom to tell her that I was moving to Florida. She was very upset asking me why and not to go. Mom didn't know what I was going through. She knew things were hard, but she had no clue how hard.

Do I tell her, Mom, I have to go; I'm addicted to cocaine and have been for the past two years? Do I tell her, Mom, I have to go because I've been sleeping on the subways for the past year, and when I wasn't, I would sleep on the job? Do I tell her all the shit I've done? There were things I couldn't tell her then, for fear of my life and freedom; there are things I can't share even now.

I could never tell her the truth because she couldn't handle it. I just didn't want her worrying about me because I knew she would go crazy. Besides, why allow her to stress over something that she could not control? Shit, it was hard controlling it myself.

"So when are you leaving?"

"I am at the Port Authority as we speak, about to board a bus down south right now."

They had made the last call for boarding. I said good-bye and hung up the phone. There was no way to talk me out of it. What could she do to save me? Put me in a rehab center? It had to be done my way. It felt right.

We boarded the bus and were out of there. I had never been out of New York. New Jersey didn't count because it's right next door. My window seat provided a great view of the scenery that got more beautiful the further south we went. It felt so good. It felt like I was sitting on the lap of G.O.D and She was telling me that "You will be okay now" and that I had made a great decision. I knew that as long as I remained as strong and determined as that very moment, I would beat the odds.

While still looking out of the window, I smiled at the reflection of myself in the window and said, "Thank you." Those two words, thank you, spoken out of my mouth, caused a small area of the window to fog up. Looking at it, I drew a small heart in the middle of it. As the heart faded away, I knew at that very moment I would never use cocaine again.

We had to transfer buses once we reached the Carolinas. Man, was it beautiful there. On the next bus, I noticed a white girl sitting there looking at the both of us like we were pieces of meat. When I sat down, a white guy immediately sat next to me. I don't remember if Gee sat next to the girl or if she got up and sat next to him, but I do know that, before we got to our destination, he had her playing with his dick on the bus. It was obvious to me by the way her shoulder was going up and down and Gee had his jacket on his lap. And I was stuck sitting next to a dude who would chew tobacco the whole ride. Even though we had a good conversation and he appeared to be a cool guy and all, that damn Gee was one lucky mothafucka.

After being on the road for nearly twenty-eight hours, we finally stepped off the bus in Jupiter, Florida. The station was on a dirt road. It felt like we had been dropped off in a real life ghost town, but still it was beautiful. Beautiful because it felt like I was closer with nature the look, the smell and I could actually see the many beautiful stars dancing in the sky.

Gee's mom met us at the drop off area. I had never met her before, yet we had spoken numerous times on the phone. She was driving a big blue van, and she got out and greeted the both of us with hugs and kisses. I thanked her for her help getting me down to Florida. She then made a joke about us stealing that car. We all laughed, yet I was surprised she wasn't angry. If she was upset, she appeared to have gotten over it or hid it very well.

She had a nice house in Jupiter, and the backyard was huge. She had about twelve dogs on her property that she loved to death. She groomed dogs for a living at this nice place in Palm Beach, and owned a couple dogs trained to be in dog shows. Gee's mom was definitely a dog lover.

Not too long after my arrival, I had given Helen a call to let her know I was in Florida. She acted as if she thought I had been joking about coming.

Her response was lame. "Oh… I didn't think you were coming now. Alley's boyfriend and his cousin are here, but his cousin will be gone in a week."

I wasn't trying to hear all that. I thought this fool knew I was coming. Now here I am at the bottom of the map and she telling me some wait a week shit. I simply told her, "Don't worry about it, I'm going back to New York" and hung up the phone.

Gee's moms had already told me I could stay there with them, so I never went anywhere.

There really wasn't any room there for Gee and me to stay, since it was only a two-bedroom house. Gee's sister Giley, his mom "Aunt Dale," and his two nieces and one nephew—Tia, Kala, and Ryan—also stayed there. Gee and I stayed either on the floor in the room with his sister, in the living room with his mother, or in the hot garage with the ants. Trust me, I had no complaints; this was better than what I was doing the day before. Plus, his mother was so very kind to let me stay as family.

That Monday, we rose early in the morning to look for work. We filled out applications any- and everywhere. I didn't care where I worked. I really wanted to be able to give Aunt Dale something to help around the house. The phone wasn't ringing at all for work for a good while. Finally, we received a job working at the Palm Beach Dog Track. This was a gratifying job. It was real hands on with the dogs. Personally, I was into more aggressive dogs, like my little brother who I missed so much, but greyhounds were cool.

We were hired to walk the dogs onto the field after putting their numbered jackets on them. Then, we would stand there with our dog, so all the gamblers could get a good look at each of them. We would walk them to their individual cages where they would then wait for the sound of the whistle, at which time their cage doors would open. The dogs would chase a fake bone around the track, and the dog that got to the finish line first would be named the winner. It was our job to grab the dog we originally brought out to the track, and escort him or her back to the kennel. Easy-Money. We didn't make a whole lot of money, though, but Aunt Dale only wanted $20 a week from the two of us, so it was all good.

Although we stayed in Jupiter, there wasn't a thing to do there for fun, so we would go down to West Palm Beach to hang out, not too far from where we worked. There was a lot to get into in West Palm, like going to the mall. New York didn't have any malls, well, maybe a few, like Brooklyn's own Al B Square Mall but there was nothing like these Florida jump-offs (a place where the happenings be happening). Not that we would go to be shopping or anything like that; however, the place was crawling with females.

Also, when they throw a party in the South, it is a time to remember. For instance, there was this block party that we went to, and to this day, I have never experienced anything like it. Everybody was in the street enjoying themselves dancing, singing and enjoying life. At one point, the police came to tell the DJ to bring the volume down. The DJ turned it down, and before the cops could get a block away, the DJ played that NWA joint, "Fuck the Police" and raised the volume even louder than it was originally. Everybody on the block started pumping their fists and screaming the words, "Fuck the police!" It was crazy. What was even crazier though, was that was the first time I ever heard that NWA joint being yelled out of the mouths of them crunked-ass Floridians, on Tamarind Avenue and Grant down there in West Palm Beach.

Yeah, I had a lot of fun that day. I noticed there were three garbage cans full of Heineken bottles. There were some people going to the cans, but I just thought that beer was for certain people.

Then the DJ got on the microphone and yelled, "What the fuck is going on? I can't drink all this fucking beer myself? Come on ya, I need some help here!"

I was like what, buckets of free beer? I never heard of such a thing in New York. This was southern hospitality for real; however, all the fun was interrupted by gunfire. Smiling faces turned frightened, and formerly dancing bodies ran for their lives. Shit, I remember running, and as I jumped over this nearby wall, I felt something hit me in my side, which took my breath away. I just lay there and relaxed my body to die. I don't know why I didn't try to fight for my life. I guess everything was going so good for me in Florida I must have felt it was too good to be true.

Well, it turned out that a bullet didn't hit me; it was more like an elbow or something from someone else also running. Once the shooting was over, I heard Gee's voice yelling my name.

"Smallz! Smallz!"

I checked myself for any wounds, got up, and jogged toward the direction of his voice. I was glad to see that he too had no holes in him. I heard one guy did get shot in the finger, so he should have been okay considering.

Hanging with Gee and his family was real cool; however, it was to come to an end once I received a call from Helen one afternoon.

"Howard, I thought you were in New York. I just spoke to your mother she's tells me you never left Florida. Why didn't you tell me you stayed?"

"Yeah I thought I'd stay to work on my tan."

"Whatever! Like your black ass need a tan. If that's the case, you do know Ft. Lauderdale does have the sunniest beach."

"Is that right? I never knew?"

"You know what I'm saying Howard. Come down here and stay with me."

"How do you suppose I get to Ft. Lauderdale?"

"Call a cab, and I'll pay for the ride here." (In a sarcastic manor) I asked:

"You'll pay for the ride there?"

"Howard I want you down here with me you don't have to worry about anything. I'll give you the address, you catch a cab and I'll pay for the cab once you reach my apartment."

"Ok I'm coming I'll call for a cab now."

As soon as I hung up, I called 411 to get a number for a cab company. Finding the number wasn't an easy task since I was from New York.

"Sir, without the name of a company I can't give you a number."

"It doesn't matter, I'll take any cab, only need a number to call." That didn't help either.

"Sir, I am not at liberty to choose one company, out of many; it just wouldn't be fair to all the others."

Damn, this bitch is fucking up my vibe. I explained that I was not from Florida, that I was from New York and didn't know any cab companies to give her a name.

"I am sorry sir but I cannot give you this information. Maybe you can give me a name of a cab company in New York and then we'll see what comes up."

"Yellow Cab."

I don't know why I said "Yellow Cab" since there is no way I would choose a Yellow Cab in New York, they are just too damn expensive. Nevertheless, Yellow Cab did show up, and she gave me the number.

Before I called the company for a cab, I thanked Gee and his mother for allowing me to stay in their home as family. Next I explained that I was going to go and stay with Helen and her sister in Ft. Lauderdale. They seemed a bit disappointed that I would up and leave. However, after living there for two months, I felt it was about time for me to go. The original plan was to come down there to stay with Helen.

I then packed my bag, called the cab, and I was Ft. Lauderdale bound.

I'll Smile Tomorrow

> Sometimes in our lives
> we all have pain
> We all have sorrow
> But if we are wise
> We know that there's
> always tomorrow

-Bill Withers

I'll Smile Tomorrow

Lesson 12

"The flower that follows the sun does so even on cloudy days."
Robert Leighton

The ride seemed like it took forever, and once we reached the area where I was to be dropped off, we could not find her apartment. The meter read $78.00 and I was thinking *this is not good.* I was riding with a big, black, mean-looking driver, and I didn't have enough money.

"Where in the hell does this fool stay?" I thought to myself.

We were in a housing complex, so I left my bags to go look for her apartment number. When I reached the last apartment in that section, I spotted Helen in the window washing dishes. I knocked on the door. She opened the door, we hugged, and I got to the business of the money to pay for the drive. She motioned to the back of the apartment.

"Go in my room and look in the closet, you will see a shoe box at the top, take the money out of there."

I took the shoe box out of the closet and opened it. My eyes widened; it was full of money. I removed the money I needed for the ride and paid big man. Helen and I exchanged more hugs and kisses when I returned to her apartment. Damn, I missed her. I really felt like this was where I belonged, right there with her.

When her sister Alley came home, she immediately ran to me, and we shared a big hug and an even bigger smile; she was also very happy to see me. Alley informed me that she was with child.

I congratulated her and gave her another hug. This is when they also informed me that they were strippers. Helen explained how she needed the money and that it paid well. She then added the fact that she didn't plan on doing it much longer. I didn't like it, but what the hell could I do? I had neither money nor a job. I couldn't tell her shit. That night Helen wanted me to come with her to work.

"I've seen your body before and plan on seeing it tonight, so I'm good."

She went to work without me. Alley wasn't due to go until later on that night and kept asking me to go with her, so I agreed to go. At the front door, I took a deep breath then entered. The first girl I saw was Helen. We made eye contact as she looked at me with that look that begged me not to be mad; a look that was fondly familiar. I wasn't mad, but I damn sure didn't like it. Even though it was hard to admit, she was pretty good at it. About ten minutes later, Helen came over and handed me a plastic cup full of Hennessey and sat down with me for a while. Helen and Alley then introduced me to some fine ass females, I wasn't mad at all.

Yeah, I was feeling the vibe in there, but, no matter what, I was not feeling the fact that she was running around in a thong. Then, something happened that really startled me. Some dude came in and sat with us, and I knew that if he wasn't a pimp he damn sure was trying to be one. I immediately didn't like him: he reminded me of Rich Blacker so much. The way he walked and talked was identical, and Rich was full of game.

Helen and Alley introduced the dude to me as Ron. Helen introduced me as her boyfriend Smallz and told him I was from N.Y.C. Dude looked over at me.

"Hey cousin, do you smoke weed?"

Coldly I replied, "Yeah, I smoke weed."

"You want to go get some?"

"Nah, I'm good, I already have some."

"I don't mean that New York shit, cousin. I'm talking 'bout that good bud."

At that point, Alley looked at me. "Go ahead, Ron is cool."

I looked over at her and said loud enough for him to hear "Fuck him."

He didn't seem to let that faze him a bit and continued to talk about smoking some weed.

"Howie, he's cool, for real." Alley tried to assure me.

By the conversation he had with the girls, I kind of felt he couldn't be pimping any of them because they didn't speak to him like he had any power over them at all. Confident he wasn't my girl's pimp, I finally accepted his offer, and we headed out the door. Ron had his cousin with him, and we jumped into a nice two-door navy blue "4 Runner" Jeep and rolled out. While we were on the road, I was like Whatever, I'm gonna smoke this niggas weed and that's it.

"Where are we heading, cuz?" The guy inside the car asked.

Ron replied, "We going to kill the man."

Here I was, my first day in Miami, in the back of this Jeep thinking, *did this fool just say they gonna kill me?*

It was weird because Ron was still talking to me like everything was cool, telling jokes and all. His cousin, on the other hand, didn't say another word. I'm thinking this nigga is straight gangsta; I know Ron had heard me say fuck him. I wondered why I had come out here fucking with these Miami niggas anyway. I would have just jumped right out of that fucking jeep, but I couldn't. Instead,

I started scheming on how to snap those boy's necks and save myself. It would be one hell of a task 'cause Ron kept looking back, talking like he's the coolest nigga in the world and telling me stories and shit.

"Yo cuz, I'm sure you know by now what my occupation is." Looking back at me again, he continued to boast. "I'm in the business of pimping these hoes."

He reached toward me to give me dap, so I happily slapped hands with him. Man, you should have seen me, smiling when he smiled, giving him daps when he reached his hand out for dap and just trying to be as cool as possible with him. I wanted him to believe I was the coolest dude in the world so I could get out of that vehicle alive.

We pulled over to some corner, and a bunch of hookers came over to the car. A few of them handed him some money, and we were back on the road. He resumed telling jokes and laughing up a storm. I wish I could tell you one or two of the jokes, but I thought I was going to be killed that night. Ron's cousin pulled over and jumped out. I figured this was the perfect time to break this dude's neck and get away. I couldn't find the opportunity 'cause he was still looking at me, running his fucking mouth. His cousin was probably gone for only twenty seconds. He jumped in the car and passed something to Ron. Ron threw it in the back seat to me.

"Tell me if that's some New York weed cousin."

I picked it up out of my lap, and it was a bag of weed, in one of those old school brown paper bags. Stamped on it were the words "Killa man." I was immediately relieved. Killa man. This nigga was talking 'bout some fucking weed the whole time. Thank G.O.D!

Ron became my main dude after that. I guess it was because we broke so much ice in our conversation. Although I was acting the whole time, my opinion of Ron changed for the better. Imagine how silly I would have looked, if that jeep was four-door and I jumped out, not knowing where the hell I was in Miami. That would have been some funny shit.

I started hanging with Ron a lot. He took me to his house one day, and he had all his hoes there getting their hair done. He told me he closed down a beauty shop for two days and had the beauticians come out to do their hair. I started to respect his hustle because it appeared like he had love for them. Also, any of them that needed a place to stay he allowed to stay in that house with him and his girl.

One thing I couldn't understand was the fact that his girl was also a hoe. I thought that was some hot mess. I couldn't have my main chick sucking other fellas' dicks. But I noticed that wasn't a problem for some of those Florida dudes. I would see them in the strip joints while their girls were working, throwing them money not giving a fuck who they were talking to or flirting with. That's something I just couldn't get into. I even hated that Helen was a stripper. However, I was glad to know she wasn't turning tricks.

One night, while I was at Ron's house, he shared with me. "Yo Smallz, you being from New York and all, you may come across some fools out here who may not like you because you a city boy. Now you may come to me saying, 'Yo Ron, I got a problem out here and I need some protection cuz.' And I would say to you "What Smallz, you got a problem?" And Ron would just have to give you something to protect yourself with."

He then reached into his dresser drawer and pulled out a .50 caliber Desert Eagle semi-automatic handgun. I was looking at it like wow, this shit is absolutely beautiful.

Ron continued talking to me, "But Smallz, you might say, 'Yo Ron, don't get me wrong but I'm kind of taking on an army, Ron.'"

Okay, where are you going with this?

"Then Ron will say, 'Damn, Smallz you taking on an army? I just may have something for you."

He then walked over to his closet and pulled out this great big chest, opened the chest and pulled out an AK-47 assault rifle. That was the first time I had ever laid eyes on one, and it was a sight to see. Inside the chest, he had all kinds of nice things in the event of war. If need be, he could back down the police easily.

Again, I began looking at Ron a bit differently; I guess you can say I respected his gangsta. When we went to the clubs together, I noticed some of the guys would look at him with pure hatred in their eyes. Yet Ron never paid those fools any attention. He would just look past them even though he was capable of taking it to a level most dudes weren't able to go. I guess it's safe to say he wasn't a thug. He was just able to take it there if necessary.

Yeah, I was having a lot of fun in Florida and was so glad to get out of New York for a while. In fact, I never wanted to leave the Sun Shine State. However, staying with Helen and her sister got rocky. They were bringing in all the money, and I had no job. I tried to contribute by doing most of the cooking.

At first Alley had told me, "You don't need to get a job. All you got to do is cook and we are straight."

Alley had a boyfriend named Roger who was, at the time, incarcerated. He and I would spend nights talking on the phone. He didn't want me to work at all; he was happy I was there keeping an eye on Alley and his unborn child. And, as for Helen, she was cool with me not working. In fact, she encouraged it. The problem was that Helen and Alley had a brother who wanted me out of his sisters' apartment. He was their half-brother from their father's side. He was some kind of sergeant in the police force or corrections or something. The thing is they never knew him before they came down to Florida. They knew they had a brother out there, but they had met him not too long before I came down.

One day, he and I had a talk. He explained to me

"Eventually my sisters are going to kick you out. Alley came to the door and said, "Don't listen to him. You don't need to work; besides how are you going to get to work? You can't drive and there's only one car between the three of us."

Once she left the room, he whispered to me, "I know my sisters; they are not going to have it."

"Homeboy, you just met them recently. I've known them for years, so stay the fuck out of my business." I got up and walked out of the room. His problem with me was that he was trying to fuck them; yes, his own sisters.

He was probably telling himself, "Man, fuck that sister shit, these bitches are strippers and they both look good. Fuck that, I didn't know these hoes until recently." The dude was a real fucking creep. I saw how he looked at them, and it wasn't anything like a brother looking at a sister. Plus, Helen told me herself that he had been trying to fuck when I wasn't around. She made me promise never to confront him about it. His motive was apparently to get me out the house, so that they may be more receptive to fucking his grimy ass.

A little while later, I could tell Alley was starting to want me to go. It wasn't so much the brother at this point. It seemed to be more because she may have felt I took her sister's attention from her. Plus, she was seven months pregnant. The whispers in her ear from the brother didn't help.

Even before the whispers from her brother, though, I had learned that I needed to defend myself from Helen's violent ways. I guess she was having some type of control freak syndrome, because she wanted to fight every day. Man, she had me jumping even when she wasn't trying to hit me. At any given moment, she would just punch me in the chest for no reason.

In an effort to scare her, I would say to her, "Helen you gonna make me hit you back one day. Please, just chill, I don't want to hurt you."

She didn't listen. Actually, one night while lying in bed, the subject of her hand problem came up. You won't believe the silly shit that came out of that sexy mouth.

"You should have gone upside my head, for real."

Two nights later, she was on her bullshit again. I don't remember what she was beefing about. However, I do remember her standing up out of her seat, walking over toward the hallway, grabbing an umbrella, walking back over to me, swinging it like a baseball bat, and hitting me on my left arm. That was it! I'd had enough of that bullshit! I grabbed the umbrella out of her hand, and she ran into the bedroom. Things had gotten out of hand and something had to give. It went from her hitting me with her hands to picking up objects and hitting me. I didn't know what I was gonna do, but first I turned the door knob, and the door was locked.

"Open this door, before I kick this mothafucka down." I was just talking shit. There was never any intent to hurt her. I loved her. She just needed to stop fighting me. She opened the door, and to my surprise, she had a steak knife in her hand, moving it as if she was gonna stab me. I wondered why there was a knife in our bedroom since we had never eaten there. Anyway, her behavior pissed me off, and I swung at her face with the umbrella. I wasn't going to hit her with it, but I wanted her to believe I would, although I would have if it became necessary. It wasn't like she hadn't stuck a knife into someone before.

As she ducked, I managed to grab her and get the knife out of her hand. Now that the threat was gone, I threw her onto the bed and climbed on top of her. She was going crazy, so I slapped her in her face twice. She looked up at me and started screaming.

"Get out! Get the fuck out!"

I got off of her and went into the living room. She entered the living room and gave me $75 after telling me she had called the police, and they should be there to escort me out of the house. She marched back into the room and closed the door. She came out again and threw the phone on the couch.

"Your father is on the phone. Ask him for the rest of the money you need for your ticket back to New York."

I picked the receiver up off the couch and hung up the phone. Pops had told me himself that he wanted nothing more to do with me. Remember when I took one of his necklaces and pawned it? The pawnshop had called the house one day and informed him that a chain they had in their possession was close to expiring, which would allow them to sell it if I didn't come in with the money. Pops asked them to describe the chain to him, and he soon realized that it was the necklace he had been missing for months. I was still in Brooklyn when they called him, so I had to go to the house to sign some paper which would allow him to get the chain back once he paid for it out of his own pocket. So that's why I didn't want to speak with him. I didn't think he would give a shit about any drama I was going through.

I called a good buddy of mind named Fritz and explained my situation. While I was on the phone with him, Helen emerged from the bedroom dragging a luggage bag with all my belongings inside and placed it by the front door. I heard keys at the door, so I peeked out the window and saw Alley with their punk ass brother. The knife I had taken from Helen was in my back pocket. I took it out.

While talking to Fritz, I told him, "If he says anything to me, I'm killing him. Can you believe this fool has been trying to fuck his own sisters? I'm killing this mothafucka Fritz if he says one thing to me."

I could feel the killer in me coming to the surface. It was all happening so fast. Fritz told me to relax, but his words were going in one ear and out of the other. It was way too late. A picture of the way I would do it was clear. As soon as he spoke in my direction, I would plunge the knife into the middle of his chest. Then I would take the palm of my hand and ram the knife in as far as it could possibly go. A high school buddy was murdered in that manner. I remember thinking damn, dude really wanted him dead.

I felt so much anger towards Helen's brother, I could taste it. My anger had been held in too long. It was time to let him know how I really felt about him. The door opened, and Alley entered first. She could say anything she wanted to me. No matter how harsh her words may be, I would not harm her. Alley passed by me.

"You and Helen had a fight?"

I ignored her, but I asked Fritz, "You heard that? You heard that, right?"

Fritz kept telling me to be cool, yet that's like telling the sun to be cool—it's not happening. Their brother came through the door. I took a deep breath while holding the knife behind my back in my right hand, and the phone up to my ear with my left. He walked straight to the back to where Helen was, never once looking in my direction. G.O.D was so with the both of us.

I told Fritz how scared that fool was and how he couldn't even look at me.

"Good. Stay calm, give me your address and I'll Western Union you the rest of the money. Don't do anything stupid."

Hearing him say he would send the money made me feel much better. At least I knew I could make it back home. About twenty minutes later, the police came to the door and started asking a bunch of questions. I had no words for them. I let her do all of the talking. They told me to get my belongings and to come with them. I did as I was told. They fucked my mind up when they walked me to the curb, told me not to go back to the house, and started walking toward their squad car.

"You just going to leave me here? What am I supposed to do? I'm not from out here, where am I supposed to go?"

Man, I thought I would be taken to the precinct or something, not just put out on the street. One of the cops did go back into the house and asked them to call a cab for me. He came back out and told me so.

"Do you really believe they will?"

"You sure better hope so." He got into his squad car and slammed the door.

Once the cops drove off, I saw Helen fighting her brother and sister trying to get out of the door.

This fool still wants to fight. Helen had my leather jacket in her hand, and the brother snatched it out of her hand and pushed her back into the house. He walked outside, gave me my jacket and informed me that a cab should be there shortly. It was just so weird to me that he was still alive. He never knew how close he was to death. I was happy nevertheless because I wouldn't have had the chance to get back to the Big Apple if I had killed him. You know, going to prison and all.

The cab came, and I was Greyhound-bound and it felt really good. I felt in my heart that the drug addiction was over, so it was time to get back to New York anyway.

Mission accomplished.

Once I reached the bus depot, I picked up my money out of Western Union and paid for my ticket. I had to wait a few hours for my bus, and once it arrived, I jumped aboard and made myself comfortable. It was a 36-hour ride back to my Big City.

I'll Smile Tomorrow

> Sometimes I feel like I'm
> My own worst enemy.
> I make things harder
> When it's really elementary.

-Pitch Black

Lesson 13

"As a dog returns to his vomit, so a fool returns to his folly."
The Proverbs of Solomon 26:11

When I was still in the bus depot, I called a few people to vent my feelings about how Helen threw me out into the street. While I was on the phone with Cee, he put me on hold.

When he returned, he told me, "Dee Dee said you could come and stay here."

Dee Dee is Cee's mother, and she was always cool with me. *Yeah, Dee Dee was good people.* After receiving such good news, I felt like everything was going to be okay, so my ride was very peaceful.

Did I just say peaceful? Well, that feeling was soon to be tested. What happened was, somewhere in Atlanta, this heavyset brother got on the bus and sat next to me in the aisle seat. We discussed a bunch of interesting topics. We were laughing and carrying on like we knew each other for years. I think it was in North Carolina when the bus stopped for us to stretch and get some refreshments. That's when he explained that he had some rock cocaine and was offering me to get off and get high with him.

Ain't this a bitch? I'm on my way back to New York to start a new life. Shit, I ran Down South in order to escape these types of temptations. Here I was sitting on a bus with a dude, with the drug of my choice on his person, who was practically giving the shit away. I had left New York exactly four months and six days before this bus trip. Could I possibly be ready for this type of pressure?

I looked him in his eyes and replied, "Nah, I'm good, homeboy."

As he walked off the bus, I thought to myself, what the fuck was that about? Man, I'm so focused right now that you can bet your bottom dollar that I will never return to that messy vomit I left in my past.

Some may say, "That was a test from G.O.D." I think I would disagree with that, for the reason that I'm under the impression that G.O.D is all wise and all knowing, which means that G.O.D has the wisdom to know I would tell that dude to go ahead with his bad self. That drug foolishness is over.

> Let no one say when he is tempted,
> "I am tempted by GOD"; for GOD
> Cannot be tempted by evil, nor does
> He himself tempts anyone.
> But each one is tempted when he is
> Drawn away by his own desires
> And enticed.
> **Holy Bible, the Epistle of James 1. 13-14**

Once I reached NYC's Port Authority I felt really good to be home. Florida was a great place to live, and I promised myself to one day go back to stay, but there is nowhere like N.Y.C. And, no matter where I go in the world, I know I will always return, even if it's only for a visit.

I got on the #2 train and headed to the Boogie Down Bronx, 219th Street to be exact, where Cee stayed with his mom. When I got to Cee's house, I put my bags down, rang the doorbell, and his mom Dee Dee answered. She seemed happy to see me,

"Hey Howard!"

She looked down, and after seeing my bags, she looked back up with a very confused look on her face.

After seeing her expression I asked, "Dee Dee, did Cee ask you if I could stay here?"

She invited me in. "He never mentioned a thing to me."

As I walked in behind her, I apologized. "I'm sorry Dee Dee. I would never have come if I had known you didn't agree with it."

"You know how that boy is. But it's fine. You can stay. You just have to stay in the basement with him."

"Thank you, Dee Dee. I'm going downtown to see if I can get my old job back, so I can give you something for your trouble."

I went down to the basement where Cee was, feeling embarrassed and ashamed. So I started cussing him out.

"Why the fuck did you tell me that you asked your mom if I could stay, when you know damn well you didn't ask her shit."

"Fuck you talking 'bout? I did ask her."

"Cee, she didn't know anything about shit when she opened the door and saw me with those bags."

Trying his best keep from laughing in my face Cee replies:

"She knew. She just fucking with you."

I walked toward the steps to call her so I could get this cleared up, because I knew Cee was fucking lying.

"Okay, okay, I didn't ask her, but I knew she wasn't going to say no once you got here. You know she loves you, so just calm down, it worked."

I was pissed, but I didn't have a Plan B, so I did what Cee said and calmed down. Both of us walked to the train and shot down to 34th Street to see about getting my job back. As soon as I walked into the building, I saw my Uncle Lee (I love you, Unck. Rest in Peace). He was really happy to see me because he gave me a big smile and an even bigger hug. I explained to him that I was there to get my job back. He was still a jokester.

"I could have told you that much, 'cause I know darn well you didn't come way down here to see me."

He was wrong though because I felt I might need him to get my job back. I went upstairs and spoke to a few people and then was issued a lie detector test. I lied on every question to which I felt a lie would be the best response. I had come up with my own little system. The tester had a nice sweater hanging up on his door, so, before responding, I would look at that sweater and immediately tell myself how nice it was. Trust me, there were many questions that called for a lie. I am not saying my system works, as I truly don't think it could be that easy. However, I will say this I walked out of that office with a job which I was to start that next day.

We headed back to Cee's house. Dee Dee was happy for me, and we came up with an agreement that I would give her $50 a week to stay in her home. Cee and I then walked up the block to the pizza shop and started beefing with some dudes from his block. The arguing was all in fun. We had a little hip-hop rivalry with them. When we turned to leave, I noticed my Moms walking up the stairs of the subway. I was so happy to see her, and we embraced tightly. She didn't know I was back in town. I had tried to call a couple of times at rest stops on my way back to the city, but couldn't get through. She had told me Helen kept calling the house and was begging her to have me return her call, declaring it was very important.

Moms told me that she had expressed to Helen, "There's a thin line between love and hate."

Changing the subject, I informed Moms that I got my job back, and I would be staying with Cee and his family. We spoke for a little while, until her train was in sight. We hugged and exchanged kisses, and she boarded her train. I used a pay phone to call and find out from Helen what was so important.

When she picked up the phone, my intention was to hear her out and then tell her not to call my mom again and to stay out of my life. It didn't actually happen like that. What was so important that she had to tell me was that she was pregnant with my child. All the bitterness I had toward her went right out of the window once she uttered those words. I was so happy. I honestly couldn't stop smiling.

"I am going to be a daddy."

She also explained to me how she was trying to get out the house to tell me she was sorry and to beg me to come back; her sister and brother wouldn't let her get to me. My mind instantly flashed back to when I noticed her fighting to get out of the house and them pushing her back in. I wasn't even sweating that foolishness anymore.

Hearing how happy I was to receive such good news, she informed me that she was coming to New York to be with me in a few days. We then talked about finding a place to start a family. I told her I could probably sell some weed to make some extra cash, and she offered to Western Union me $300 to get it started.

That didn't work. $300 was not enough to make money hustling weed. After I bagged it, I probably had something like $100 profit, and that didn't count the weed Cee was taking from me when I wasn't looking. One day, I was in the bed asleep, and for some reason, I woke up. I heard the music playing. Cee was dancing to the music and rolling a joint right under the spot in the ceiling where I had my shit stashed. That's Cee for you. I loved him like a brother, and he would do anything for me and me for him. Still, I had to remember I couldn't trust him when it came to certain shit. Regardless, Cee is my boy. He would smoke my weed, but I wasn't mad because I was happy to see him not smoking those woos anymore, since it was I who started him in that cocaine nonsense.

When Helen did show up, she checked into a women's shelter until we could get a place together. Although this really wasn't the type of thing she was used to, as long as it was short term, she would be okay.

She would visit me all the time, and on one particular day, I decided to open up to her about my prior addiction. It was she, Cee, and I in the basement—she and I sitting on my bed and Cee on his own.

"Helen I want to tell you something about me that you never knew."

"What?" Confusion spread across her face.

"I used to mix rock cocaine with weed and eventually became addicted to it."

"Stop lying. Don't forget, we used to live together, so I know better than that."

"He isn't lying, it's true; for real it's true."

Cee used to have a crush on Helen, and as I watched him become so excited about being in this conversation, I knew he still did. I imagine Helen realized the truth was written all over his face and looked back at me,

"Say Word!"

Before I could respond, Cee yelled out again, "Yeah, it's true."

But Helen was still looking me in my eyes waiting for my answer. I just nodded yes, while looking back into her eyes. "Trust me, I'm okay now."

She reached over and gave me a big hug and a kiss. "I'm glad you're okay."

Man, did I need that, and I was so happy it went that way. We just went about our lives from that day forward, and never once did she doubt my recovery. Nah, my baby never worried about me relapsing although there was some who thought it was very likely. Like my brother Mobes. I remember one day we were waiting for the #1 train on 125th Street heading down town.

"Do you believe you'll never smoke woos again?"

"Mobes, that's over fam."

"Yeah, wait 'til you get that first check then we'll see what happens."

I didn't have a reply to that. Out of everyone, Mobes should know, I was through with that shit. Then I began reasoning, why should he believe it was over? This is a powerful drug that I'm saying I put behind me; he couldn't possibly know how emancipated I feel. It didn't even feel like it was going to be a fight. Shit, the fight was over; I done knocked that coke shit the fuck out. The thing was this revolution wasn't televised. It took place in my heart, so how was one to know its outcome? And by the way, there would be no rematch. Although I didn't reply to Mobes verbally, my soul was screaming, "Trust me man, it's okay."

Not too long after my return back to NY, my boy Fritz called me with some very great news.

"Okay, Smallz, I gave you a couple of weeks to get settled in. Now I need you to meet with a couple of homies of mine who own a recording studio not far from where your parents stay up in the Bronx."

Fritz was probably my biggest hip-hop fan and was my acting manager, so he wasn't asking me to go and meet with them. He was telling me to meet with them.

Before I rode down to Florida, Gee had a meeting with a fellow at Delta studio in Times Square. I went along with him to a meeting for our music. The guy we were dealing with didn't appreciate what Gee was bringing to the table musically. The thing with Gee was that he had this very lyrical style that was maybe before its time, so the dude didn't know where to go as far as marketing him. I remember thinking how stupid he was for not wanting to deal with Gee. However, once he heard my demo he fell in love and wanted to work with me A.S.A.P.

At the next meeting with him, I brought Fritz along with me. They put me in a recording booth which was bigger than the room I had at my parents' house. He basically had me rap over a couple of tracks for a group of his partners, and they fell in love with me.

There was this big fat guy who sat behind the mix boards who would really go crazy for each lyric that I spit. I was soon told that was Dr. Dre, but not the Dre from California but the one from NY. Some may remember him with his partner Ed Lover. They were huge at one point in their career. After our meeting, the main guy took Fritz and me downstairs to a restaurant for lunch and gave me a contract for a production deal. That next day I took the contract to Mary. She sent me to a lawyer who she claimed she had taught the ropes to in the beginning of his law career. Mary was a paralegal back in her day.

The lawyer didn't like the contract and printed me up a new contract to return back to the dude. When I did, he gave me a cassette tape of some beats he wanted me to write some songs to. He told me the tracks were from the legendary producer Clark Kent. It's said he was the one who first discovered Jay-Z years later.

It all was looking real good and was looking very promising to Fritz and me, save for it was way too much for me. I never stayed to learn where this all was headed. I believe it was a week later that I escaped to Florida. Now that I was back, Fritz saw it was time for me to get back to my business of song making. When I went up to see his homies, they were soon to become my homies too. They were Charlemagne and his partner Vidal. Char was the main producer and Vee was the engineer, producer and businessman and I can't forget Seth who would come in sometime to produce tracks for us as well.

When they heard me spit, they loved my style and this made me the first of many MCs they had down with them on Fortress Ent. Other talent followed me: Dante, Tim-X, MR. Voodoo, Gee-Blast, L Swift, KA and Kev of Night Breed, to name a few. Every Saturday, we would all meet up at the studio and engage in some real sessions. We all went home with a finished song. If I wasn't in the studio or working, I would always be in Harlem hanging with my squad from my 'hood, and it was the same shit going on. I would still run around and be in the project staircase while my partners would get high right in front of me. Not once did I judge them, nor did I ever look down on them—it just was what it was. Only months earlier, I was passing those coke-filled blunts around with them. I just had the same feeling for them that I once had for myself and that was that this was just a fad, and someday, we would all laugh about the destructive shit we used to do.

Friday, which was payday, had come and gone many times with no problem. Dee Dee would get her $50 on time, and when Monday rolled around, I would go back to work.

I was hired to work with the phone company again, though, this time, my job duties were to escort the telephone men around the Bronx, as they installed and repaired phones. All I had to do was hang out with them. The company apparently felt safer if they had people escorting their employees. That made sense because it could be dangerous going in and out of some of those buildings and in and out of strangers' homes. We would go in some very drug-infested buildings, where it seemed like the tenants were imprisoned in their own homes. There were times when we walked into buildings and had guns pulled on us. We'd stand with our hands up, pleading:

"Don't shoot! We're from the phone company."

For instance, one day we were walking up the stairs, and on the third floor, this Spanish dude jumped out with an Uzi assault weapon pointed right at us. He was yelling at us in Spanish, but neither of us could understand anything he was saying. Yet his body language was perfectly clear:

"I will murder you! Who the fuck are you and why the fuck are you in this building?"

Another dude ran up behind us in the staircase carrying a .357 handgun. We were sandwiched in the staircase between two gunmen.

"We are with the phone company!"

The guy on the bottom step told the guy above something in

Spanish after we showed them the tools we had on us. Whatever he said caused the other one to lower his gun and motion to us to proceed up the steps to our business.

The job was kind of crazy, but it wasn't like that every day, and besides, I needed the work. Like Snoop Dogg proclaimed:

"My Boo Boo's having my baby."

It felt good to be giving Dee Dee that money every week. The whole family had much love for me. It was she, her husband Bunkie (who has since passed. RIP Bunkie we will always love you), Cee's little brother AJ, his baby sister Porsher, and soon-to-come lil Bro, JT, who was lodged in Dee Dee's abdomen. I enjoyed staying there with Cee's family, plus I wasn't in anyone's way in the basement. It also made it easier to have Helen come over for a little sexual healing.

Staying with Cee's family, though, was soon to change. It had nothing to do with them and me. The problem was with Cee and his mom. What happened to change things was the day when the two of them had a very heated argument. Cee said something he had no business saying, especially to his own mother, which caused her to tell him to leave her home. She then noticed me packing my stuff.

"Howard, don't you leave because he has a smart ass mouth; you stay right here."

So I found myself in this weird situation. The way I remember it, Cee wouldn't even come in the house unless I was there. Can you understand where I'm coming from? He would wait up the block for me to get back from work and come into his own house as my visitor. I knew I couldn't stay there if this was how it was going to continue. It just didn't feel right.

Once, Helen spent one night with me in the basement since

Cee was gone. The next day, when she went back to the pregnant women's shelter, they kicked her out for three days and told her to go back to wherever she was the night she didn't show.

Now with my pregnant girl homeless, I started to sneak her in Dee Dee's house until her three days were up. They didn't know she was staying there, but she was. At night, I would just act like I was taking her to the train, when she really was still in the basement. That shit only worked the first two nights, 'cause the third night, when I told them I was walking her to the train, I returned to find Bunkie in the basement washing clothes and Helen looking at me with that funny face she wore when she knew she was wrong.

I just kept the lie going saying to Helen, "Come on, I just called, and they're home."

She was just looking at me as if to say, Howard, he knows everything. I already knew we were busted, once I'd seen them standing there together. There were more than enough places for Helen to hide, which meant he knew she was there and must have gone looking for her.

Still sticking with the script, I motioned to Helen. "Come on, they said we have to hurry up."

She walked over to me, and as we walked up the steps, she confirmed, "He knows what's up. He came looking for me. He must have known I never left the house when you did."

Walking out the house, I replied, "I know, I just can't explain this to them right now, I'm way too embarrassed. I'll think of something. Let's go."

Even though my pops and I were on bad terms, I called my parents' house from a pay phone. My mom answered, and I explained the situation and asked if we could stay there for one night only. She spoke to my pops, and they agreed and that's where we went.

The next morning, my sister called and offered to help me in any way she could.

"I need $300 to find us a place to stay."

"Come down to my job this morning."

Helen and I went down to meet with her, and she blessed us with the money. We both thanked her and immediately left. We had business to attend to.

Other than getting the money from my sister, it wasn't a good day at all. It was snowing and very cold out. But, that didn't stop us. We went to the store and picked up the Daily News and went hunting for a furnished room. We started calling numbers from pay phones and traveling to different places to see rooms. Either we didn't like the neighborhood, the room, or the price, or they wouldn't accept a couple.

We found one spot on 167th Street in the Bronx, near the #4 train line. It was nice, but we were told we would have to come back because the landlord wasn't there to let us know the amount of the rent. As we waited, we decided to call a few more places, which meant going back to the pay phones, in that cold New York City snow. I called a spot in Harlem and spoke directly to the landlord.

"Come check it out. I have a nice place for you."

"I plan on moving in with my girl, and she's pregnant."

"That's not a problem. Bring her with you; just hurry up. My name is James. I'll be waiting."

I was feeling the vibe I received from James, so we jumped on the train to meet up with him. The building was on 119th and Lenox, but the entrance was in the block going towards 5th avenue.

It was a seven-floor building, and the room we wanted to see was on the top floor. It was one of those buildings with two separate sets of stairs to climb per flight, and of course, there were no elevators.

James was the landlord, but someone else showed us the room. It was bigger than I ever thought it would be and had a queen-size bed with a big dresser with a mirror. We liked it a lot, yet there was a downside—we would have to share the bathroom and kitchen with four other couples. However, since we liked the place, we took it and were given the keys. I was so happy to be back in my hometown of Harlem. I doubt if there's another town on the globe like it.

In fact, when Mandela was released from prison after serving twenty-seven years as a political prisoner, he chose to come there to visit all of the beautiful people of Harlem. Yes, Helen and I were right there on 125th Street to witness the historic event.

It seemed like the whole world was out there. While listening to Mandela speak, I felt myself getting a little choked up, as my mind quickly flashed back to the TV movie Mandela when the legendary actor Danny Glover portrayed him. I thought, "Damn, he's been through so much, fighting for the rights of his people, and here he is in Harlem with his extraordinary wife still by his side proving that she is still with the struggle."

When it was over, we decided to take it in, so we headed back to our building. There were a bunch of dudes that would hang in and outside of our building selling drugs. As we passed them, I noticed that oh-so-familiar smell of the mixture of rock cocaine and weed in the air. I also noticed one of them sprinkling this mixture into a split cigar. I then thought about how Mandela was just up the block speaking to us about uplifting ourselves. Even though those brothers seemed to be cool with what they were doing, nonetheless, I said a prayer under my breath for them. Man, don't I know what they were going through.

> "But a room is not a house
> And a house is not a home
> When the two of us are far apart
> And one of us has a broken heart"

-Luther Vandross

Lesson 14

"Tears poured down my face, as I separated them becoming family"

H. Keith McAdams

The Author

It felt good to have a place we could call home, even though it was just a room. When I came home from work every night, we would be stuck in that room just looking at each other or watching TV. If not, we spent half the time having sex and the other half fighting. To this day, I don't know what her problem was with me, but I do know she always wanted to fight. I figured it had something to do with her being pregnant, you know, some hormone shit.

One night I slapped her up a little bit because I felt like I couldn't allow her to repeat the same abusive behavior as in Florida. That next morning, I woke up to go to work, and she was lying there asleep, like a beautiful angel. On the other hand, I noticed bruising on her face; her light skin made it easy to notice. That day I promised myself not to ever put my hands on her again; unless, we were smashing, of course. I went to work feeling so bad for hitting her, especially with my baby in her stomach.

My refusing to fight, though, didn't stop Helen from wanting to fight. My strategy was to grab her, get her on the bed near the remote control, and hold her down. Then I would get the remote, flip through the channels, and watch TV until she calmed down.

Sometimes I would start to release her, and she would try to jump up fast to start fighting some more. Yeah, she could be a handful.

###

Gee didn't stay in Florida either. After I left his mom's house to go stay with Helen, he went to New Jersey to stay with his father. After a while he left his pops' home and came back to NY. He would do his own thing during the day, and at night, he would come and crash on the floor of the single room Helen and I had. The word then got back to the landlord somehow, and he came to my room and spoke to Helen and me about the situation.

"It has come to my attention that your friend is staying here with you."

"Nah, that's my cousin. He only comes around once in a while; he doesn't stay here."

"I was told a couple of days ago of his staying with you, then I started seeing him for myself. I just want you to know, you all will have to find another place if this continues. However, you can let him know that, if he wishes, I do have a vacant room down the hall that he is more than welcome to rent."

When James left, I thought, damn, how do I tell him this? I suspected when he left Jersey to stay with us in a one-bedroom, it would eventually be a problem. Helen had already told me there wasn't enough room for us all. I understood her and felt the same, but Gee and I had struggled together, and I figured I could let him stay with us until his situation changed. He would and have done the same for us both. James was offering him a room down the hall from us. He couldn't beat that.

I saw Gee that day and informed him of the situation with James. Long story short, I can't remember what his exact response was, but, knowing my dog, I think he probably said "Fuck James," or something in that ballpark. Later, around midnight, there was a knock at the door. Helen and I both looked at each other like "damn." There was Gee, standing with his bag in his hand. He didn't say a word. He just stood there like, so what you gonna do? I had a big choice to make: let him in and risk having Helen, our unborn child and myself thrown out on the street or telling my good friend he couldn't stay.

I just couldn't chance it.

"Gee, I told you what James said. I can't let you stay anymore."

Still not saying a word, he just turned around and left. I'm sure he thought I was wrong, but I had a family to look after. I couldn't have my pregnant girl running around homeless on the street. There was no animosity between Gee and I. Rather, a couple of days later; he did take the room down the hall. Gee didn't stay long though. Being from Brooklyn, he decided to go back to the BK.

When Helen was six months pregnant, we were advised that she should be doing plenty of walking. So we would walk up to Harlem hospital, which is on 135th in Lenox, from our place on 119th in Lenox, for checkups with her doctor and her Lamaze class.

Lamaze class was a lot of fun, and a great place to obtain the knowledge I would need to help in the delivery room. I paid close attention because I wanted to do all I could to make the delivery easier for my woman and my unborn child, who I couldn't wait to hold and kiss. I remember just lying with Helen, with my face down at her big stomach, kissing it and holding one-sided conversations with my baby.

It was the morning of September 10, 1990, and it was time for me to get up to go to work. Helen and I both seemed to wake up at the same exact time with confused looks on our faces as we lifted up the covers feeling the mattress, blaming each other for pissing the bed. As I continued to tease her, a funny look came over her face.

"My water broke!" she yelled.

I looked at her and yelled back, "Your water broke!"

Sure, we had spoken about what we would have to do when this day came, but, I swear, all that shit went straight out of the window that day. I didn't know what to do. You should have seen me running around the room grabbing shit that didn't have anything to do with nothing.

When we finally calmed down, we got dressed, went downstairs, and caught a cab to Harlem Hospital. They took her upstairs right away; however, she wasn't quite ready for delivery. We simply had to stay and wait it out.

During our wait, I had so many different emotions. I remember feeling so very nervous, and my stomach felt like it was tied in a big knot. I don't know why I was feeling so nervous, but that emotion suddenly turned to fear. Becoming a father for the first time frightened me, as much as it made me happy. I wondered if I would make a good father to this special life that would soon be joining us, on this very emotionally disturbed planet.

At one point, when they believed she was almost ready to deliver, they gave Helen a laxative to prevent her from shitting all over the place during the delivery. Once that laxative began to kick in, the nurse placed a bedpan underneath her. Whew, when she dropped her dump, I couldn't believe my eyes. I never knew a human being could hold so much crap inside of them. Trust me, it looked like a baby mountain of horse manure; it was definitely unusual.

The time for delivery was upon us, so they gave me a hospital gown, head cap, and face-mask so I could be there for this wonderful experience. Let me tell you, when my baby started to come Helen was yelling and screaming like she was possessed. I felt sorry for her, but that was something I was told to expect. I tried my best to coach her like I learned in Lamaze class.

So here I was, coaching her when to push and with my face in her face breathing with her. Still she was beefing with everyone in the room, screaming for more meds.

Then I heard the doctor say, "I see the head." After a few regular pushes, he coached Helen. "Come on, I need one more big push."

And then it happened—there was a new soul sent here to experience life on this planet we call Earth. The doctor smiled with his proclamation.

"It's a girl."

When I laid eyes on her, I just started crying uncontrollably. I was so happy to be that little girl's daddy. The doctor handed me some scissors.

"Would you like to do the honors?"

Still crying like a baby, I took the scissors from the doctor and cut the umbilical cord which separated mother from child, and we became family. I walked back over to Helen, pulled the tear-soaked face-mask off, and gave her a big kiss.

"You did well, love. "I whispered in her right ear.

I was so shocked to see she was back to her old self so quickly. As she lay there with a big smile on her face, she blurted out, "I want some Wendy's."

At her request, I walked to the Wendy's over on 7th Avenue

between 139th and 140th, where a McDonald's stands today. I took that back to her and watched her as she ate, thinking to myself how beautiful she looked stuffing her mouth and how lucky I was to have her on my team. I then noticed a little ketchup in the corner of her mouth, so I leaned down and gave her a kiss to clean her mouth.

Gazing into her eyes, I told her, "I love you."

The nurse interrupted us to tell me, "You can go up to the maternity ward to see your baby girl now."

When I got there, she was lying there in a little crib. I just wanted to pick her up and give her a bunch of big kisses but a big window stood between the two of us. So I leaned up against the window and just stared at her, full of joy. I would just stand there staring at her for what felt like hours; then the nurse came and said:

"She's beautiful isn't she?"

Still looking at my baby girl, I nodded. "Yes, she is."

"I am so sorry to be the bearer of bad news, but I have to take her and feed her. Rest assured, you will be able to be with her tomorrow."

I went home alone that night but not before I called and informed everyone I knew about the good news of my baby girl.

That next morning I had to go to work, and I was assigned to work with this white guy who was a very religious person. That was a Tuesday, the day he went to church instead of lunch. One of my fellow escort workers, who was basically a street type dude like me, told me how he went to his church with him. He told me that, while he was listening to the pastor's sermon, something came over him and he caught the Holy Ghost.

This white guy appeared genuinely peaceful and didn't allow anything to aggravate him. So, this being the day after the birth of my child, I felt like it was time for me to have a relationship with the Most High. So for the first time in years, I went to church.

When we arrived, I noticed I was the only black person there, which didn't bother me. They all greeted me with a big smile when I entered. The sermon was okay, although it was boring. It wasn't nothing like any of the black churches that I had attended in the past. You know, black pastors be up there doing their thang and the choir be jamming. I sat there waiting to catch the Holy Ghost. I was praying to G.O.D, to show me a sign that this was his true house, yet it just wasn't happening. At the end of the service, the pastor asked:

"Is there anyone who would like to give themselves to their Lord and Savior Jesus Christ?"

I quickly raised my hand and stood up. Okay, maybe this is it, maybe it will happen now. They beckoned me to come up to the front, and I recited some words with the pastor. When it was over, everyone in the church came up to me saying, "Peace be unto you" then embraced me. I did respect the brotherly love that they displayed; however, I just didn't feel the spirit had hit me at all.

I always felt something wasn't being said in every church that I had ever attended, like something was taken out of its doctrine and deliberately kept from us. I later learned that the stories of the Bible were all allegorical.

As soon as the workday was complete, I shot down to Harlem Hospital to hang with my two girls. On my arrival, Helen had my daughter in her arms and quickly passed her to me. Ahh, it felt really good to hold her in my arms and give her so many kisses. Indeed, I love that little girl.

This may sound kind of crazy to you since I had just left a

church, but we ended up giving her an Islamic name. You see, the Muslims were always in the streets of New York talking to the people about Allah, which is the name of G.O.D in the Islamic faith. I would sometimes stop and speak with some of the brothers. Even before I went to Florida, I would purchase some reading materials from some of them.

In those days, you had two different types of Muslims that were out propagating the religion of Islam. They were the Nation of Islam, well groomed and wearing bowties. The other group was known then as The Ansarullah "Helpers of Allah" Community, recognizable by their long white garb. There are many other sects in this faith, but, in those days, I never noticed any of them in the hood.

I always believed in G.O.D, even if I was doing things which could be seen as ungodly, so we named our daughter after the name of the G.O.D of the Muslims. Since they call their G.O.D Allah, I added "ia" to it and came up with Allahia, pronounced Ah-lay-a. This wasn't an official Islamic name, although today I interpret it as Allah in All.

So Helen and Allahia had to stay in the hospital for two to three days and my parents and I picked them up and brought them home. I was so proud to be a father that I would sometimes strap her in one of those baby harnesses and walk with her on my chest to my housing projects across town on Amsterdam, to show her off to my people.

The room in which we stayed wasn't cutting it anymore; we needed a bigger place. Helen's stepbrother Will and his girl had a nice studio apartment in Mount Vernon, NY, that they would be leaving soon. They put a good word in for us with the landlord, so maybe we could move in once they left, and that's what we did.

Our landlords were a nice black couple with two children. They owned a two-family house with an attic at the top, which we rented. It had a big bedroom and an even bigger kitchen area that could be used as a room. We could only take showers in the bathroom. What I really liked about it, was the neighborhood, it was nice, quiet, and in the cut.

A few days later, it was Thanksgiving of 1990; we were getting ready to head over to my sister and her husband's house in Co-op City in the Bronx. Helen was holding Allahia in her arms and suddenly threw my two-and-a-half month old daughter in the air to her right. I dove on the bed to catch her from bouncing off the bed and hitting the floor. Once my baby was secure in my arms, I looked over at Helen to curse her out but noticed that she was lying on the bed shaking. I then rushed Allahia to her bassinet and placed her in it, then ran over to Helen because she was having a seizure.

She used to tell me stories about her having these episodes, but, out of all the years I'd known her, this was the first I'd witnessed for myself. I remember her telling me that, if it ever happened, to roll her on her side, to keep her from choking or gagging to death on her own saliva and that's just what I did. Her eyes had rolled up into her head and her arms were all twisted up and stiff. So I just held her there on the bed on her side until she came through. Once she did, I was still shaken up a bit.

"Are you okay?"

With a blank look on her face, Helen asked, "Where am I?"

Considering she had never enlightened me on the possibility that she may also experience amnesia, her not knowing where she was kind of pissed me off.

"Stop fucking playing Helen!" You had a seizure and threw Allahia in the air."

Her reply upset me even more.

"Who's Allahia?"

"Who's Allahia?"

"That's your fucking daughter!" I lashed out.

Her eyes looked disorientated as if to ask, "What are you talking about?"

"Stop fucking playing! This shit isn't funny." I then asked, "Do you know who I am?"

When she looked into my face, her expression changed from confused to understanding.

"You're Howard."

It struck me that she wasn't playing. This made me extremely nervous. Thank G.O.D moments later she came back to her senses. I recounted to her all that had just happened.

"Yeah, whenever that happens I was told that I lose my memory. The doctors say it's normal."

Normal? I then felt sorry that she had that condition and even worse that I thought she was playing with me. That was one hell of an experience, witnessing the one you love go through. That was the first time however, it wasn't the last.

I'll Smile Tomorrow

> I keep thinking how young
> Can you die from old age?

-**Drake**

I'll Smile Tomorrow

Lesson 15

Don't look back. Something might be gaining on you."
Leroy Robert "Satchel" Paige

My only complaint with the area in which we stayed was the distance it was from the train. We had to walk seven long-ass blocks: four in Mount Vernon to 1st Street. 1st Street turned into White Plains Road of the Bronx, where we would need to walk three more blocks to the #2 train. We would have to do the same when going back home.

One day I saw my boy Andy, who I knew from high school standing outside of this little Chinese spot in route home. Remember, he was my home-boy in high school that would bang the beats for me while I displayed my lyrical skills to the onlookers. Wherever and whenever I saw him, we'd talk for a while. He would always tell me to come out and hang with him when I got a chance.

"No doubt, dog I will." But I would always keep it moving. Not that I didn't want to, because I considered him a good friend of mine, but, after work, I would just want to get home to my family. Furthermore, hanging out in the streets had begun to become old. Why look back?

After a few weeks to a month, I would end up standing on the block a little longer sometimes, just talking with my dude. He started to introduce me to his boys here and there who were from the same area of 241st in the Bronx. Now I'm not one to be trying to make a bunch of male friends. My squad that I grew up with and loved dearly was in Harlem; I didn't need any more friends. However, Andy, being my dude for years, I started dropping by more often. His team showed me much love.

There were a couple of fellas in his crew, Curry and Ray, who I had also known from high school. Their boy Rich didn't attend my school, but he would often come, though, and hang with us afterwards. The rest were Joe "Flip," Cujo, his brother Al, Justice, and his brother Rick, Skeeta, Tee, and the homie Joe Grime. Like I said, I couldn't hang out a lot because I did have to work five days a week. Then, one day, what started out as a rumor at the job became a reality: the phone company didn't need as many escorts watching their employees' backs anymore. Eventually, the security company I worked for lost that contract, which abruptly left me unemployed.

Being unemployed gave me a lot of free time to hang with my second team, who, at the time, called themselves the Hard Pack. It wasn't a gang, just a group of guys hanging on the corner who would hold each other down if need be.

Flip had a nice small studio apartment in a house that his mom owned. During this time, Flip's place was the hangout where we would go to burn trees and listen to music on his monster stereo system. Out of the whole team, Flip had become my partner; I don't know why, it just happened that way. One thing we had in common was we both shared a love for cooking. Yeah, Flip could definitely burn.

I think my love for cooking came from watching my pops as he prepared meals in the kitchen. My moms cooked as well, but pops really loved to cook and it showed. I really enjoy cooking Italian, Caribbean and soul food dishes.

I did all the cooking in my house. When most guys come home from work, they would be upset if their dinner wasn't cooked. Me, I would be disappointed if I came home and dinner was cooked. It wasn't that Helen couldn't cook; I just preferred to come home and do it myself. All she had to do was have the meat defrosted.

Flip was also laid off from his job, and he informed me where to go to get unemployment, so I applied and received unemployment. Though Helen had a job in a supermarket in Yonkers, my unemployment checks would help out a lot.

Flip and I had a plan to go to cooking school together. He knew of a place in midtown called NY Food and Hotel Management. Although Flip changed his mind at the last minute, that didn't stop me. I went to that school Monday through Friday for six months. It was very exciting. Mondays, we would have a theory class, Tuesdays were cooking for catering, Wednesdays were pastry and Thursdays were creating menus and cooking dishes. On Fridays, the teachers would break the class into two groups, and every other week, one group would cook for the whole school. So we would have to cook for the hotel section of the school, all the teachers and staff members, plus the other half of the future chefs. Everyone in the school enjoyed great meals with all the trimmings, at a low cost of something like $3.25 per person.

While I was going to school, Flip hit the block with those cracks and wasn't trying to do the school thing anymore. I wished he had come with me. All was going well for me at school until they gave us a two-week vacation. I used to come through the block, and Flip would be sitting on a crate fresh from head to toe.

"Man, you getting all this money, I'm gonna have to come

out here and get a piece of this action." I jokingly said to him one afternoon I was coming home from class.

He removed his sunglasses from his face and looked up at me.

"Come on dog, pick up some shit and get money."

Now I didn't expect him to say what he said, '

Most dealers wouldn't want you to get any of their money. Now I know I said he was getting money even though I knew the block wasn't popping like that. Being from Harlem, I had seen blocks that were popping where dudes were really seeing money, so, when Flip said what he said, I respected it. I then took a little money and hit Broadway the next day to pick up like seven grams of coke to start with.

When I got back home with the shit, the coke was still wet, which meant it would be hard to get it off. So, that next day, I started to go downtown to get my money back. As I was walking to the train, I saw Flip. I told him what my intentions were.

"They ain't gonna give you shit back and then you gonna have to kill someone. So what I'll do is give you ten dimes, and once you finish and re-up, you just give me my ten back."

No one had ever offered me such a thing. First, he told me to come on the block, and on top of that, he gave me the money to get on so I wouldn't get myself into any unnecessary trouble. I took him up on his offer, paid him back like we agreed, and it was on. To take it a step further, he introduced me to all his customers.

"If you don't see me, you see my boy right here." He pointed in my direction. "This is Smallz. He'll take care of you."

If that wasn't enough, when a customer came for five or more dimes, he would let me get a part of that deal. So he really became my partner at that point. Reggie and Mobes would always be my main dudes, but Reg was locked up and Mobes was due home soon from his rehab treatment. Flip was up there with them as a true homie. Now I don't want to come across like my whole crew from Harlem were out of the picture, but they weren't running the streets as much in those days.

The short vacation the school gave us came to an end, so that's where I would be during the hours from nine to five. As soon as school was over, I hit the block, trying to make back all the money I once spent using cocaine myself, by exploiting the addictions of others. You see, being a user before, I felt like I knew all of their weaknesses and exploited that. Yeah, I swooped in like some type of vulture.

There was so much money in the area, even though we weren't seeing much of it. The problem was the block of 241st and White Plains Road had been established for many years on the drug tip, and we were a block up on Penfield. Since most of the heads were creatures of habits, they kept going to where they knew best. I knew we were gonna have to change that in order to see some real money. On the other hand, I didn't put too much thought into that because I really had plans to finish school and start a career in the culinary arts.

All was well at the home. Helen didn't mind me hustling, though she didn't like the fact of not seeing me as much anymore. Helen had lost her job at the Key Food Supermarket because the boss was trying to get into her pants. Or she might have lost her job after I threatened to kill him right there in the store if he didn't apologize to her.

After the Key Food gig, Helen started working for my sister, babysitting my niece Amani. When she left my sister's house, she would take a cab home. On her way home, she would make a stop on the strip and I would give her whatever money I made to take back to the house with her.

One day, Helen didn't show up for her pick up. When I got home that night, I noticed all my shit was packed in bags. I turned the lights on to see if my eyes were playing tricks on me. Yes. All my belongings were packed in bags. She was lying in the bed acting like she was sleep.

"Helen, why is my shit packed?"

She turned over and said, "Turn the light off and get the fuck out."

I was in shock as I stared at her. "What did I do?"

She jumped up and flipped the light switch off. She lay back down and said again, "Get out!"

I hit the switch again, and she jumped up once more, but, this time, she grabbed a Heineken bottle which was sitting on the floor next to the bed. She smashed the light bulb with it. Glass flew everywhere.

In the dark, she shouted, "Go stay with that bitch I seen all up in your fucking face, when I came through earlier to pick up the money."

Before I could ask her what the fuck she was talking about, I found myself defending myself from her oh-so-familiar attack. As usual, I subdued her until she was calm. Once I released her, she walked right out of the apartment. I didn't give chase. I went over to the crib where my daughter lay in the next room; thank the most high, she was sound asleep.

I did have an idea what she was angry about. There were some

Spanish girls from the area who hung on the block with us. The thing that got me was that Helen would always see them out there and never felt a way about it. Secondly, I knew I wasn't in any of their faces like she claimed. Nonetheless, there was this one Spanish mommy named Eve who came out there to hang with me sometimes. Maybe that's who Helen was speaking about. Yet I don't remember her being in my face either. Now Eve was one sexy mothafucka, so I could see why Helen would get a little jealous about her, and maybe, she had every reason to be.

Helen came walking back in the door about twenty minutes later. She was calm now, and I was able to speak with her. She told me she went to the phone booth up the block to call the police to come put me out of the house, but they wouldn't come because I lived there also, with our child. As she tells me this story, I couldn't help but think to myself, did this fool really call the police on me again, after that incident in Florida, almost two years ago? I dismissed the thought, and the two of us proceeded to clean the room of all the broken glass.

Not long after, Helen decided to join the church her stepbrother attended. I had no problem with that, except the women in the church were telling Helen it was a sin to live with me out of wedlock. After a while, they had brainwashed her to leave me, telling her that, as soon as they got a room ready for her in one of their homes, she was welcome to stay there with her baby. She was also advised to stop having sex with me completely.

Now, I really didn't want to stop her from leaving if she thought this was her spiritual calling because I believed things like that do happen. The tough part was not having sex and still lying in the same bed. Considering that I was used to sexing every night, after a couple of days of this, I spoke to Flip about my situation at home. His advice to me was to just hold out until she came to her senses.

That next day, I ran into my old flame Nicole, the girl who briefly lived with me when I left my parents' home. We talked briefly and made arrangements to meet at a hotel on 233rd and Webster the next day. Again, I looked at it as destiny or something because just like the last time I broke up with Helen, Nicole popped up and here she was again, as Helen was about to leave me to be down with some crazy church ladies. I don't mean to disrespect them, yet sometimes they would hold meetings at our studio apartment, and I would hear the foolishness they would speak about.

One day, one of them said to me, "Please don't think we are taking your daughter away from you. You will be able to see her any time, but Helen wants to bring her child up with her, in the church."

She also spoke about how she could introduce me to some of the brothers to help me. What I gathered from that was, "If these brothers are as crazy as you all, please, keep them away from me."

This may have been for Helen, but it wasn't for me. Those church members would be running around the streets harassing people who didn't want to be bothered. I never thought that was a wise way to propagate your religion. You can lead a horse to water but you can't make him drink.

I wasn't interested in her offer and just started to see more of Nicole. I didn't see it as cheating, since Helen would be gone once her room was ready. However, I kept a very low profile with Nicole whenever we would go out to eat. I would choose a seat somewhere in the cut, so no one who knew me would notice me. Nicole hated that I was so discrete, but, until Helen really walked out of the door, it had to be that way. I thought it was funny on the account that Nicole had a man, and she couldn't care less if anyone saw us.

I don't want to come across like I wanted Helen to leave because that was the furthest from the truth. It was just that Helen believed in something dealing with her own personal salvation and I didn't, and in order for her to pursue it she couldn't be with me. I couldn't get in the way of that; besides if the shoe had been on the other foot, I would have done the same.

One night, while we were lying in the bed, Helen rolled over and started kissing me very passionately, and that may have been the last I heard about her leaving me. I really don't recall how Nicole and I stopped seeing each other, but we did with no hard feelings. It was exactly two and a half months later; when we met again, I was going into the check-cashing place on 241st Street and White Plains Road.

Nicole looked into my eyes. "I think I'm pregnant."

Without skipping a beat I said, "It's Sam's right?" Sam was her boyfriend.

She chuckled. "Yeah, let's blame it on him right?" She displayed no attitude. We engaged in idle conversation, said our goodbyes, and kept it moving.

I saw Nicole again a few months later on the same block sitting in the passenger side of a sky-blue Acura. As I spoke to her at the window, I noticed she looked a little fat in the face. I asked her to step out of the car to give me a hug. I really didn't want a hug; I just wanted to see if she looked pregnant or not. She refused to get out of the car no matter how much I asked, yet she was still as cool with me as she'd always been. Her girlfriend came out of the store, we said our goodbyes again and they left. That would be the last I'd hear from Nicole for years.

It was a week later when Helen and I got into an argument about who knows what. What I do remember is she took a tuna fish can and threw it at my head as hard as she could. I moved out of the way just in time, and it slammed against the door. Thinking she tried to bust my head wide open really pissed me off, and we started fighting. I punched her on the top of her head. I immediately felt bad for hitting her and went back to my holding-her-down routine. That was the last physical fight we ever had, but we did argue here and there.

I want you to know that Helen and I loved each other a lot. Even after a big disagreement, we never held grudges; we would go right back to being best friends. Yes, it was weird like that, but I knew I wanted to be with Helen for the rest of my life. That being said, I'd been saving some money which I took to a jeweler to pay for an engagement ring for Helen. That following weekend at my parents' house I got on one knee, pulled out a little box and opened it.

"Helen I've known you for quite some time now and I have developed strong feelings for you. We have been through so much together and we still manage to be together. Helen I want to spend the rest of 'my life with you; so will you please take this ring and become my wife?"

Helen looks at me with tears in her eyes and a smile on her face reaches out and hugs me, as she whispers in my left ear with a trimmer in her voice answers.

"Yes Howard I will, yes, I will."

I know that girl loved me because I had a very bad case of

eczema. The first time I noticed the rash developing, I was staying with Gee's family in Florida. It started at the middle of my arm on the other side of my elbow and eventually spread all over my body. It looked like I was some type of reptile or something. I was so stressed I lost weight and started feeling very insecure. Helen never cared how I looked. She'd just help me put moisturizer over my entire body while assuring me, "It'll be okay."

There was one medicine that I needed to help with my skin condition which cost $75 for a tube of cream. After a while, I figured I'd go to public assistance and see if I could get some type of help with paying for the medicine. You may ask why I didn't just continue paying for the medicines myself. Sure, I could afford it, but, on the other hand, I figured why not allow this government to lend me a hand? This would be a crumb of the forty acres and the mule they promised my ancestors.

When I went to the human resources office, they wanted me to work in order to get my assistance. So the next thing I was made to do was go to the health department for a checkup. That was to see what type of work I was capable of doing, if any at all. While I was at the clinic, they found that my blood pressure was extremely high. If memory serves me correctly, it was something like 200 over 100, so they didn't put me to work until they got the results of my blood work. It may have been five days later when I returned for my next appointment and learned that my kidneys appeared to be failing due to my hypertension.

I was given a prescription for some blood pressure medicine, but the truth was that I was in complete denial about my health issues. I looked at that doctor like he was sick, trying to tell me that I was the one sick. Man, I felt like a million bucks. I mean, for real, I was working out and looked good. In my opinion, that doctor needed a fucking doctor. I didn't know a person could feel and look great and still be suffering from high blood pressure. No wonder they call it the silent killer.

At this time, we got word that we were having our second child. It became apparent that I had to really get some money. I had come up with a money plan, but I was going to need Flip to be down with it. The problem was that the police had snatched him up and he had to go up north to do a bid. During the same period, I had finished culinary school, and this crack head I used to supply had gotten me a job with a catering company downtown. They started me off with $11 per hour, and it was on. This didn't stop me from hustling, though; I still was on that block after work.

Since this was a catering gig, we would prepare food for huge parties for very rich white folks. If you were lucky enough to be asked by the chef to work at a party, he paid double your hourly rate, which was a beautiful thing. I had two months on the job when he asked me to tag along for a party. The location was some big mansion downtown across from Central Park. There were a bunch of celebrities at this party, or so I heard from the waitresses. A big screen blocked off the people in the kitchen, so the partygoers wouldn't see the help. And I couldn't see anyone.

After the party, we all went back to the job to return the equipment we had needed for the party. At some point, I was way in the back counting my money because I planned on going to re-up on some coke after work, so I was getting my money together for the transaction. The chef happened to come back to where I was.

"Hey McAdams, let's wrap it up because…," He looked down at all the money in my hand and looked back up at me. "We're getting out of here."

I was never to hear from that chef again. Well, that's not totally true. On Mondays, we had to call him to find out our schedule. Whenever I called, he would have the same answer.

"Listen Howard, because of the change of weather there are less parties, which means less work. I won't need you this week, but I have your number. So if anything pops up in the weeks to come, I will give you a call."

To this day, he hasn't called.

Now, I took what he said as the truth because I'd always known that, when the seasons changed, work got slow. However, his statement coming right after he saw that money in my hand seemed a bit coincidental. Rob, the guy who had hooked me up with that job, did inform me that the chef had let other people go. On the other hand, the chef kept him, which wasn't hard to believe because Rob might have even been a better cook than the chef.

Rob had called me to work with him on another occasion for a party at Columbia University on 110th Street in Harlem. It was a good gig, and afterwards, we got paid in cash, so I was a happy camper. What did trouble me was Rob's homeboy met us after work, and all they could think about was smoking crack. They wanted me to go here and there with them, and it was getting on my nerves. I didn't want to see him spend all his money on drugs because I felt Rob was a cool dude. They asked if I had anything at the crib they could buy, but all I had was that wet shit that I had copped a year ago. I ended up jumping in a cab to the Bronx and leaving them on 125th Street to deal with their addictions.

About two hours later, they called me telling me they were in front of my building and wanted to cop something. I grabbed some of that old shit and went downstairs with one of my pistols. I took the pistol because I knew they were high and what they were capable of. I thought to myself I wish they would act stupid. People thought crack heads were soft, but I knew different since I was once in that same boat. I came downstairs and pointed the gun right at the both of them.

"What do you want?"

Startled, they replied, "Give us five."

I did so, and they returned about three more times that night. They said they liked it in the powder form because they rolled it up in their weed. They were whoola smokers and that would be the best for them. I had never tried to sell it before on the grounds that most of my costumers wanted rocks. Rob ended up buying it all over a course of three days, so I actually never lost out with that very first package I copped.

Helen and I figured we were going to need a bigger apartment to raise two children. We went to a real estate office for their assistance in finding the apartment. The deal we had with the real estate company was that we would pay them one month's rent on any apartment they found for us. Knowing the landlord required one month's rent and a security deposit equal to one month's rent from potential tenants meant that we had to pay a pretty penny to move in.

One company found us a decent two-bedroom apartment. It was one of those railroad apartments. You know an apartment where each room is connected to each other, so if all the doors where open you can see straight though the entire apartment. What I liked most was the beautiful kitchen with nice counter space to prepare meals. In addition, there was a big indoor patio; Helen whispered in my ear, "I want this apartment." Once we left with the real estate agent, Helen and I made a U-turn and spoke to the landlord on our own behalf and got the apartment. Doing this, we cut out the middleman and saved $750 cash.

I had decided to take a little break from the block for a while. At least, I didn't go on the strip to hustle. I just wanted to hang back and watch for how I could take over the whole area. I wasn't really interested in running all the dealers off the block by force. I was interested in how I could corner the market. Like I said, there was a lot of money out there, and I wasn't really getting my share.

The days turned to weeks and the weeks to months, and I noticed how some of the other dealers would slowly start migrating to Penfield Avenue where I was. It was cool with me because they had a bunch of steady customers and that would bring more money to that area, so I kept that in mind, while I thought of my next move.

I'll Smile Tomorrow

" Got to get this cash right but last night,
Some fools ran in the spot,
Guns and flashlights.
You know I showed them how we pump in the fast life.
"You blast right?" "No doubt son, "That's right".
Truly I don't wanna live this way.
Boy am I in trouble on Judgment Day.
I need to take my ass to the Mosque and pray.
Why I'm playing with these streets when these streets don't play?
Well it's that part of me, which started me,
And made the God in me so hard to see.
I probably be this way for life —
No lovely wife, just my rusty knife. I know it ain't right.
I struggle and I fight. Yet seem to fall back to the streets at night.
I tried falling to my knees, but that ain't work.
I always smoke trees, but the trees don't work.
Made moves, got cheese and the cheese ain't work.
I'm back to Lord help me cause the devil —
He's at work.

-CHORUS-

(YEA) I'm in too deep. I can't sleep.
When the devil speaks, I get weak.
Will I ever escape these rough streets?
Or will I be young covered with white sheets.
~
One minute, I'm almost the courts defendant.
The next I'm, fed up with crime.
Seems like this goes back and forth sometime.
So when the night falls, I pray for Sun-Shine.
I'm sure there are a million others like I —
Ready to die, just don't know why.
Sometimes I hear chicks say "He's so shy".
Then other times, "Let's get away from this guy".
It seems like the devil done stole my soul.

I can't control. Yet I did try though.
And Yo I got two lil girls that need Popz.
But he flows in this tangible world and can't stop.
I believe we were born Righteous.
Then soon our enemy invites us.
To the evil which excites us.
While he strives to be just like us.
Some know the truth and some believe lies.
Some like me are at war with both sides.
A brotha wanna chill 'cause it will be wise.
But why do I always tote the 4-5?
-Chorus-
One doctor blamed this on my mom duke.
Neglected as a child, into this he grew.
But nah, she raised me the best way she knew.
You walk in my shoes, even you'll lose your screws.
Yet, there are a few who know my position.
But there either dead, thugged out, or in prison.
Seems like no one else wants to listen.
Until the heat's pulled, and it won't be in the kitchen.
G.O.D! Why does Satan invade my space?
Is it true he got beef with my race?
Please Lord can you put him in his place?
Or did you make two of me with one face?
Or is this the hell that you told me of?
It can't be the way that you show me love!
My niggas say, "There's no Lord above.
We alone on these streets. We will always thug!"
Though there's many signs that prove your there.
That voice in my mind goes and ask "But where?"
It's said that, you're alone on your throne.
Allah, us thug nigga's need ya home. ""

-Chorus-

The Author

Lesson 16

"The only real sin is to be ignorant of the universal, timeless principles of existence. Such ignorance is the root of all evil and all misguided behaviors."

Morihei Ueshiba

My boy Flip was still in jail and would be there for a year or so. But before he left, an O.G. from the neighborhood had come home from doing five years in prison. I had heard a lot about Shizzy Raw from the rest of the team. Yeah, the entire crew was happy their dog was back. Shizzy and I eventually became cool, and he became my partner. Shizzy came home trying to do the right thing, so he had jumped from job to job, in hopes of making a living.

I used to see Shizzy out on the block running taxis, trying to make ends meet while keeping out of trouble. Sometimes, he would come by and talk with me,

"Man homie, this shit is really tough out here. I'm telling you Smallz, I've been really busting my ass trying to make an honest living dog."

"Yeah Shizzy, I feel you fam but what's happening with the taxi thing?"

"Man that's some Bull-Shit. It's like thirty niggas on the block Smallz, each-of- them, scheming for customers." I look in his eyes nodding my head.

"Things will come around for you. It's like a law or something."

Now he's nodding his head up and down.

"Yeah you right Smallz, something's gotta give. By the look in his eyes, I could tell it was just a matter of time before Shizzy hit the streets again. Then it happened.

One day, he approached me about some dudes he knew that were getting money and would hit him with some weight of that cook up (rock cocaine) on consignment. He had run the idea by Andy, and Andy told him 'bout a spot out in Pennsylvania that he knew of, through a friend of his from Boston Road. So Andy, Shizzy, and Cujo went out there to see what was up on the cocaine tip.

Two days later Shizzy drove back to New York to re-up and snatched me up to go back with him. He would tell me how cheap homes were out in PA. That caught my attention. Listen, I would have loved to buy a home for my family. I went to the crib and explained the situation to Helen; she didn't want me to go. Knowing she would love the part of how cheap houses were out there, I explained that part of the story. Just as I thought, that got her attention as well.

"You can go, but, if you don't come back telling me that you got us a house, that's it, you can't go back again. Okay?"

I agreed to her terms because I thought they were fair, besides I was going on the word of the next person. I figured once I got out there, I'd see what's really good. I left the next day and was going to only be gone for three. Shizzy and I took this smoker chick named Kim we knew with us, so she could carry the coke. Shizzy got 300 grams from his connect and gave it to Kim, and right in front of us, she pulled her pants down and stuffed it all up in her twat. Then we hit the road to Pennsylvania.

I don't recall the details, but Andy fucked up some of Shizzy Raw's money, and the whole drive down, all Shizzy talked 'bout was how he was gonna fuck Andy up. Those who really knew me knew that I wasn't down with drama between team members, yet outsiders could always get it. So, the whole ride down I tried to convince Shizzy not to harm him, because if Andy did fuck up some paper, there had to be a reason. I was worried for Andy because Shizzy was the type of dude that had lost it on many occasions, and Andy wasn't cut from the same cloth.

Once we arrived at the house where Andy and Cujo were trapping out of, Shizzy did something that showed me just how dangerous he really was. He walked in the house and just pretended like everything was cool between him and Andy. I mean, there were no signs of him having a problem with Andy whatsoever; it was damn near scary.

Cujo, Andy, and Kim went back to New York, and Shizzy and I stayed. Once they were gone, Shizzy confided in me.

"Andy is lucky you're his dog 'cause no one else would have gave a fuck if I'd kicked his ass or not." I was glad on the strength of me he let it go, at least for now.

The owner of the house was a big, tall, dark-skinned older lady, who we called Big Momma. Big Momma was a really nice lady. She would let us sell drugs from out of her home for a small amount of the product. She also informed us about other dealers who would hang around, trying to sell their product, near the house. Shizzy had already known about two dudes he saw hanging around the house. Later on that night, we exchanged words with them, letting them know that they couldn't be out there cutting into our bread. Without any argument, they left the area. We didn't see them again, well, at least not around Big Momma's house.

We were pushing what would go for nicks in New York, for twenties out there in PA, and I loved those numbers. The problem was that the money wasn't coming in as fast as we would normally like it to; nonetheless, it was coming, slowly but surely. That's when Shizzy told me about this little housing project, which its inhabitants had happily named "The Jungle." According to Shizzy, that's where the real money was.

So, that next afternoon, we went to see what was popping in The Jungle. And, like Shizzy said, it was a little gold mine there. Every time you turned around, someone was asking, "Are you holding?"

Even though we were getting money and everything appeared to be good, I sometimes saw things as too good to be true, so I developed an eye for details. I watched the dudes who were watching us, as if to say, about us "I know these mothafuckas ain't out here getting money." I didn't bother telling Shizzy about this because I knew he would think I was overreacting, so I just kept up with the program with my eyes wide open.

Shizzy had really been gung ho ever since I had stated that I wanted to buy a house in PA for my family. He loved the idea because he knew if I was out there every day, business would run smoothly; in addition, I could keep my eyes on any workers we would bring out there. Now that we had made a couple of dollars that afternoon, we decided to go see if we could find a home for my family.

After looking at a couple of houses, I finally came across this inviting three-story home with four bedrooms and two full bathrooms. As I looked through the rooms all I could think of was how much Helen would love raising our children in that home. A white family was looking at the same house; Shizzy Raw and I left the house and shot straight to the real estate office. That's when we learned it just wasn't that easy to buy a home, 'because this real estate dude started talking about credit. I looked at him like "Nigga! Do you see this cash money here?"

He didn't care 'bout that shit; all he wanted to know was a simple thing: how good my credit was. My bubble was burst when we left his office. Later that night, we returned to The Jungle, and there was even more money out there, which cheered the both of us up. After being out there for just a few minutes, I noticed there were even more eyes looking at us as well as if to say, "Who the fuck do these niggas think they are?"

I spotted twenty to thirty guys walking north through the middle of the projects while we were walking across them headed east, to the other side. Our plan was to then walk south on the east side of the development; I discretely pointed toward the group of guys who are now walking east, in our direction.

"You know this is for us right?"

Shizzy looked at them. "Those niggas ain't thinking about us, come on."

Checking out the scene down the street where he wanted to walk, I knew that was not the wise thing to do. Shizzy didn't want to take any guns with us on that trip due to his quick temper. He had gone on about how it wasn't that type of area and how everything would be cool. I went along with it foolishly because I knew in my heart, it's always best to have the hammer and not need it, versus to not have one and need it. So I knew walking down that street was a bad idea.

There was an organization out there named March, and their movement was to get all of the New York drug dealers out of PA. The group's headquarters stood right across the street from where we were.

"Shizzy, let's stand right here 'cause I know for sure, these fellas are coming to have some words with us."

Up the block, from behind us, four more guys were walking and two more riding bikes towards us. By the time I pointed this out to Shizzy Raw, damn near thirty guys had surrounded us.

"Are ya out here hustling?"

Shizzy got a bit tongue-tied when he tried to answer him.

"Alright listen, you can't be getting any money out here."

Shizzy spoke up. "What are you talking about, we can't get any money?"

"Nah, this is us out here."

I was tired of dude's mouth. "So, what are you saying, you're controlling this entire housing development?"

"Yeah, from right here…" He pointed in the distance. "… To way up there, where you see that grey building."

Shizzy asked, "So you saying we can't eat at all?"

Another one of them chimed in. "Nah, you can go three blocks that way; all that is freelance."

We kept moving, and walking down the block. We talked about how we liked how they handled that; they weren't beefing at all. Even though we were extremely outnumbered, they just explained what was what and let us pass right though. The only thing was that we weren't completely finished running around their turf because we had this smoker hustling out there for us. That presented a problem since we didn't know where he was and thought he might have run off with our product.

Smoker dude was probably six feet four and weighed around 240 pounds and talked a bunch of gangster, while we walked to The Jungle, to set him loose to get money. He wasn't talking shit to us, but I knew how dudes like that operated. They liked to put it in the air hoping you would feel intimidated by them. That was not the case because, as we were walking back though those projects looking for him, we debated how we were gonna murder his punk ass if he didn't have our money.

At that very moment, we noticed the same thirty dudes walking back through the opposite way from when I first spotted them. In about forty seconds, we would be face-to-face once again. A few of them reached in their coats, like they 'bout to pull them thangs out.

"You see them reaching right?"

Shizzy replied with pure understanding, "Yeah, I see them."

At that very moment, my mind flashed back to when I was kissing my daughter, who was about a year and some change in age at the time. So I'm telling her I'd see her in a couple of days. She said and did something that seemed very strange at the time. All she did was say goodbye as she waved her hand. She did this three times. Yeah, that's something she did all the time, but the way she was waving and saying bye made it seem as if she knew she wasn't going to see me again.

There we were, in some Pennsylvania housing projects called The Jungle, with no guns. As we all met up, I looked in the first three faces closest to us, and as our eyes met, they all turned and looked the other way. At this point I thought to myself, these niggas are scared. But there were just too many of them to be certain.

As we passed each other, moving in opposite directions, one

of them jumped out from the group of guys and yelled, "What's up man?"

The voice wasn't aggressive at all. I looked, and it was one of those dudes that had tried to hustle around Big Momma's house. Now, he was actually speaking to Shizzy, and then he hollered to the rest of them saying, "Nah, they cool."

Taking a page out of my big homie's Richie Blacker's book, I put my hands in the pockets of my hooded black Carhart sweatshirt like I could be packing that thang. I heard the dude tell Shizzy that they were talking 'bout getting the Uzis to use on us. I wasn't really feeling this dude being cool because this would be the first time for it. I then stepped closer to stand right next to Shizzy, to really pay better attention to the words he spoke with his body language, more clearly.

Once I walked up to get closer, another one of them walked up also. I guess he was trying to tell me something, plus he had his hands in his coat pocket as well. I was a bit nervous but I didn't let them see it. Dude with his hands in his pocket just stood there watching me, as I positioned myself to watch them all believing this was the end of my journey called life. To my surprise there weren't any problems and Shizzy and I continued looking for the guy who was working for us. We didn't find him.

That next day, Big Momma started beefing, wanting more coke from us, and when we agreed, she wanted more. She pissed off the both of us because not only were we allowing her to get high, we also filled her fridge and cabinets up with food. Later that afternoon we decided to drive around PA and like Beanie Segal once said, "Pick out a quiet town and tie it down."

We found a couple of spots which looked like they had great

potential. Yet, not knowing much about the area, we figured we would come back and try to meet some females that stayed there to gain some inside knowledge. With this as our intentions, Shizzy and I went shopping for some new gear and kicks 'cause we didn't come down with any change of clothes. That's how it was when you grinding on the streets.

I was out there Friday, Saturday, and Sunday, and I was supposed to be going back to NY on Monday, so that's what I did. We really couldn't get our shit off like we thought in The Jungle, plus Big Momma got really greedy.

As a result of not getting a house, I knew Helen wouldn't want me to go back, so I decided that, once I finished the work that I had, I would just stop and play broke, so she would want me to go back. There were two reasons why I didn't follow through with what I had planned. First, Helen and I had made an agreement. Secondly, I knew I should keep my ass home with my family. All that running in and out of state shit was a single man's game, not for me.

Shizzy would come back and forth to the city asking me when I was coming back and explaining to me how he's getting money out there.

"I'll be there soon, real soon."

Shizzy's gear was always tight, and he owned three cars. I decided to hit the block again, not out of state but right there in the Bronx. My specialty would be nicks and dimes, and I would ride my bike and give out some samples to some of the customers. Whenever I saw another dealer trying to make a sale, I would give that customer a sample and ask them to try it before they tried theirs.

Rumor had it that some of the other dealers on the strip thought

I was wrong for giving out samples. How I saw it was, if I want to give my shit away, fuck you, why can't I? Then they were mad when they found out I had nicks, the word was I was fucking the game up because everybody else had dimes. I couldn't argue with that, but, fuck that, I had to see some paper; shit everyone else was.

I had hired a couple of workers, one I had met two years before when Helen came home with an attitude. She eventually told me that some light-skinned dude had grabbed her arm and began calling her out of her name, when she wouldn't holla back. I was sitting in the house with my daughter and Cee when she walked in. At first she didn't want to tell me her problem, but, once she did, I quickly grabbed the hammer, and then Cee and I ran out the door.

I didn't know which dude she was talking 'bout, but I was aware of the group of guys that hung on that block, so I stepped right to them. I counted five dudes and one chick out there; usually, there were a lot more, not that I cared. I would have preferred if they all were out there.

I was highly upset because these niggas saw Helen and me together all the time. I approached them, with Cee playing his position on my right, not saying a word.

They all copped a plea; it was almost pathetic. Months later, I met up with Freedom on the train we got to talking and he started working for me. Freedom had been one of the brothers out there that day, and since the guy who disrespected Helen was bright-skinned and Freedom was dark, he was cool.

I started to like Freedom a lot, because he had respect for me and for the game, plus he was about getting money, which made me money. During the '93 NBA playoffs, I was at the crib in front of the TV. I would just hit Free off with some work, and he would continually get my attention by yelling toward the window to me whenever he needed to re-up.

I also put a young gun named Chuck to work, and then Andy got on board. I didn't know why Andy wanted to work for me when he could just pick up some shit and work for himself. In any case, I gave them all the dimes and I would work the nicks, so I still was out there risking my freedom. This was my way to help feed those who wanted to eat and to see who I could trust once things started to pop off.

It had come to my attention that everyone on the strip was getting their coke from the same person, and that same person came to me with an offer I couldn't refuse.

But I did.

See, I figured that, if every dealer had the same shit, all I had to do was make sure mine was better, so I started to inquire about some of that good. (Good product for the fiends) People on the strip were starting to think I was getting some real money, so this was when I started to collect guns 'cause like the late, great B.I.G warned, "Mo money, mo problems."

Yeah, I had a team, but none of them was hustling, and I wasn't really certain they would really get dirty, if it came down to it. Plus, I hadn't known them that long to depend on them to step in to help protect me and my business. All things considered, bullets were more reliable.

Flip was soon to come home from prison, and I knew he was down to get this money again, and he was for certain a gunman. Shizzy Raw had ended up catching a body out in PA and couldn't attend this takeover because he was back in prison. If I hadn't followed Helen's wishes I'm certain I would have been incarcerated with him on a murder beef. My boy Reggie from Harlem had returned home a year earlier and gotten pinched for some bullshit charge which he was accused of doing before he did his first bid. As for Larry (Mobes), he came back on the scene clean, getting that money and then was locked up for some shit he didn't do. I know he didn't do it because my worker Chuck and I were standing right there with him, when police snatched him off the street. He had just told me that he took his work to the apartment and I should stash my own since we were shooting dice. Later I had to let Chuck go 'cause he wasn't making any money and kept asking for a raise.

I had found another worker named Carlito. Carlito was a forty-something, muscular Cuban dude. He was a good worker, and if he came up short, he always got it back to me on the next package. Also, if I was around and a Spanish person was to speak to him in Spanish and knew English, he would hip them.

"Listen, this is my homie Smallz; when you see him with me, you speak English."

And if it's someone he wasn't comfortable telling that to, he would allow that person to speak Spanish but he would respond in English in the conversation out of respect. I felt he was very loyal, and he was a true tough guy. I watched Carlito stab a few dudes right in front of me, plus he always had the pistol stashed in the bushes. Smokers would run up to me trying to divide and conquer.

"Carlito is running around telling everyone you and him are partners."

That didn't bother me at all. Man, he could have told them he was the boss. As long as he knew who to pass that paper to at the end of the day, we were cool. But when it came to my attention that Carlito was smoking that shit, I had to stop fucking with him as well.

Without any workers on deck, it seemed like my whole operation was falling apart. I was smoking over $50 dollars worth of weed a day and drinking, approximately eight 40oz of St. Ides (malt liquor) on a daily basis.

Being paranoid, wherever I went, I would almost always have a gun or two on me.

One day I was in my parents' home, and my pops offered to drive me back to my place. Pops was speeding through the streets.

Very reluctantly, I pleaded, "Pops, can you slow down a bit?"

I forget what he said, but he continued to speed.

More nervous as he drove, I spoke again. "Pops please slow down."

"Why?"

"Because I have a gun on me, and I don't want the police to stop you."

He quickly slowed down while giving me the third degree.

"Boy do you mean to tell me you brought a gun to my house."

Not knowing what to say, I shamefully put my head down and said nothing. Pops continued: "What in the world are you carrying guns for anyway? Have you lost your fucking mind?"

Still I sat their looking stupid, saying nothing. He concluded.

"I tell you this; there bet not be any accidents in that house with my grandchildren."

I felt like my days were numbered, even though I didn't have any direct beef on the streets. I would go to bed feeling that premonition and get out of bed in the morning feeling the same way. I knew I should be living better; however, I was ignorant to the true meaning of life which left me emotionally in too deep.

> But they don't know about
> The stress-filled day
> Baby on the way
> Mad bills to pay
> That's why you drink Tanqueray
> So you can reminisce and wish
> You wasn't living so devilish.

**-The Late, Great:
Cristopher "Biggie Smalls" Wallace**

Lesson 17

"The same thing that makes you cry makes you smile."
H. Keith McAdams
The Author

The date was April 27, 1993, and Helen and I figured we should head over to Mount Vernon Hospital. We had been given the ninth of that month as a due date for the delivery of our second child making Helen damn near twenty days overdue for delivery.

When we got to the hospital, the doctors performed some tests and decided to induce labor by sticking this funny-looking stick-like object inside of her in order to pierce the amniotic sac which would cause her water to break. Not long after, Helen was once again sweating, breathing, yelling, and pushing another beautiful baby girl out of her womb to join our family. And yes, once again I was right there, wiping the sweat from her forehead, instructing her in proper breathing, being yelled at, and with the doctor's help, informing her when to push.

Although I didn't cry as I did with the birth of our first child, I did cut the umbilical cord separating my second child from her mother. All I could do was smile uncontrollably. Since I named our first child, I allowed Helen to do the honors. This was not as easy a task for Helen, so, with the help of my homie Gee, they came up with the name Kiyanah Simone and, of course, McAdams. However, I call her Keyz.

###

It was maybe a month after Keyz's birth that Freedom had gotten locked up trying to pass some countrified money off for the real thing. So it was just Andy and me on the block. I then decided to start going out during the day to see how the money looked at that time. It was definitely bubbling on the strip in the mornings. The thing is, I didn't know the comings and goings of the strip during daylight hours and found myself being handcuffed by the police.

I was out there doing the hand-to-hand thing myself, which was my second mistake. My first was being in the game in the first place. Denise, a female customer of mine, approached me with this strange white guy with her. She asked me for four dimes, and the guy reached out to give me the forty dollars.

Feeling something wasn't right, I asked him, "Are you the police?"

Before he could answer, Denise said, "Trust me, Smallz; *he smokes more coke than you re-up with.*"

I thought to myself, He smokes more coke than you re-up with. Damn. Hearing her vouch for him in such a way gave me the confidence needed to make that sale. The two of them went on 'bout their business. About two minutes later, out of nowhere, someone rushed into the store I slung drugs in front of. I and a couple of other fellas were standing right there. That was the distraction because seconds later, we were all on the wall being searched by the police.

One of the officers pulled money out of my pocket and said to another officer, "We got it."

As he handcuffed me, I thought, you ain't got shit. I kept the drugs between my ass cheeks, and I knew I would get rid of that before they got me in any precinct. A van pulled up, and I was escorted onto it. That bitch Denise was sitting on the ground in the back also cuffed. Considering I didn't see the white boy she was with, I automatically realized that she had helped them set me up. Now some may feel if she is arrested as well wouldn't it be more likely that she had been set up as well. My mentality was since she spoke for him when I asked him, if he was the police. For the reason that she vouched for him in a way that would seem like she knew for a fact, that he wasn't the police, she helped them set me up.

A strange thing was that the police also arrested this Jamaican dude named Steve who lived in the building over the store I worked in front of. It was strange since he didn't even hustle. If anything, he might come and talk to us for a minute, and afterward he would keep it moving.

I couldn't dwell on why they were taking him with me because I knew my next move was to take this shit out of my ass and get rid of it. That's when the cop pushed me on the floor right next to Denise who was looking at me as if to say "sorry."

Once the police drove off, I immediately pulled the cracks out of my ass and stuffed them under the rug of the van. I could feel Denise struggling to reach it with her cuffed hands, I didn't care if she got it; as a matter of fact, I wanted her to. It was a great relief when I knew she had it in her possession. All of a sudden the van stopped, and the cop who was in the passenger seat got up and walked directly towards us. At that very moment, I heard Denise's handcuffs rattle and felt the bag I kept the drugs in hit me on my side. The cop then pulled us apart, picked up the little drug-filled bag, and walked away pointing at me.

"That shit ain't mine," I declared.

He paid me no mind, as he walked back to his seat, and we

proceeded to travel around the northeast Bronx packing that van with plenty of arrests. I couldn't believe the amount of people they stuffed in that van; we were literally on top of each other. Once they were finished their four-hour arresting spree, they took us to the 161st for booking. The next day, I saw the judge and learned that I was being charged with selling to an undercover narcotics officer and was being held on a $1,500 bail. I also learned that the guy Steve from the block was my co-defendant. To this day, I don't know why he was arrested with me.

I had no idea where I was going to get $1,500 for bail because I didn't have it. All I had was a house full of drugs. The money they found on my possession was taken for evidence. We were taken from the courtroom to the Bronx House. The Bronx House sat right there in the heart of the Bronx, and it had a terrible reputation. I sat in the cage; I, Steve, and a bunch of other unlucky souls were waiting to go upstairs with the rest of the population.

Before I could be sent upstairs, a corrections officer yelled my name and informed me I had posted bail. I walked through the cracked gate. Once the gate slammed back, Steve, my Jamaican homie, ran behind me. He seemed to be very distraught.

"Smallz, what about me man?"

He stared at me with his mouth wide open, face pressed between the gate and both hands wrapped around those cold bars. He looked so sad, and I didn't blame him. It had been a real nightmare for him. Yet I could tell he needed to hear me say something positive to him, so I did.

"I'll try to get you out too, don't worry." I said that to give him a ray of hope, despite the fact that I didn't even know how I made bail. While I was waiting to be released, Steve had also made bail and was sent to wait with me. As we waited, I made a comment about how fast it was to put you in jail but how long it took to release you. After hours of waiting, we jumped on the train to the Bronx. Once I hit the block, everyone was happy to see me.

"Yeah Smallz!" They surrounded me with hugs. Andy was also there. When he tried to hand me some money, I grew really nervous.

Yo, I'll pick that up later." I didn't take the money he gave me because I didn't know if he just made a sell to police or if it was marked money. So just getting out of lockup, I thought it would be best if I didn't touch any paper. As that was happening, I thought I saw my pops' car pass by and thought, Why am I standing on this fucking block? So I took my black ass home.

When I got home, I called my parents, and they informed me that my grandmother had bailed me out (Rest in Peace Grandma. You are truly missed). Once my pops got the money, he repaid her. I also told them a big lie about how I didn't do anything, and they believed it. Once I got off the phone, Helen started yapping.

"I told you we should go to Florida because Roger said he'll let you hustle for him and would pay you one hundred a day."

Months before my arrest, Helen had taken a trip to Florida to see her sister and her children. I didn't like the fact that she was taking my daughters on a long train ride, so I gave her a pistol to ride with, just in case. Once out there, I guess she and he got to talking, and he offered me a position on his team. She came back telling me her great idea.

"Hell no!"

She just wanted to be near her sister, so she couldn't see how much of a bad idea that was. That next day, when I saw Andy, he didn't have any money for me. He told me a sob story about his girl and said he'd work it off on the next package. I tried to avoid the block and let Andy do his thing out there but then he had another story about the money. The next day I decided to ride my bike around and watch him. There was no problem with my money, but he still had to make a few more sells to pay me back all that he owed. Police were all over the place back then, patrolling the block on horseback.

"Smallz, it's way too hot out here these days. I can't risk it right now."

I understood his concerns. Plus, the money he owed me may have been a little over two hundred dollars; on the other hand, for the amount I got it for, it probably came up to sixty-something dollars that I actually lost. The problem I had with Andy was that, when I was in police custody, he had gone to my apartment and picked up some work from Helen, and I often wondered if it was his intention to beat her for the money, thinking I wasn't returning home. Although it was a suspicion I could never prove, and one that may not be true, the thought left a bad taste in my mouth.

I was offered five years probation which meant I would have to stay out of trouble for five years. However, getting that probation was an obstacle in itself since my dude Steve didn't want to take the probation. You see, the judge wouldn't let me plead guilty to receive probation unless my co-defendant Steve pled guilty as well. The day we were to go to court to see the judge again, I pulled Steve to the side outside of the courtroom.

"Yo, Steve, you know you have to plead guilty today if you want to get probation?"

"Smallz I didn't do shit, so I'm not taking any plea."

Even though I understood his logic, I still needed him to cop that plea of guilty. "Listen Steve, I understand your reasons, but these white folk ain't trying to hear that shit. Do you wanna go to trial with this and lose or what? Do you really believe you will win?"

It truly wasn't my intention to try to scare him, but it was what it was. Steve pled guilty also and we both accepted five years on probation.

I tried to find a job, but nothing was happening, and my rent was due soon. Feeling trapped and not knowing what else to do, I took it back to the streets alone because I no longer had any workers.

Two weeks later, we had some small drama with a Puerto Rican smoker named Pablo from Mount Vernon. Actually, Calvin this little Puerto Rican dude that used to hang on the block with us every now and then had a problem with Pablo, and Calvin's big brother came and put a little Kung Fu move on him. So Pablo came back an hour later with his hand in his pocket calling me from a block away to come holla with him. At the time, I was coming out of the Chinese joint shoveling some shrimp fried rice into my mouth. I wasn't feeling the situation at all; besides, that guy might get high but he wasn't anybody's punk. Then I noticed his girl off to the side with a worried look on her face, which got my spidey senses tingling. I motioned to him to come to me as I walked off to where my crew was and where I had my pistol stashed in the bushes by the church. When I turned around, he wasn't in sight.

I wasn't feeling that dude at all, even though he had once been considered cool. About a year or so before the latest incident, he was on the block trying to sell me some herb. I was with Cee and Cujo when he showed up, so I was gonna let him make a couple of dollars since I was gonna pick some weed up anyway. Then dude gave me a bag of some weed shavings, which looked like straight up sawdust. In the most polite voice I could muster, I handed that bullshit back to him.

"Nah big man, I'm looking for some bud, so I'm gonna pass."

Now that was very respectable wasn't it? But this fucking guy, while standing on my block, where I got my money, had the balls to say some crap to the dude he was with.

"You see, shit like this is what makes me want to go get my gun."

The words that came out of his mouth 'caused me to black out. No, I didn't do anything to him; I just kindly pulled Cujo to the side.

"Go to your house and call me a cab. I gotta murder this fool"

Cujo jogged up the block to his house.

I told Cee, "Go home; I'm 'bout to kill this dude." Cee tried to talk me out of it except I wasn't trying to hear that shit. All I could think of was how could this dude come on my block and say some shit like that? So I walked up the block, and the cab was there waiting.

Me and Cujo jumped in and shot to my house. He waited in the cab as I grabbed this nice little .32 caliber, eleven shot automatic, put it in the pocket of my jet black army coat and ran back out the house and jumped in the cab. There were no words between Cujo and myself during the cab ride back to the block. We both understood what had to be done and that was to lay dude down. I also understood that this drug shit was a business, and it would be bad business to do it right where I got my money. So I had to wait for him to walk off the strip which he always did as he walked back to Mount Vernon where he stayed.

The cab pulled up, and I tipped for the ride. When we got

out, Pablo was not in plain sight, but Cee was there waiting. Still in battle mode, I began to scan the strip for him and then Pablo emerged, walking down the strip toward me. He was walking with his hand in his pocket.

While still looking at dude, Cujo coaxed, "Finger on the trigger, Smallz, finger on the trigger."

On the other hand, I had Cee telling me to calm down and chill. I wasn't trying to hear that shit Cee was talking. I put my hand in my pocket and my finger on the trigger, as Cujo warned. Now I was hoping he'd cross the street and go up Cujo's block, or up 242nd, toward Mount Vernon, but he did neither. All of a sudden, he opened the passenger side of a gray mini-van and jumped in. The guy he was with jumped in the driver's seat, and they sped off.

I tell this story because there was a little drama with Pablo the day before, so I was gonna bring a pistol since I knew I was going to be on the block alone that night because the squad was talking 'bout going to the movies. When I headed to the door, for some reason Helen stopped me.

"Do you have a gun on you?"

"No."

I couldn't believe it when she patted me down, found the piece, and took it from me. I wasn't gonna stand there arguing 'bout that shit. She just didn't want me running around with a gun and selling drugs while being on probation. I then walked out the door and, as I skipped down the steps, a whisper within me warned, "You're going to jail tonight."

And I will say, within a half an hour, I had police around me with their guns in my face, telling me not to move. My heart was racing so fast and all kinds of thoughts ran through my head; I suddenly knew this was the end of my rope. The cops gave me a quick pat down and I started to think, okay they are searching for guns. Thank G.O.D Helen stressed me not to carry tonight.

That's when this other plainclothes hopped out of a car.

"Hey Mr. McAdams, or should I call you Smallz?" He grinned. "Yeah, I heard a lot about you from my buddies in the Bronx. Didn't you just get popped not too long ago for drug sells?"

I said nothing; I was hoping that they would just let me walk off, without any handcuffs. However, it didn't work out that way. He told the other officers to search for drugs, which they did; not coming up with any, they still handcuffed me.

As they walked me to the unmarked car, I was beefing to them about my rights, knowing they couldn't care less about my rights. I knew if I went to the station, they would find the bunch of drugs stashed in the crack of my ass. Once we got to the car, that one officer who was speaking disassembled the back seat of the Jeep.

"You see, there is nothing back here, so, when you get out we will check again and if there is anything here, I will consider that as being yours."

Now that fucked my whole plan up because I most definitely was gonna kindly take that package out of the crack of my ass and stuff it in the back seat. So I figured, I better hold it in my hand and when I get out the car then figure out how to get rid of it. The car came to a stop. They let me out and then they made a very thorough search of the back seat. I then was thinking *I should just drop it on the ground in the street as they searched the Jeep, but I felt I wouldn't get away with it with police all around me.* That's when they rushed me through a little door, and once inside, I knew I had lost my chance to dispose of the rocks.

I eyed a garbage pail and tried to walk over to drop it into it, but, at that point, I heard a voice behind me.

"Open your hands."

My heart started beating, and my mind just became numb just thinking how busted I was, yet I still had to try something. I opened the hand that didn't have anything in it, and then another voice barked an order.

"No, the other hand!"

So I transferred the drugs to one hand to the other and opened that hand. Then with a chuckle in his voice, I heard one of them say:

"Okay, now open both hands."

And that was the end of my rope. I opened both hands, and it dropped to the ground, and all the police started laughing and pointing at me. At moments like that, you wish you could rewind time and not even get involved with the stupidity which you find yourself in at that moment.

> "Cause we were put here to be
> Much more then that
> But we couldn't see it because
> Our minds were trap
> But I came to breakaway the chains
> Take away the pains
> Remake the brains
> Reveal my name."
>
> **-Rakim**

Lesson 18

"When the ears of the student are ready, then come lips to fill them with wisdom."

Ancient Egyptian Proverb

After I was stripped searched, they ran some good cop/bad cop shit on me. One cop would start telling me how I was going down for an "X" amount of years while the other one would try to get me to give them someone who was holding weight (a large amount of coke), and in return, he would help me. Although I could give them that info, why would I? My situation was my problem, and no one else would have to deal with it but me. They were as stupid as they looked; I said nothing.

During the search, they found a WIC card in my wallet which was used to get formula for my baby daughter Kiyanah.

"We're going to your house to give your wife this card, and while we're there, I'm going to tear that fucking place apart; if there is something there, I will find it."

That's when the good cop said, "Yeah, buddy, if there is anything in the house, this will be the best time to tell us 'cause, if we find it later, we are locking your wife up. As for your children, they will be placed in foster homes."

I can't front, he definitely had my attention when he said that foster home shit about my children. All I could think about was how Helen grew up under those conditions; I couldn't allow that to happen to my babies. Even though the thought boggled my mind,

I just couldn't admit anything to them. Shit, these mothafuckas went to the police academy, so they were gonna have to figure this one out without my help. You see I wasn't as worried about them finding drugs (although there was plenty in the house) as much as I was worried about them finding the few firearms I had stashed throughout the apartment.

They left for my place, and I was shook the whole time they were gone. When they finally came back, I knew I was in the clear for the simple fact that they didn't walk through the doors with what I called my black pear in their hands. There was no concealing that mean bitch. (A firearm that is.) One officer says.

"Lucky for you no one answered the door; but I left the W.I.C card in the mailbox." I felt very relieved, although I knew I was surely going upstate anyways; as long as I didn't drag my family into this shit, I was cool.

Damn! Did you hear what I just said? As long as I didn't drag my family into this shit, I was cool. Could you believe that simple-minded shit? *Smallz, you've already dragged your family into this shit and now you'll drag them down even deeper, because, what the fuck can you do for them while you're sitting in a goddamn cage?*

They allowed me to make that one phone call; I chose to call Helen.

"Hello."

At that moment, I didn't know what to say. I remembered once hearing someone say hello means just what it sounds like—"Hell - low." The emotions that ran though me at that moment tortured me and made me feel so low; I was now dwelling in hell. I was very ashamed, but, after a long pause, I answered her.

"What's up?"

Now let's take a look at those two phrases: hello and what's up? If Hell is low, then what's up? I was always instructed that Heaven was up. It's funny how both terms could be used literally as a sincere greeting, yet allegorically means something totally different.

Helen heard in my voice that I was in trouble. I could hear in her voice that she was worried.

"What's wrong?"

"I'm locked up."

"You are?"

We both shared a long silence, and then I broke in.

"You know I'll be gone for at least three years, so I want you to go to Florida, to your sister's house and I'll see you when I get out."

"Howard, I am not leaving you. I'm not going anywhere."

I thought it would be best if she went back to Florida; however, it was like music to my ears to hear her say she wasn't leaving me. I told her to inform my parents about my situation. I also told her that I loved her and our children, and then hung up the phone. At this time, I was put into another cage, while those pigs watched the television debut of that pig program *NYPD Blue*. 'Till this day I can't watch that show.

I remember sitting there, watching through those bars, thinking *if I just would've left the house a half hour later, I wouldn't even be here, since they were gonna lock up anybody to get back to the station to watch this program while doing paperwork.*

Once the program was over, I was placed in another cell for the rest of the night and told by the supposedly good cop that I'd be going to my new home in Valhalla County Jail in the morning.

Sure enough, I was transferred that next morning and was housed in the new building. The new building was a closed-in area, with about forty cells. It had a day room area, a universal gym, an indoor basketball court, and showers. Our food was even sent to us in trays. They made it so there was no reason for us to leave the area. Soon as I walked through the doors I heard someone scream out:

"Smallz!"

I looked around to see who the fuck was calling my name, and I saw my dude Freedom. Freedom was a good worker, and I learned he was an all-around good guy. He was the only person I would deal with while in there. When my family sent me packages of cold cuts, cookies, and other goodies, I'd allow Free to help himself to whatever he wanted.

After sitting in that joint for a month, I was sent to court, where I was released on my own recognizance because the D.A. still hadn't tested the product I was arrested for to determine if it was definitely real cocaine or not.

Helen and my children were in the courtroom, and we all walked out so very happy. My youngest daughter Keyz was four months old, and I remember taking her into my arms, pacing back and forth hugging and kissing her, while waiting for the elevators doors to open. I knew it wasn't over; however, it was definitely good to know that I was able to go home for a minute.

My mom and sister felt they were going to throw the case out because they felt I wouldn't have been allowed to go home if they had anything on me. I tried to keep them focused on the fact that I would eventually have to go away, so they wouldn't be surprised the day it happened. However, my words seemed to fall on deaf ears.

I was given another court date, for two weeks later. When that day finally came, I remember Helen, our children, and I were planning to go to my court appearance together, but it so happened that the carpet guys were scheduled to install our carpet. It had slipped our minds until they knocked on the door, when we were all getting ready to head out the door.

"Plan B" was for Helen and Kiyanah to stay back with the carpet guys while Allahia and I go to the courthouse. I thought, *after court the two of us could go to Baskin Robbins for ice cream.*

Just before we were to leave the house, the phone rang. I answered. It was my mom.

"Are you ready to go?"

"Oh yeah, Allahia and I are walking out in one minute"

"Didn't you tell me the carpet guys are there?"

"Yeah they here, Helen and Kiyanah are staying here?

"You better not take that girl with you to no court; leave her right there with Helen. I'll come with you."

I didn't appreciate the fact that my mom was ruining my plans, but I did as she said. Allahia stayed home, and I met my moms at the bus stop going into Mount Vernon where I was due in court.

I met with the same lawyer that I had when the judge released me two weeks earlier and everything seemed to be okay. However, once we stepped into the courtroom, everything seemed to fall apart. The D.A. had evidence of what I really had on my possession that night in question. To make it worse, everything my lawyer would say on my behalf, the D.A. would object and the judge would rule in his favor. At one point I looked over at the D.A. and he looked back at me with this little devilish smirk on his face, as if to say, "It's over for you homeboy."

It got to the point where my lawyer would look at me. Her eyes were saying, "I don't know what else to do." She then asked me, "Is there anything you want me to say to the judge?"

Now that seemed to me like they all were in cahoots against me. How in the hell was she gonna ask me for help? I didn't have any law degrees. There was something that I asked her to say but I don't remember what. However, once she did, the D.A. quickly objected and won, and then he returned to his seat.

"Homeboy, give it up. Game over," was written all over his face. In actuality he was right game was over. Then it struck me, how can these people be in cahoots against me, when it was I who purchased the drugs, sold the drugs and ultimately, it was I who was caught and arrested with possession of the drug. I mean really; maybe I was in cahoots against myself.

I don't know what happened next but I do know that out of nowhere the court officer came up behind me and slapped cuffs on my wrist. I looked back at my mom who was sitting in the back of the courtroom weeping. I felt sorry that she had to see that, but it was a good call for her to tell me not to bring her granddaughter.

While I sat in the holding cage in the back of the courtroom, I thought, Damn! What if I did bring my daughter, how would they have dealt with that situation? I was sure they would have still taken me into custody but how would they had gone 'bout it? Would they have called some type of social worker to take her before I went into the courtroom, or would they have let her sit there and watch her father being led out of the courtroom in handcuffs first?

I was busy telling my family to get ready for the fact that I was one day going to have to do a bid for the decisions I'd made;

however, I wasn't prepared for them to take me back into custody on my first date back in court. I had known plenty of homies released on their own recognizance, but they had stayed out for much longer than two weeks. I guess it's true, "different strokes for different folks."

I was sent back to Valhalla and put back into the new jail. I really started getting into my working out and reading books. Keeping busy seemed to make the days shorter, but that was only a figment of my imagination.

My parents had found me a paid lawyer to help me get out of that situation. My case was moved from City Court to County, and at my next court date, I was charged with criminal sell of a controlled substance to an undercover police officer. The new charge was added on top of the two-month-old original charge of criminal possession of a controlled substance.

I thought it was crazy that they could arrest you for one thing and say something else so much later. My new lawyer came in, and I was so happy that he was there because he was from the city, and I figured he would show them some real law up here in White Plains. I came to find out that dude had no pull in that courtroom whatsoever, and it seemed like the judge wanted to rub this fact in his face. I ended up having to go back and forth to court on many different occasions on dry runs. That meant I kept going to court but most of the time was never sent upstairs to see the judge. We also called that tactic bullpen therapy.

You see, this was used to make you tired of having to go back and forth to court in hopes that you would just cop to a plea bargain. On the day you were scheduled for a court appearance, you were awakened early in the morning and sent to an area to be strip searched, shackled, and put on a bus for a long bumpy ride to the courthouse. Then you were unshackled and thrown into a cell with a bunch of other convicts awaiting their fate, which often wasn't good news.

While I was in the bullpen, so many emotions and negative vibrations came from every direction, and often violence broke out, and people got hurt. To top it off, a great majority of the humans in the cell never get to see the judge and were given another date to repeat this routine over again. And, don't forget that after leaving court, you were again shackled, and put back on the bus, for the long bumpy ride back to the prison. Once stripped searched, you were returned to population to deal with all the emotions brewing there.

My paid lawyer was an ex-cop, and I hoped that would be good because he knew all of their tricks. As you will see, I learned that, once a cop, always a cop. Once he learned that the judge didn't care about his city ass, he started trying to get me to cop a deal. I tried to explain to him that he should challenge them on the fact that my initial arrest was for possession and much later I was being charged with selling. It just started to feel to me like he was dragging his feet and really couldn't care less what happened to me.

One afternoon I was expecting a visit from him, and when I was notified by the CO that my visitor had arrived, my partner Mike gave me some strange counsel on what to say to my lawyer. Mike was what some called a little person, others called him a midget. I think he was taller than a midget; he was more like a dwarf. Nevertheless, he was a cool dude, who I would eventually call Brother. The advice Mike gave me was to tell my lawyer

"You couldn't get me out if the government pardoned me."

I looked down at him. "What the fuck are you talking 'bout Mike?"

"I once heard a guy tell his lawyer that on some mob movie. Just try it out."

Still thinking Mike was crazy, I went down to see my lawyer. We were given our own little room to hold our visit. He then started to say shit that started to piss me off, like asking me if I did sell drugs to the police. I answered him like I always did.

"No I never sold drugs to any police in Mount Vernon."

I couldn't understand why he kept asking me the same thing over and over again, with me telling him the same shit over and over again. He never asked that when my parents paid his retainer, yet now he wanted to throw in the towel and wanted to ask questions like he had some type of microphone in his fucking pocket or something.

"Did you make a sell to police?"

"No! Not in Mount Vernon, where they said that I did."

"But you did make a sell that night?"

"No, that was my first arrest in the Bronx, that night I didn't make a sell to the police."

"But you did sell to the police right?"

"No I didn't, not that night."

By now, I figured he did have some type of recording gadget on him, to play back to my moms, so she'd hear me say I did do the crime, so he could step down as my lawyer. That's when I thought about Mike's advice, although still thinking it was insane. I looked that paid lawyer in his eyes, as I rose from my chair.

"You couldn't get me off, if the government pardoned me."

I'll tell you what—I swear I hit the jackpot. Man, he jumped up out that chair and started yelling.

"What did you say? What did you just say?" At this time the meaning came to me. You see even if the government let me go home he probably screw that up because he was so incompetent.

I just looked at him with a baffled grin on my face. I was baffled because I didn't expect such a reaction from him. The grin was because I was very pleased, knowing I could get under his skin, at the level which I did. I didn't care; I knew he wasn't on my side, so screw him. I just couldn't wait to get back up to population to thank my boy Mike for the wonderful advice.

Before I was thrown in jail, I had taken a bit of an interest in Islam. I bring this up now because, before this incident with that insane lawyer, which happened in my seventh month of incarceration, I had attended an Islamic studies class in my second month of incarceration. I was in the dorm lying down on my bunk, when a voice came over the loud speaker announcing some type of Islamic studies class. A couple of days before this I was transferred from the new building, to H-block. I rushed downstairs to see what it was all about. H-block was nothing like the new building. Unlike the new building where everything you needed was in this one confined area, in H-block, everything was wide open. Here, our living quarters were dorms, we went and ate in a real mess hall, and rec was in a huge yard with the rest of the population

Once I walked into the class, I immediately felt the positive vibrations the brothers had, and within the next two months, I had taken my oath to Islam, which declared me Muslim. One of the main reasons I accepted Islam was for a plan that my boy Mike and I came up with a plan to escape from that jail.

There was a crack head that I used to supply on the streets

that had a way to get me into a garbage truck which would leave the jail. His only concern was that he didn't know where the truck went to dump its trash. He worked in the mess hall, and one of his job duties was to get all the trash onto this truck. My main concern was if it was one of those trucks that crushed its garbage, and he assured me that it wasn't. I told Mike about the plan, and we agreed to go for it.

Not too long afterwards, I was sitting in Jumah, Friday's Islamic service, when the inside Imam's lecture seemed to be about me. I watched him, and with an attentive ear, I listened while he stood at the podium speaking.

"Brothers, I'm sure there may be some of you in here today that feel like you just have to escape from this place. Yeah, you just might be scheming on a way how to because you may be facing five to ten years."

That was the amount of time I was looking at. I listened as he continued to speak.

"Hey, you may be married and even have two daughters out there you want to get home to." As you know, I left my two baby girls behind. He then went on to talk about how Allah is the best of planners and how we have to trust in him that all will be good no matter how things look today.

I sat there with tears in my eyes, knowing Allah was speaking to me through him on the grounds that every word that came out of his mouth was right on point, with my immediate situation. After services, I walked over to him and complimented the brother on his sermon. And he gave it all to Allah.

"Al Hamdullilah, meaning 'All praise due to Allah.'"

I then went back and informed Mike about my change of heart

in our escape plan. He didn't like that I was bailing out on him, but I had made up my mind not to go. I mean, really, what would I do once I got out? I would've had to completely cut my entire family off, plus I would need ample cash to make any moves. We wouldn't last three days out there, if that. The more I spoke to Mike, the more it sounded like all he wanted was to get home to sex his wife, and after that, it was whatever happened, happened.

Later on that night, when we all were supposed to be sleep, I found myself just lying in bed wide awake. Then I just happened to sit up, and in that position, I noticed Mike trying to quietly tiptoe away from his bed. When he noticed me, he quickly lay back down like nothing happened. I too lay back down wondering why he was trying to sneak out of the bed. After about five minutes, I popped my head back up and saw him pop his head up to look in my direction. Is this nigga trying to kill me?

I mean, the same night I told him I wasn't down with the escape plan, he's acting all sneaky in the wee hours of the morning. I was certain that he was still going through with it, and since I was the only one who knew the plan, he had to quiet me. I got up and grabbed my blade out of my stash and propped my pillow up so I could sit up and watch him all night. As I sat there and watched, he popped his head up again and I said to myself, if this fool comes over here, I will slash his fucking jugular.

But all he did was look over at me and put his head back down. In around five minutes, Mike simply stood up and walked toward my cubicle. My heart rate started to speed up 'cause all I could think was how to kill him before he killed me.

Once he reached my cubicle, he whispered, "Hey Jihad" (That was my Islamic attribute at the time meaning War. Some see it as a physical war, though it is more like a spiritual war, which one must fight within) "Can I get a cigarette?"

I gave him one, and he proceeded to take a seat at the foot of my bunk. I moved up to the head of the bunk, as we both sat there talking. I believe he was talking about how stressed he was, which I could surely relate to, but, at the time, I was busy watching his hands for any false moves.

Without any problem or signs of any problem, he got up and walked back to his cube with very little of his cigarette left. I sat there and watched him as he put it out and lay down, not to pop his head up again for the rest of that night. Yes, I kept my eye on that fool the entire time.

That next day, Mike too had come to grips with the reality of us not making it too long on those streets if we had escaped. All was well. We never spoke about that night of peek-a-boo again. Well, at least not right away.

So that is how I really began to take Islam seriously. Then, a month later, the outside Imam informed me that Helen had taken her Shahada, her oath also, out in his mosque in Mount Vernon. I wasn't really happy that Helen became Muslim because I really didn't think she was ready. In addition I was almost sure she was doing it for me and if that was the case I knew it was only a matter of time she would denounce the faith all together. Afterwards I thought, Hey, maybe it was a good thing, because Allah makes Muslims. She would visit me dressed in three-fourths of cloth and her head wrapped in a Hijab. I thought she looked good in her outfits.

Now back to me and this going to court shit. I was trying to get a bid that would allow me to go to shock camp, a boot camp for criminals. I wanted shock because it would enable me to get back to my family in six months. The problem was that I would have to be convicted to a sentence of three years or less to be capable to enter the program, and my lawyer was telling me that there was only an offer on the table for four and a half to nine years. He and the D.A. were talking, and he said that was as low as she would go. I glared at him like he had lost his fucking mind.

"I'm not copping to any four and a half to nine; they'll have to come lower than that."

I couldn't imagine being in prison for that amount of time. They had to be fucking crazy. Yes, I know I was out there hustling, and I also know I could have been doing something more productive to make ends meet. Yet, I also knew that there were bigger fish in the sea that supplied the little fish in the pond. I guess my question was why had the fishermen set all their nets in the ponds, knowing the root of the problem was out at sea? That squelched any talk of taking that so-called deal.

I was incarcerated a little over three months when a new brother came into my housing unit. He went by the attribute of Abdun Nur which, in Arabic, meant Servant of the Light. I was soon to learn that he was a very knowledgeable and spiritual being, for some reason, he took a liking to me and we became like true brothers. Our relationship was that of a master and a student. Since I'd been incarcerated, I had a couple of teachers who taught me Islam according to their own knowledge. Yet, when it came to Nur, the knowledge that was bestowed on him was very deep and mystical.

Nur didn't consider himself a Sunni nor a Shiite Muslim. Nur and the inside Imam knew each other from previous bids.

So Muhammad would tell me to be careful about what Nur was teaching because he was known to have some off-the-wall teachings. I didn't care what anyone said, because, many a day, Nur and I would be in the back at my cubicle, with Bibles open, Qur'ans open and various dictionaries in Greek, Hebrew, and Arabic in hopes of bringing me closer to what those scriptures were actually saying to us. He would often break things down, proving to me that most of these writings were allegorical, while the masses would take them literally. I would lay down for bed at night looking up at the ceiling, finding myself sort of frightened because of the things he would shed light on. Yet, I would rise in the morning in hopes of picking Nur's brain for more.

One afternoon, he was breaking down some things in the ancient book Coming Forth by Day, which some know it as the Egyptian Book of the dead. I remember looking around the dorm area, at the rest of the Muslims and non-Muslims, just doing whatever, like watching TV, playing cards, talking on the phone, etc.

"Why Me?" I assumed he would want me to explain myself further.

"Only the privileged know." Seeing that I was somewhat confused with the answer he gave, he continued. "Once I walked through the doors, I noticed how you would hang on to every word the other brothers would say in hopes to find the truth. That is what showed me that you had an attentive ear because of your thirst for knowledge."

There were many things which he would tell me not to speak to the others about because everyone wouldn't see the light. Then he would quote a passage in the Bible, John 1:5:"The light shines in the darkness and the darkness comprehended it not."

Nur began to teach me how to read and write Arabic. The one thing about the Arabic language was that every letter in the alphabet has a beginning form, a middle form and an ending form which could be confusing at first, but, within three days, I was able to read the Qur'an in Arabic. Nur was proud of me.

"Jihad, I have had a lot of students but you are by far my best."

Now I didn't know if I believed that. Yet, on the other hand, I did know that he was the first teacher I had who would hand me the tools, which if used properly, would allow me to begin to build and free my mind.

During Islamic classes, it was said that I would shine like a star. It was obvious that I had excelled in understanding. The learned in the class would speak highly of me.

"You, brother, are living proof that Allah makes Muslims."

Abdun Nur sat on the sideline, with his cool and calm mannerism, looking at me, nodding his head, while he stroked the hairs on his chin.

Later that week, the Imam was giving his first class on Arabic. No one knew I was being taught already by Nur, and at this point, he was beginning to get me a bit familiar with the language's grammar. This class was a very basic class, and I was ready to show the brothers what I had already learned. So Imam Muhammad went into the back, and within seconds, he returned with a chalkboard. He then began to write down some Arabic characters in their beginning form. Once he was done, he asked, as he pointed at the board with a point stick:

"Can any of you brothers tell me what letters of the Arabic alphabet these are?"

I waited to see if any of the other brothers would answer the question. Looking around the room, I noticed no hands went up. So I looked over at Nur and he never looked back at me, so then I raised my hand to answer the question. Imam Muhammad looked in my direction with a disturbed look on his face which said to me, "Don't tell me Nur got you in the Arabic already."

He pointed at the board to the first letter of the Arabic language. "So, what's this letter brother?"

Sitting back in my seat I looked at him standing there anticipating my answer. "That, brother, is the first letter of the Arabic alphabet and it is called Alif"

Still looking a bit surprised, he then asked for the answer to the next, which I answered correctly, as I did the next two. I then noticed him look over at Nur, so I did the same. Nur was just sitting there playing with the hairs on his chin nodding, with a slight grin of approval on his face. Then Imam Muhammad wrote down some words on the board and asked me to pronounce them, and I did so. He then scribbled his name on the board and asked me to tell him the word. You see that was a trick. What he did was kept the Shadda character out, which would tell me to double the letter it was over, which were the double letter m in Muhammad. I then pointed the mistake out to him. At that time, he just lowered the pointer, looked over at Nur, and said to him:

"I see you really have been working with the young brother."

Nur continued playing with his chin hair, nodding his head, grinning. After class, he threw his arm around my neck in a playful headlock.

"That's my boy. You got them all confused right now; they won't get any sleep tonight."

It was funny because the learned would tell me not to deal with Nur because of his mystical teachings, but now, they saw with their own eyes the things he had taught me that they didn't, and it was all in the guided lines of orthodox Islam. Yet, in secret he did have me studying teachings that they probably thought were off the wall but couldn't dispute with actual facts if they tried.

Muhammad was due to be released in two weeks, and Nur explained to me that the community would have to vote another brother into the seat of Imam. I immediately reacted with a big smile on my face and much hope in my heart:

"That should be you; I'm voting for you for sure."

The next words out of his mouth left me standing there, looking at him for the first time like he had really lost his mind. All I could muster as a response to his comment was, "What?"

Looking at me like I was the crazy one, Nur replied, "You heard me, I want you to be the next Imam."

We argued for a minute, before I walked away from him because he was talking crazy. Later on that night, we were sitting in my cubicle and the subject resurfaced.

"There is no way I could be Imam. I mean, first of all, I haven't even been Muslim more than seven months, so I'm not ready. Second there are other brothers in the community who are more qualified to lead."

The whole time Nur was looking at me, as he stroked the hairs on his chin, nodding and grinning at the same time, then he replied, "Maann! You are ready, plus this would be a great experience for you when these people send your ass up north. And what are you worried about? I'll be right there at your side. Trust me; you'll be a good Imam."

"If the brothers do vote me into that position, I would only accept if you agree with me right now that you will teach all of the advanced classes. I'll handle the less difficult classes, plus I'll speak during Jumah services."

He agreed.

The night before Muhammad was to go back to the free world, instead of class, we voted for an Imam who would succeed him.

Muhammad opened up by saying, "Asalaamu Alaykum. Brothers, as you all know, I will be released tomorrow morning, and you all will have to vote a new Imam in to lead this community. As you may also know, I can't participate in the voting. However, I will take this opportunity to say, I think the brother Jihad is someone you all should consider to lead this brotherhood."

Hearing him give his speech really surprised me. I can't begin to say how it made me feel. If I had a mirror in front of me, my face would have been bugged out. Another brother in the circle spoke.

"What about Abdul Nur?"

Nur quickly responded, "No brother, I believe the brother Jihad is the wisest choice as well, so I won't go against him."

Right after Nur said his peace, my brother Shu-ab spoke. He was someone I would have chosen if Nur hadn't been there.

"I agree, so don't vote for me either."

At that time, Muhammad walked out of the door, and when he returned, there was a new Imam to succeed him and that Imam was me. I made Abdun Nur my Niybu, which would be the equivalent to my vice president, and together we would build our community to a level that it never before reached.

As Imam, I had all the brothers give whatever they could afford such as food, soap, clothes, cosmetics, stamps, etc. to the charity box. This was done so that if any Muslim or non-Muslim came into the system and needed anything, we could help them get on their feet. Those who were not Muslim didn't have to replace what they had taken, but Muslims would have to replace all items back to the box, if they were capable. I also had fliers made, telling the other convicts that we were holding classes introducing Islam for all who were interested in learning more.

###

Meanwhile, back in the courtroom, my lawyer was telling me that he thought we should sever our attorney/client relationship. I told him no and that he had to stay and finish what he started. You see that dude had caught a little attitude and now wanted to leave me for dead, and run off with the money my family paid him to defend me. So when the judge spoke to us, my lawyer was buzzing that nonsense in my ear.

"You tell him that you wish to replace me as your attorney. You tell him, you tell him right now, tell him." He then blurted out to the judge:

"Your Honor, my client would like to address you."

He may think that he has just put me on the spot, but I actually did have something that I wished to address to the judge. So I just calmly cleared my throat. "Your Honor, I would like to be granted a court order to be able to leave the facility in order to receive a marriage license."

The judge granted me the court order, and I walked away shackled, leaving the lawyer standing there looking stupid. Well, maybe not as stupid as I looked, walking away shackled. Shortly after that court date, I had yet another court date after which I walked out of the courtroom having copped out to a five-to-ten prison term. That judge wasn't budging, and my lawyer gave up on me soon after he got paid. I returned to the jail, and Nur immediately pulled me to the side asking me what happened in court. The look in his eye led me to believe that he already knew the answer to that question. It amazed me sometimes when he seemed to know how I felt before I told him.

I told Nur how the judge offered me a five-to-ten and that I accepted it. During the following days, I walked around like I was lost. I wasn't making all my prayers, nor studying like I should. Nur would give me words of encouragement; nonetheless, I didn't want to hear that philosophical crap at that time. Not long after my sentencing, Nur went to court and came back moping, and when I asked him 'bout it, he replied:

"They gave me a five to goddamn ten."

Now this may sound crazy, but, when he told me his bad news, it instantly made me feel a bit better about my situation. Go figure.

On the other hand, I was extremely joyful that the judge had granted me permission to get married. Helen and I had spoken about getting married even before my incarceration and we figured why not now? At least when I got up north, I would be able to receive conjugal visits, her being my wife and all. So, on a set date we made that happen.

It was far from a fairytale wedding in a great big church. Our marriage was held inside the walls of a jail with CO's watching our every move. We managed to make the best of it. I had my brothers Nur and Mike there with me. Mike was now Muslim. Helen was with her friend Shrilly, and an outside Imam did the service. As you may have guessed, we weren't allowed to consummate our marriage. We weren't granted much time after the ceremony before we had to separate and go our own separate directions. Helen went back to the freedom outside of those confining walls and I went behind them back into population.

Back in population, I was fighting a small war. The former Imam, Muhammad, who I had replaced was rearrested and was back in H-block, and he wanted his title of Imam back. He paraded around like he was a righteous Muslim, so all the new brothers would think he was better qualified for the position and vote him in. That was something that I learned he had an infamous reputation for: going home then coming back to overthrow the current Imam.

Muhammad would pull me to the side and ask if he could address the community by giving a Friday lecture. I had no problem with it, but Nur would advise me not to allow it. Nur's reasoning was that Muhammad couldn't come back to jail and just expect to jump right back into the mix of things, 'cause apparently he needed to sit down and listen. Maybe he would learn something that might prevent him from going in and out of prison. It made sense, so I agreed not to allow him to address the community.

Muhammad then tried to get some of the brothers on his side, in hopes that he would be able to overthrow me, but I had the loyalty of the Islamic community; so that didn't work. Nur seemed to like the fact that Muhammad was coming for my position. Let him tell you, because it kept me on my toes and sharpened my skills.

Nur would encourage me daily. "This is a life lesson for you; things like this are happening every day. What doesn't kill you makes you stronger."

I had heard that term before, but hearing it come from Nur, in my present situation, seemed to open my mind to deeper depths. However, even though I still considered Nur my brother and teacher, he had begun to really get on my nerves. I felt he wasn't holding up his part of our agreement. He was supposed to teach the more advanced classes, but he had started abandoning those obligations.

Nur had become a barber at the jail and he would literally start cutting hair two minutes before the class he was supposed to teach. I would be pissed at him because I would subsequently need to have to go down there and instruct a class on topics that I had yet to fully inner-stand myself. (Understand being the first step, over-stand is the second and higher step and Inner-stand is the third step which happens within when all three become one.) By the end of the class, Nur would stroll in like all was good. He would do this all the time, and I would always tell him off about it. It even came to the point where I stopped speaking to him. I know that's a little extreme, but I didn't want the position as Imam in the first place, until he talked me into it and agreed to teach certain classes.

Once, when I was instructing a class on the Arabic language, the Brother Muhammad entered the class. He wasn't there two minutes before he started to challenge me in the language's grammar. Now he was much more advanced than I in Arabic and was asking me many questions in the language's grammar, for which I had not many answers. At one point, I noticed that he had a smirk on his face, which I took as he felt he was on his way to overthrowing me. That's when the door to the classroom opened, and Nur walked in. I don't know if Nur was dealing with telepathy, intuition, clairvoyance or what have you, but it took a mere second for him to figure out what Muhammad was up to. Nur took control of the class and dominated Muhammad in the Arabic, right before my eyes. Muhammad got up and left the class, knowing then, if he didn't already know, that he was no match for my Brother/Educator.

Today, I believe I know why Nur wouldn't teach some of the classes he said he would. I figure maybe he wanted to put me in situations of panic and fear, so that I could face those emotions and overcome them. He knew that I was able to teach those classes without him; the problem was that I needed to know that for myself. As I think back, I never had a problem until that day with Muhammad, and Nur was still there to hold me down when I needed him, just as he promised.

Although Muhammad didn't prevail in his quest to overthrow me, that would be the last day of my leadership as Imam and Nur's last day as my Naiybu. You see, that next morning we were told to pack our belongings on the grounds that we were being transferred to State Prison in the morning.

That night Nur and I were sitting in my cubicle, and I was telling him the story about Mike and me planning to escape and how, when I backed out, we spent that night watching each other. Soon after, I decided to get up and ask Mike about that night in question even though Nur suggested that I not bring it up again. Still, I proceeded to walk the couple of paces to where Mike who we now call Malik meaning King was seated studying the Holy Qur'an.

I asked him, "Mike, do you remember that night when the two of us were up to the wee hours of the morning watching each other?"

He informed me that he remembered that night well.

"Man, I thought you were gonna try to kill me that night

because I backed out of our plans to escape this place."

What Mike said next, I often find myself thinking about to this very day? Mike closed the book, placed it on his lap, and looked up at me with shame in his eyes.

"No Brother Imam! I was hoping to kill myself that night, but you kept watching me."

Allah works in mysterious ways.

> If I could buy one thing,
> I'd purchase time
> Go back before the birth of crime
> Abort it
> Cause it hurts my kind
> Life's a road test, learn the signs
> Cause most crash and burn
> In their prime.

-Brownsville Ka

Lesson 19

"I seem to have been only like a boy playing on the sea-shore, and diverting myself in now and then finding a smoother pebble or a prettier shell than ordinary, whilst the great ocean of truth lay all undiscovered before me."

Sir Isaac Newton

I was sent on a bus ride to a prison called Down State. I guess it was called that because it wasn't as far north as the other prisons; in fact, it was still in the County of Westchester. I was placed in what they called reception, which was where they gave us tests and evaluated us for what prison we would be going to from there.

My second day there, I saw my big brother Nur. We weren't allowed to greet each other, so, from afar; we greeted each other with the hand sign for peace. Though this sign of peace was given with both fingers together, symbolizing our bond in unity. Unity being the offspring of peace. As I walked away, I gave a look back, and he was still looking at me, though, this time, he had his right hand up to his face, pulling down the skin of his right eye, making it wider. That was something that he would always do, symbolizing that G.O.D would always see and be with me. I turned back around happy that I got to see my big brother once again, even though, the day before, I wasn't even speaking with him.

G.O.D is the best of planners.

Things were going well, excluding the fact that I didn't have any soap, deodorant, socks, or underwear. I was in dire need of a package from home. I had already asked my parents for those items, and they sent a package to me. The only thing it was shipped to another jail about eleven hours away from my home in the city.

I was being housed in Watertown, New York, and Watertown was also the name of the facility. That first day was kind of scary. Well, maybe scary is a bit extreme, but it was definitely unusual. They called for recreation, "rec," so I and this brother named Born walked together to the gym. In order to get to the gym in Watertown, you would have to walk through the yard. Now, as I traveled through, all I could see were hundreds of convicts, many dressed in army jackets, sweat suits and Timberland boots. To top it off, Born and I walked pass a rather large congregation of Puerto Ricans who called themselves The Latin Kings. They were all throwing up some type of hand signs as they greeted one another.

When I looked to my right, I noticed Born wasn't with me anymore; then, I noticed him at least thirty paces ahead of me. I remember thinking, *damn*.

I wasn't allowed to go to the gym that day because I didn't have any sneakers to wear. So I stayed in the yard and did my daily work out of pull-ups, pushups, and dips. Afterwards, I went back to the housing unit, got my clothes together to do laundry, and walked into the little laundry room. So far, everything was going well, except the part about the dryer. You see, when I walked back into the laundry room, I saw my clothes on top of the dryer still wet and some other douche-bag's shit was in its place. I figured at that very moment that someone was testing me, and I was determined not to fail. So I took whoever's clothes that were in the dryer out, placed them on top, and returned my still damp clothes to the machine. I then went back into the dorm area to lie on my bunk awaiting the conflict that was sure to come. After a few minutes of lying there, I noticed this brother who appeared to be somewhat agitated approaching my cube.

"Can I have a word with you?"

Maintaining eye contact, I hopped down off of my bunk "Yeah, what's up?"

Getting straight to the point he asked, "Did you take my shit out of the dryer?"

"Indeed so," was my reply as I sized him up, in case this conversation went to something more physical. "My shit was still wet, so I returned them to the dryer."

He seemed pissed when he declared, "Your shit was dry when I took them out."

"If that were the case, we wouldn't be having this conversation."

As he walked away, he nodded his head. "Okay. You're right, okay."

I felt a bit disturbed, not knowing if he had any hidden agendas that might come up later. After all, I was in prison. Looking at homeboy, you could tell he'd been locked up for a while, so I figured I had to go get me a sharp piece of something soon.

Earlier that day, I had met a Muslim brother from outta Buffalo, NY. I asked him if he could get me a banger. He asked me what I needed it for, so I briefly explained to him the situation. He then got all hyped, talking 'bout calling him into the bathroom and murdering him.

After I calmed him down, he gave me a nice sharpened piece of Plexiglas. It was a Friday, and in that particular jail, they had what they called late night, where you could basically stay up watching cable from Friday to Monday, as long as you got yourself out the door for work detail on Monday.

So, later that night, better yet morning, around 3 a.m., I called dude to the back of the dorm area, where it would be just the two of us. With that banger in my back pocket, I asked him:

"Do you still feel any particular way about that situation with the laundry earlier, because you walked away like you're still harboring some type of animosity towards me?"

"Are you still thinking about that? Man, I forgot all about that."

As he walked back to the front where everyone else was watching TV, I wasn't really satisfied that it was over; nonetheless, I let it ride because if it was really an issue, we could have handled it right then and there.

I only stayed in Watertown for a week, and then they sent me to a spot named Governor, in Governor, NY. Governor was a decent spot to do time, since that was all I had to do. Once settled at Governor, I figured I would drop a slip in the infirmary box to talk to a doctor about this kidney problem that I was told I may have. I figured why not let the state pay for fixing my condition? The doctor ran some tests and found that it was true that I might need treatment due to kidney failure. Hearing the doctor in the prison confirm what the doctors on the street had said fucked my head up. The infirmary doctor explained that the treatment I would have to receive was called dialysis.

To keep myself from going insane I enrolled in a trade school. I took up floor covering, which I liked a lot. It was in that class where I met a Dominican brother named Zook. Zook approached me when he noticed me writing a note in Arabic and asked me about it. In our conversation, it came to light that he, too, was a

Student of the Mysteries. It was then I remembered Nur telling me:

"If you are who I think you are, you will meet someone upstate who will add to your teachings."

It turned out that Zook was the man for the job. He took me much deeper into the wisdoms of the teachings. I would sometimes wonder if Nur even knew the things in which I was now dealing. I then would feel silly thinking such a thing, then dismissing it by telling myself of course, Nur knows this. He had just walked me through elementary. It was for me to allow Zook to take me through to the next level or degree.

He taught the same way I was taught by Nur—one-on-one. We would meet up during rec time and spin the yard, (walking around) building on this Divine Truth which, if used correctly, could and would destroy all negativity in the one who wishes to tap into it.

In my studies with Nur and Zook, it came to my attention that the people of Ancient Kemet or "Egypt" developed a very complex spiritual system, in which people all over the world would come to that beautiful civilization in Northeast Africa in order to learn from the Kings and Queens that inhabited the land. In fact, if one were to truly investigate ancient history, they would find that many of our religions today find their roots in this Ancient Egyptian Mystery Schools of the Nile Valley.

Although I still wore the hat of Islam, the average Muslim would probably disagree totally with my new-found knowledge. Yet, I can find a lot of these same teachings hidden between the lines of the Holy Qur'an as well as the Holy Bible. However, I have run into many Muslim brothers who do over-stand the teachings and see true Islam as a vehicle to obtaining that divine peace in oneself.

Many of the brothers didn't want to listen to anything that may challenge their faith. My point was tested one day while we were in congregation in the mosque. The Imam spoke about this book that was floating around the jail that challenged the Orthodox Sunni Muslim. He went on to say that he wanted the heads of anyone who was found in possession of that book.

I looked around the room at the faces of the brothers and noticed many different expressions. Some had looks of anger, some looked puzzled, and many seemed not to care one way or the other. As I write this, I sit here wondering how my face looked that day in the mosque when the Imam basically put a hit on the person who was found in possession of the book in question. Did I look angry, puzzled, or uncaring? Or did I look worried? Why worried? Maybe because the book of which he spoke was lying under my pillow, back at the housing unit. No need to be worried; I was respected at that facility for teaching Islam to the brothers, so I would be good regardless. Besides, no one ever found out about it.

The Islamic community at Governor was tight. The administration would let us have Islamic Festivals which allowed us to invite our families. We were allowed to cook all kind of good foods that we normally would only dream about. Don't get it twisted—we had to fund these events ourselves with the money we would receive from fragrant oils. We were allowed to purchase these oils from an outside merchant and sell to General Population. So the Islamic community had its own bank account. There was one festival when Helen and the girls came up to hang with me. I remember seeing Allahia and Kiyanah from afar, and I called out their names. I watched Allahia as she looked in every direction and then she spotted me. Man, she took off running down this small grassy hill in my direction with a big smile on her face with her baby sister running right behind her. Allahia then jumped into my arms and I switched her over to hold her in my right arm and after that bent down to catch Kiyanah in the other. Do you know, lil' Miss Thang stopped, looked at me, and ran straight back up the hill to her mom who was watching and smiling. Everybody laughed because it was too cute.

The reason why she ran back was probably because she had no idea who I was. Though I, too, wore a smile on my face, this truth entered my mind and under my breath all I could say was

DAMN!

At some point in the visit, Helen had to walk back to the lockers in the building with Kiyanah to grab some more diapers for her. So, in their absence, Allahia and I sat on one of those picnic benches and engaged in a very emotional conversation. My whole family had told her that I was in a hospital because of my kidney problem and would have to stay until I received one. So Allahia, who was almost five at the time, sat on my left and asked me:

"Daddy, can you get a little child's kidney?"

I looked down at her and said, "I don't think so, why?"

She then looked up at me, "Because I want to give you one of my kidneys, so you can feel better and come back home."

I reached out and gave her a hug, and we both shared in a nice little cry together. It was beautiful. Helen told me later on that night on the phone that Kiyanah had asked her:

"I see my daddy?"

And there I was, smiling again. Though this time I thought to myself YES!

###

Zook's time was getting short, so he was transferred to a different facility. There was no one else in that jail that I knew of who could help guide me in my spiritual travels. At first, I figured I was on my own. But according to scripture, "The body is the temple of the living G.O.D." So if G.O.D lives in the body, with true Inner-standing of this, how could I ever be alone?

I'll Smile Tomorrow

> How you gonna win,
> When you ain't right within?
> How you gonna win,
> When you ain't right within?
> How you gonna win,
> When you ain't right within?
> Uh uh come again.

-Lauryn Hill

Lesson 20

"There is no power greater than my-self. However, I do bear witness that this power is greater than me."

The Author, **H. Keith McAdams**

PRESENT DAY

It's July 3, 1995. The sun is high, clouds are few, and the skies are blue. Some may say it's a beautiful day. Normally, I would agree, but I'm currently incarcerated and have been for the past twenty-two months.

There is talk of some type of Fourth of July festival that the facility is allowing us to have in the yard. I hear they were really cool in the past. You see, we would get to eat many of the things we could only dream about under different circumstances, so why not participate?

I'm day dreaming about tomorrow, sitting in the day room with a few other prisoners watching Master P's video "Ice Cream Man" on B.E.T's *Rap City* when a brother named Church came busting in the door, all riled up, hollering: "Them boys out there about to kill each other."

###

As I sit here in this box, looking back at my life, I decide to concentrate on my present and that is to get out of this prison, inside of a prison because this could not be my future. Like the streets, when accused of a crime, you are entitled to your day in court. So I am entitled to a hearing with the superintendent or one of his deputies. I am also entitled to call witnesses at this hearing. Most dudes would call other convicts as witnesses; G.O.D knows I have a whole bunch of them who could honestly testify on my behalf, but I choose to take a slightly different approach. I have one person in mind that I would choose to testify for me, yet I understand that it could be a great risk. You see, I'm calling down that racist CO who was on duty the night of the riot. To tell the truth, the whole truth, and nothing but the truth, so help him G.O.D."

So, after two days in that hole, my gate cracks and two COs lead me into a room where one of the deputy superintendents is sitting eagerly awaiting my entrance. As I walk in, our eyes connect. Now I don't know what she sees in my eyes at that very moment, but what I see in hers I can only describe as freezing cold with, a bit of anger, and an obvious hint of revenge.

If she is trying to intimidate me, it is working; regardless, I decide to focus on the task at hand. It helps knowing that this is just the hearing in which I am to give a plea of guilty or not guilty and, if not guilty, name my witnesses.

She gets right to the matter at hand, turning on the tape recorder, which was lying on her desk in clear view. She then states her name:

"This is Deputy Superintendent Rachel Bad cocks, and I have an inmate Howard McAdams DIN# 93A5336 sitting before me." She then asks me to state my name and DIN# for the record, and I do as she asks.

Then she goes on to read my charges, and after each, she asks if I plead innocent or guilty. It goes something like this.

"Mr. McAdams, on the date in question, July 3, 1995, you were charged with inciting a riot. How do you plead?"

I sit there and tell the truth.

"Not guilty."

"Attempted assault on a New York State corrections officer."

Again, I reply, "Not guilty."

Still looking down, writing on the papers lying on her desk, she then asks, "Weapons?"

This was my third and final charge, and for the first time since I first walked into her office, she looks up at me with pure disgust. With only her eyes, she dares me, "Go ahead. Not guilty right? I'll teach you a lesson you'll never forget, asshole."

She is right. I look her in the eyes and proclaimed for the third time, "Not guilty."

Lowering her eyes back to scribbling on the papers on her desk, she goes on to ask if I have any witnesses. So, I tell her the name of the officer who was on the dorm the evening of the riot. I am returned to the box moments after the hearing to sit and await my fate.

Later on that afternoon, I hear a commotion outside of my cell, so I get up and find a small area to peek out of the gate. I catch a view of two officers, pleading with the guy locked in the cell to the left of mine.

"Please. Put the pencils down guy, calm down, it's okay."

Getting a good look at the officers, I notice that they are two of the pigs who put their hands on me the other day. Then I hear a voice screaming out of the cell.

"I'm not putting down shit! Fuck you! The first one of you walk in here getting poked the fuck up."

I just grin to myself and go back to the bunk to lie down, thinking *I knew they were bitches.*

Two days later make a week in the box and that is when I am

called to meet with the Deputy Superintendent for the second time, for, what I hoped, is the verdict of the hearing that I had with her. This time, when I walk into her office, she offers me a slight smile and asks me to have a seat. Her behavior makes me a bit more nervous than I already am, but, nevertheless I do as she says and take a seat though I just cannot accommodate her with a smile in return.

Once seated, it feels like someone turned the temperature up in the room because I suddenly begin to feel sweat building up on my forehead. Moments later, she starts reading papers on her desk while babbling. All I could manage to understand were the words, "Not Guilty," which she repeated for each charge. I then ask her if I am free to go and she replies:

"Yes, Mr. McAdams, you are free to leave."

Damn, it feels like a big weight has been taken off of my shoulders, and I believe I could fly, even if that means I would simply be flying from one part of the jail, to another. Just before I stand to leave, I have this sudden urge to ask her what she would have given me if I was found guilty. She looks up at me and, with the most serious look on her face, she replies:

"Well, I was thinking about transferring you to South Port for five years."

Man, was I happy that the truth prevailed, because South Port is a jail where the State houses all of its solitary confinement convicts on twenty-three hours lock down. There, inmates only get one-hour recreation which was in a small outside cage.

So I stand up from my chair, walked pass her desk and walk out of her office without saying another word. I notice that she gave this wide eyed, wide mouth, head twisted with hand on her chest look like:

"So you're just going to walk out without a 'thank you' or anything huh?"

Yeah Miss Lady that's just what I'm doing. Deuces.

Everything is good now, even considering being locked up fucked everything up. I am sent back to population, but not back to C dorm. Instead, I am transferred to F dorm. Same set up as C dorm, just different people. I didn't like the vibe there, but, fuck it, send me wherever, as long as these years keep passing.

While I am unpacking my shit, the CO calls me up to his desk and tells me that my fellow inmates had approached the officer in C dorm about me returning back and he had agreed.

"Pack your shit, you're heading back there."

I don't have much to repack, so I'm back in C dorm within five minutes. Soon as I walk into the dorm, dudes start telling me how they stepped to the CO and got him to see things their way. Shit, I am indeed impressed and feel good that I am loved and respected in such a manner by my fellow convicts.

The jail was never the same after the riots. We walk everywhere in line and wear our green, state-issued uniforms unless we were at recreation. Plus we only get five minutes to eat in the mess hall. Yeah, the joint is being run like a maximum security prison. Yet, there is one thing that still worries me. That CO who believed I assaulted him still believes it was me and was a bit pissed off when I was found not guilty.

I see him in the yard, and he just sits there, staring at me while I work out. One morning, to my surprise, this asshole is the officer on duty. He just sits there staring at me as I get ready to go to chow and then to my job in the gym. Here, I experience the most fear

I'd ever felt since my incarceration. I booby-trap my cubicle in order to know if any one stepped foot in my living quarters. I put match sticks in out-of-sight areas so if, anything was opened or moved, the little match would fall. That would be the first thing I would look for, before I even enter my cubicle. I also made my bed and took time to tuck my cover in a way that I would know if anyone lifted my mattress or otherwise disturbed my space. Who knows, he could place all kind of contraband from guns to drugs, and maybe I could have a chance if I knew someone was in my cube tampering with things.

As time would have it, that CO never tried any funny business to delay my time. So, seven months after the riot, which was February '96, I am transferred out of Governor and placed in Cape Vincent Correctional Facility.

Cape Vincent was the spot I've been waiting to get to since the bus ride into Upstate New York. Cape Vincent is where mostly all drug convictions would have to go in order to participate in the six-month drug program, which released you to return home after completion. On arrival, though, I learn that there is another six-month drug program, ASAT, which I would have to complete first before being accepted into Casat.

This information turned out to be very disappointing, because, instead of two years being shaved from my time, it would only be one and a half years shaved. I eventually figure it was better than doing the whole five. I recalled a very famous proverb: "patience is a virtue."

Every morning, we all would bring our chairs into the TV area, form a circle, and conduct group meetings. The leader of the group is this little old white civilian lady named Daisy. Daisy opened up the first meeting revealing to us that she was an alcoholic for twenty years and had been clean for forty. The next thing out of her mouth was startling. She went on to tell us that even though she hadn't taken a drink in forty years, she would always be an alcoholic. I sat there stunned. Yet, I felt my right hand rise up into the air and began shaking, thirsting for recognition.

My hand was recognized, and my voice anxiously broke the air. "Please forgive me, but are you saying that you truly consider yourself an alcoholic, though you've been clean these last four decades?"

"Yes, that is exactly what I am saying."

My eyes searched over the faces of my peers, and then thought to myself, damn. I hope these brothers aren't buying into this negative mind state. I felt obligated to rebut. Shaking my head, I looked back at Daisy.

"It's just that I am of the thought and bear witness to the fact that there is a force that dwells within us all, that is indeed capable of all things. If we are to eliminate a negative, we must always think positive. So for those of us who indeed want to have peace in our lives we may first have to go to war. And this great battle will take place in our hearts."

I noticed some confused faces within the circle so I continued.

"I guess what I am saying is, once we discover and hit our own personal rock bottom we come to know that this life will only get worse if we continue running these streets chasing after these drugs. Know that, the power for you to stop using and never turn back is within, you need only to tap into it."

"I know what you are trying to say, but it has been proven that addiction is an incurable disease, so this is the direction in which

I wish to continue these groups."

My intention wasn't to convince Daisy to change the curriculum of the group, because I Inner-Stand that she made a living off these teachings. I only spoke for the ear that was ready for a deeper wisdom, of whom they were and why they were here on this planet. Which I feel is to discover the greatest good within ourselves; drugs being just an unpleasant detour. After that day, I rarely participated in many discussions and never did I reveal that, I, too, had a problem, in which I conquered many years ago without one relapse nor a single craving to use.

I really want to make one thing clear at this point in these writings. If believing that you are always an addict once you were addicted to any controlled substance, gives you the strength to never pick up again, please continue to do what works for you. The fact remains that I don't agree with that philosophy, I feel that, that theory keeps the door open, for relapse. However, "if it ain't broke, don't fix it", and whatever your method is, remain strong.

In April, Helen and my daughters came up to see me. Man, we had a great time considering. We were talking and laughing and just enjoying each other's company. If memory serves me right, it was April 16, 1996 and Kiyanah would turn three on April 27th. I didn't know then, but that would be the last time seeing my family during my stay in prison. Though we did do a lot of talking on the phone and on one particular day Helen informed me about this guy who just moved into the apartment complex that she and the girls had themselves recently moved into. She says to me.

"Howard he reminds me so much of you the way you walk, the way you talk and the way you dress; I know for sure if you were home you two would be cool. He has 4 daughters and came to me the other day and asked if he could hire me to do their hair."

"Oh yeah, that's what's up, so did you accept the job?"

"Yes I accepted, I actually done his youngest daughters hair yesterday."

"Helen, do you still want me to come to you when I'm released?"

"Yes, Howard of course, what are you talking about?"

"I can tell you have a bit of a crush on this... what's his name?" Helen hesitated then replies.

"Terry."

"Ok Terry. So... do you have a crush on him?"

"Yes I do have a small crush on him Howard but I wouldn't act on it, no baby, that wouldn't happen, not at all."

I never asked about him again and as far as that went, I just hoped for the best and prepared for the worst. There were so many things going on around me that I thought it might be wise to focus on the here and now.

For instance, I was still going back and forth to outside hospitals to take tests, basically to learn how much longer I had till my kidneys failed and I would indeed need dialysis. Dialysis. That word alone had me shook. Just knowing that, soon, I would have to get connected to a machine three times a week in order to preserve my life.

I was in Cape Vincent for six months before the doctor told me he couldn't approve me to go home early on work release. His words hit me like a lightning bolt.

"Mr. McAdams, work release is a program that slowly allows you to be home with your family, but you will have to find a job. I don't know if you will be able to work with your health issues, so signing you out would make me responsible for you. And that I can't do."

Walking out of his office, with these two pig correctional officers, the first thing I saw was the legs on this fine woman. As I watched her walk down the hall, I thought to myself, Damn! I won't be able to be with a woman for another two years.

That next month, which made my seventh month in Cape Vincent, I was transferred out to a facility which could accommodate me with a dialysis machine. I was sent to a maximum security facility, Elmira, in Elmira, New York.

Elmira was like none of the medium security joints in which I had dwelled. It was an old prison, built a little after the civil war. Walking into this joint, you could smell murder in the air. I remember thinking to myself, *if these walls could only talk, I am sure they would tell a 'Hell' of a story.*

When I got there, I had three years of prison time served. I had passed my halfway point. If only I could keep myself out of trouble, in two years I would be back in the world.

They put me in the infirmary for a couple of days, until I could see the doctor. That Monday, I finally was able to see the doctor. He walked into the room with two nurses. The doctor explained, "Mr. McAdams, after looking over your labs, I don't see any medical reason for you not to participate in the work release program."

It was like music to my ears, so I thought I would toss another coin in the juke box and asked "Do you mean I won't need to start dialysis treatment?"

Yeah, I took it all the way there, but there was no more music, since he suddenly unplugged my juke box.

"No sir, someday you will need to be treated with dialysis;

however, I don't think it needs to be now."

"Hey Doc, will you inform the administration of your findings and that you believe I would be able to attend the work release program?"

"I most certainly intend to. I see no reason for you to stay here, if you won't be starting treatment any time soon."

Later on that day, I was released from the infirmary and sent to G-Block. Once there, one of the officers on duty informed me gallery 3, cell 4 was where my cell was located. I found myself very confused looking for gallery 3 since that was my first time in a Max. I noticed that there were four levels on either side, which made 8 levels. Each gallery had 'bout forty-two cells, maybe a few more, and on each gallery the first and second cells were double-bunked. All the others were single-bunked. Galleries 1 and 2 were called the flats because they both were on the ground level.

Seeing that one side of the block was Gallery 1 and the other Gallery 2, I wasn't sure where Gallery 3 would be. That's when I went to the officers who were congregated in their little area.

"Pardon me; could one of you please inform me how to get to gallery 3?"

They all got quiet and looked at me like I was a fool; then one of them broke the silence.

"Oh yeah, this is Howard McAdams. He has just come to us from a medium joint; however, they tell me he's one mean mother fucker."

He had just tried to play me, but he'll never see or hear of me running to him or any of his fellow co-workers for their help, bet that. Then he gave me directions to Gallery 3, and how it worked was that one side had 1, 3, 5 and 7 while the opposite side had 2, 4,

6 and 8. So I went up to my gallery, and while I was walking toward my cell, I noticed this porter mopping the floors. He looked like one of those big mean characters you would see in prison movies. You know the type with a do- rag on his head and looking like he could bench press the whole gym. As I walked pass him, stepping on his still damp floors, I noticed he had very cold eyes as he gave me a head nod. Still keeping it moving, I returned the gesture. As I walked into the cell, he spoke and the sound of his voice pierced the air. I instantly tuned in to his statement, searching each word for the slightest hint of disrespect.

"Hey bruh, do you need any supplies, like soap pads, bleach, or something to clean your cell?"

Recognizing words of respect I replied, "Yeah, that'll be cool. Thanks a lot."

He walked away, and I started unpacking my belongings, thinking to myself of the resemblance of his voice to Mike Tyson's. My back was to the gate when I heard his voice again.

"Here dog, I brought you the broom and mop also."

He then got very excited while pointing at my bed. "Are you Muslim?"

"Indeed." As I looked down at my bed to see what he was responding to, I noticed my prayer rug folded on my bed.

He then smiled and said, "As-saalmu Alaykum (peace be unto)."

"Wa Alaykum Salaam wa Rahmantullah wa Barakartu (and on to you peace, mercy and blessing)."

He then gave me a big hug and, in my right ear, said "Subhan'Allah" (Glory to Allah). In my left, he said "Alhamdulillah" (all praise to Allah), and "Allāhu Akbar" (Allah is the greatest) was said into my right. I also spoke the same words in his ears; it was all done simultaneously.

He told me his name was Shaka, and I told him my name was Habiybullah. Yes, at that point I chose to change my attribute from Jihad, the spiritual war, to Habiybullah (Beloved of Allah). Even though I was caged like an animal, I understood that every struggle in our lives was an initiation from G.O.D into deeper understanding, of life. Also I tried to change my attribute in each jail so that when anyone calls me I would know just where I knew them from.

Shaka bounced, and I finished unpacking and disinfecting my living quarters. Then a CO came up to the gate to inform me.

"You're quarantined until Sergeant Lynch comes to talk to you to see if you have any enemies here in Elmira."

Lynch showed up to speak with me just before lunch, and I was allowed to join population in the mess hall. When I was in the infirmary, I spoke to my moms on the phone and told her that this was the last spot that I knew Reggie to be, and I was going to find him as soon as they put me in general population.

"You don't need to be looking for anyone."

"Moms, how that sound? Reggie's here and I don't look to link up with him?"

Her silence told me that she understood damn well what I meant. You see my moms loved Reg; it's just that the mother in her kicked in, and she probably felt Reggie and I, especially in this type of environment, only spelled trouble.

While waiting on line in the mess hall, I saw my dog serving food on the line. I mean, I said I was gonna find Reg but never thought it would have been that easy. So I was on the line looking at Reg with a big grin, I would soon be face-to-face with my childhood buddy. I received my spoon and tray, and then, about twenty seconds later, I was damn near standing in front of him, so I blurted:

"Reg!"

He looked at me with a startled look at first and then a big smile came across his face.

"Smallz, What up homie?"

Not being able to hold a conversation at that moment, we exchanged words briefly, and I went to sit and eat my meal. Reg soon came and sat directly across from me, and we spoke up until the time my gallery was called to leave the mess hall.

"Damn Smallz, what happen why did they send you here, did you get into any trouble where you were?"

"Na Reg they got me here on some health issue madness."

"Word Smallz; what's wrong Black-Man?" I found it weird how one of my oldest and dearest friends had no idea of my illness. Man being behind these walls you can really lose touch. So I gave Reggie the low down on my situation.

However, before we went our separate ways, we promised to meet up in the yard later.

I arrive in the yard before Reg. Well, in order to get in the yard, I had to first walk through this indoor area called the Field House. Others knew it as the Coliseum, named after that ancient landmark in Rome where the gladiators fought. That's also how Elmira Correctional Facility got its infamous title, Gladiator School. Just walking through it, you could feel an aura, intense tension. So I thought to myself, I need to find a nice sharp piece of something, soon.

The yard was just as bad, but it was outdoors and more open. Straight in front of me, I noticed these great big stone bleachers, which looked like they were chiseled into shape, right there, where they sat. I walked across the baseball field and climbed three huge knee-height steps and sat on the fourth and final stone, where I could observe my new surroundings.

From where I was sitting, it was easy to spot Reg once he entered the yard. Again, a smile came across my face as he walked toward the bleachers to holla at his boy. He was dressed like me, in a fresh green army jacket, state greens, and a fresh pair of Timberland boots. As Reg got closer, he spotted me, so now we were both smiling at each other, as I hopped down the huge steps to meet my dude at the bottom.

Of course, we were sorry to have to meet each other under these conditions; however, we were glad to be together. At the bottom of the bleachers, we gave each other a strong embrace.

"When I first saw you in the mess hall, Smallz, I thought you were this dude Malik I had beef with not too long ago. Damn Smallz, you look just like this dude!"

I instantly thought about a brother Malik that I bided with, up there in Cape Vincent. So I asked, "What joint was he in before he got here?"

Reg looked at me strangely. "I think he said something about Cape Vincent."

"Yeah, I do know who you're talking about; he was in Cape Vincent with me. They must have transferred him here after that fight he had with the Latin Kings."

"Yeah, Malik mentioned something about some drama he had with them."

"What happened between the two of you?"

"Smallz, we were real cool; he even joined the Nation of Islam and all. He was my brother, but, one day, he and the brother Malcolm got into it, and he punched Malcolm in the face. Malcolm being an older brother, I couldn't let them fight, so I punched Malik in his face. We then fought and I ended up beating the shit out of him."

It was sort of funny because Malik had a little rep for his knuckle game up in Cape Vincent, yet he was no match for my Home-Boy Reg, whose knuckle game I know is tight. Spinning (walking around) the yard, we talked about all types of shit— from what we heard last of what was going on in the streets, to the things that caused us to end up in prison.

When rec was over, Reg had a plan for us to see each other again because he was in C-block and I was in G-block, which meant we would never have rec together. Somehow, he was able to sneak out here this time.

Reg told me about an HIV awareness class that we could sign up for, where we would be able to meet twice a week. We first attended the class to talk in the back about strategies to keep us out of the prison system once we returned to the so-called "Free World." It really didn't happen that way—the class was so informative, that Reg and I would be on the edge of our seats, absorbing this very important info. Then one day, months later, the guys in the class were very disappointed to learn that there were people in the group who weren't suffering from HIV. Neither Reg nor I had any idea the group was exclusively for those who were ill. Their argument was they didn't want anybody running around the prison informing others of their condition. Understanding their point perfectly, I addressed the class.

"I do understand exactly what is being said today, and if I had known this was a secluded group, I would have never come. Which now makes me wonder, *If the group was discrete, why was it so easy to sign up?* Not looking for an answer I continued on.

"In truth, my original intention was to come to this group in order to spend some time with my childhood buddy," I pointed directly at Reg. "But shit, you hardly see us talking to each other once class starts, and if you were observant, you would have noticed us sitting with an attentive ear, taking notes, and asking questions. Neither of us are lifers, and we hope to someday return to the streets. The information we receive in this class can be used as a tool to help us lower the risk of catching HIV and AIDS. This class would be useless if you didn't allow others to participate. How else could we prevent this epidemic from spreading, if some are banned from this knowledge? And one more thing; I have never, and will never, inform a soul about anyone's condition in this class, and if you all didn't have this little meeting today, I would have never known who was infected."

I made my point crystal clear, and they agreed to let us stay, so score one for the prevention against HIV and AIDS.

I had met a Muslim brother named Hakim later that day, while studying in the mosque. Although I had already met a bunch of good brothers, Hakim became my homie for real. Hakim was an older brother. He was forty-one at the time we met, yet he was a big kid, always joking around, plus he could tell you anything about hip-hop, old school or new. Though he was a big clown, he was also the go-to guy when or if the Muslims put a hit on someone.

Hakim would always ask me questions about medium security facility. While spinning the field house, I teased him.

"Stop fronting, you know you've been to a medium before."

"I can never go to a medium."

My response was. "Why not?"

What he said next I should have been prepared for, but I wasn't.

"I got fifty to life," he uttered.

I was not certain, but I think he also said, "I'll never step foot in a medium." You see, I was still stuck on, "I got fifty to life."

Unable to reply, we walked in silence for approximately ten seconds. Finally, I was able to speak.

"Damn dog! I'm sorry to hear that. What the fuck did you do?"

"Back when I was twenty-two, I robbed this gas station and the manager tried to be a hero. So I put one in him and he died instantly. I took it to trial and got twenty-five to life."

"Where did the other twenty-five come from?"

He looked at me and said, "I wasn't finished. About ten years into my bid, they sent me to Clinton Danamora, where I got into it with this dude. Dude pulled out this nice little blade; I pulled out something like a sword. Dude tries to run for it, but I catch him once in the back and this nigga goes and dies."

I began to think of all the people that survive several stab and gunshot wounds. Hakim stabbed a man once and shot another once, and both men expired. He told me about another body he caught in Auburn Correctional Facility. I believe he said he ran a razor across this one guy's throat; however, he beat that charge.

Looking at him, he never tried to come off as intimidating. Shit, he was usually smiling or laughing about something, yet he was a ruthless killer. One day he showed me this Crocodile Dundee knife, which was very impressive; what made it even more impressive was the fact that it was all Plexiglas.

"Dog, can you get me something like that?"

He then started beefing. "Habiyb, you going home soon; how I look giving you any weapons, let alone some killer shit like this?"

Though he was Muslim, that was probably the most positive thing, I'd ever heard him utter.

"If you ever do need a weapon, you got so many brothers close by that stay armed; you just get your ass home in one piece."

Don't get me wrong, I did understand his words; however, I felt like this: if I got into a problem, it should be me who had it popping, not the next dude. I mean, yes, my time was short, and of course, if I did stab something and get caught, I probably would catch an new charge and risk never going home, which was Hakim's and a couple of other brothers' point. Yet, I saw it at a slightly different angle, which was if I was in some real drama, it would be better to get caught with it, than without it.

Meanwhile, the doctor wasn't able to convince whoever needed convincing to release me to the work release program. I was told I would have to do the remainder of my time. This knowledge was a very hard strike to my heart. I desperately wanted to go home because things were really fading away between me and my wife.

I hadn't seen my wife and daughters in about eight months, and I rarely received letters. All I basically had were the phones, once she removed the block. Now that I was in a Max joint, we were able to receive conjugal visits. All we had to do was follow a simple procedure, and we could spend a weekend together every forty days. So I went and informed my counselor that I wanted to sign up for trailer visits with my family. He gave me all the appropriate paperwork to fill out; the only thing left was for Helen to call him and set a day to come in, fill out some papers, present some ID, and bring in our marriage license.

I explained to Helen exactly what she needed to do, and she said she would get right on it. In the meantime, I was transferred out of G-block and sent to I-block. I-block was said to be the most dangerous block Elmira had to offer, so it was given the name "the Projects."

I was sent to I-block's eighth gallery. As I passed each cell to get to cell 21, where I would be caged, I saw two dudes standing in front of #22. I was coming through with bags of all the things I'd accumulated during my stay in prison. I stopped in front of my cell and dropped all my shit in the front, then stepped inside to do some quick cleaning before I brought in my belongings. I noticed I didn't have a locker or a chair in my cell and, by now, I figured out that one of the guys outside in the gallery was a porter, so I stepped out.

"Pardon me bruh'" That got his attention and he looked down at me.

"Yea what's up?"

I then asked him if he was a porter.

"Yeah."

"If there's an empty cell or will be soon, can you let me know, so I could run in and take out the locker and chair because I don't have any in my cell?"

"I'm not on your payroll, homie." Then he looked down and pointed at all my belongings on the ground. "You look like you've been doing this for a while; you know how this works."

I immediately understood he wanted to be paid for that info, so I just walked away and continued with my business thinking, Okay I'll get it without you, black man.

I took that situation as a very important lesson. You see, the porters in G-block would have had no problem giving that information, but, on the other hand, "everyone's not the same," and besides, these were "The Projects."

Later on that day, I saw my counselor, and he asked me, "Did you tell your wife to give me a call so we could get these visits?"

"Yes I did, but I will holla back at her tonight 'cause I need to get this ball rolling."

He looked at me and gave me one of those I understand smiles, and we parted ways. So, later that night in the Field House, I gave her a call. When she picked up the phone, I said "Hi," and then asked if she ever called the counselor. She told me that she didn't get a chance to and that she would the next day. So, that next day, I saw the counselor and he said he still hadn't heard from her, so now I'm like "Damn! My wife is gone." Two nights later, I called her again.

"Helen, you still haven't called the counselor, babe? If you don't want to have these visits, let me know, so I could tell this dude to forget it and I could finish my time without the stress."

She goes on to say, "Howard, you let him know that I will call him and believe me, I do want to visit you! It's just that I can't call long distance so I have to buy a calling card. I'll try to do that tomorrow. Trust me honey, I really do want to have these conjugal visits with you so I will call him."

Helen did give the counselor a call and made an arrangement to handle the paperwork for the following month.

###

When you walked into the Field House, to the right was the bathroom area, then the shower area, the workout area and at the very end, there were three picnic tables that were lined up and spaced out against the wall. The first table was where the Muslims would congregate. The next table is where you would find the presence of the Latino organization -- "The Nietas". The third table belonged to the Latin Kings. There was a fourth table, not against the wall, but nearby. It was occupied by the brothers of the Nation of G.O.Ds and Earths, who some may know as the Five Percent. A little farther down, standing against the next wall, you could find a jailhouse clique who were called, the Rat Hunters. Word was that they would seek out snitches and murder them. Further down against the wall stood the infamous Blood gang. Yeah, there were Bloods, even in New York.

In the other spots where I was imprisoned, Bloods were either in hiding or run out of the joint. Not here though, because there they were congregated in the corner, about twelve deep, sporting that red. When I was in Governor, if there were Bloods there, they weren't telling. Yet, when I was housed in Cape Vincent, I witnessed a few incidents with Bloods. I'll share a couple of them with you.

There was this one young dread brother named Tony who was double-bunked with my Muslim brother whom I shared the attribute Jihad with. Jihad was a Puerto Rican brother, and when Tony had first come in the dorm, he expressed his dislike for Jihad because he was Puerto Rican.

"Man, these motherfuckers got me bunked with this punk ass Puerto Rican. I can't stand them mother fuckers."

I thought to myself, He doesn't know Jihad ain't what he thinks he is. Shit, Jihad would probably bang one of them Puerto Ricans up faster than he would. I mean, Jihad loved his nationality and his people, but, being Muslim, he was always ready to ride on any of the Latin cliques if they ever transgressed.

Giving Tony a smile like "Nigga you crazy," I calmly said to him, "That's my brother, he's cool."

I then changed the subject hoping he'd take heed and not get himself hurt. Weeks later, Tony came back from the mess hall telling me that he wanted to become Muslim. I noticed that he looked kind of nervous, so I asked something like, "Are you okay?"

He informed me that he was okay, but just wanted to know if and when he could take his Shahada. I then noticed my boy Pedro waving his hand to get my attention. We made eye contact, and he motioned to me to come over. Seeing a look of urgency in his eyes, I asked Tony to give me a minute and went over to see what Pedro needed from me.

Pedro was the top Nieta in my particular dorm. He was a young dude from Puerto Rico and learned how to speak English while incarcerated. Once I walked into his cube, he took a seat on his bunk and offered me a seat in a nearby chair and I accepted.

In his very strong Spanish accent Pedro informed me.

"It has come to our attention that your little homeboy Tony is Blood. Now you know we are not allowing any Bloods to stay in this facility. If and when we locate them we run them out."

"What makes you now say he's Blood? This man has been here for weeks."

He pointed at an old Spanish guy, who has just gotten to Cape Vincent that day. "Poppy over there said that they were on Rikers

Island together, plus there's another brother in F-unit who says the same."

I kind of laughed to myself as I realized the reason why Tony ran to me so animated about being Muslim. So I asked Pedro to give me a minute, and then walked back over to Tony.

"Does your wanting to be a Muslim have anything to do with what this Dude here is saying about you being a Blood on the Island?"

"Nah, I've been thinking about it, and I do, I do want to be a Muslim. I mean, I did hang with a couple Bloods, but I'm not Blood."

Not really buying it, I told him to give me a minute and walked back over to Pedro.

"Dog, he's saying he may have hung with a couple of Bloods, but he ain't Blood, plus he now wants to be Muslim."

Pedro eyes suddenly lit up. "Jihad, please don't allow him to become Muslim. He has no love for G.O.D's laws; he runs to you for help because he understand he's been made by my people." He paused and gave me a piercing look. "He's afraid. These guys just want to come in and gain more numbers; then we all will have to go to war with them to run them out."

"Listen, the brother ain't causing any trouble with anyone, and besides, he and I are cool. So as long as he stays peace, I can't let you harm him."

"Jihad, please understand, I won't allow anyone to harm him, if you don't okay it. Yet, I can't promise his safety when some of my other brothers from other units spot him outside of this unit, when he has to go to chow, work, school, or rec."

I understood that, in order to protect him, I would have to drag my brothers into it.

"Or what could be done is, I run and tell little Mexico to meet him in the bathroom and you tell your boy that there's someone in the bathroom waiting to fight him. Don't tell him it's Little Mexico. If he asks, just tell him it could be a monster in there. All you know is, it will be a mano a mano."

I loved the idea. I then excused myself and went back to holla at Tony. I asked again if he was Blood, and he admitted it. I told him what was said to me about the one-on-one in the bathroom awaiting him, and if he accepted, he would be allowed to continue to chill in population. Thinking Tony was a real cat, I was sure he would jump at them terms; instead, he was shook. I mean he wanted nothing to do with that bathroom.

I told him he was safe on the dorm because I wouldn't let anything harm him, but told him that when he walked outside anything could happen. Still he wouldn't walk in that bathroom. Trying not to let him go out like a complete sucker, I told him to throw a couple of cans of Jack-Mack (fish that comes in a can) in a net bag, step to one of them dudes and bust they head open. That way, he would go out like a soldier. Ultimately, Tony chose a different way out. A sergeant came to the dorm and Tony packed his belongings, carried them to the sergeant, told him that he was afraid for his life, and ended up leaving with the sergeant with his tail between his legs.

A couple of months later, there was this new dude who came into the dorm at Cape Vincent. He seemed like a pretty cool guy. It was a couple a weeks later, during a late night, when there was a great commotion going on in the bathroom. I saw a bunch of Nietas fighting the new dude. I used the word fighting instead of jumping because bruh' was most definitely fighting back. Word, he was throwing punches, egging them on with a big smile on his face. And did I mention that he was doing all this with his pants down to his ankles?

As I watched, I noticed that, one by one, they started running out of the bathroom. The cop on duty also noticed, so he ran out and caught the last Nieta, who was my bunky as he attempted to run out of the bathroom. So they both got thrown into the box. All over the bathroom floor were the pages of a "short-eyes book" (porn magazine). It was said that dude was in the stool beating off, when they kicked in the door to attack him.

Right after that incident, about fifteen brothers approached me asking if I had any intentions on mashing on the individuals who were involved in the attack. When I say brothers, I am not speaking about my Muslims brothers; I'm speaking about other "black" men, who were also housed in that particular dorm and felt the need to retaliate.

"Jihad, now you know we can't just stand here and give these motherfuckers a pass 'cause you know they wouldn't allow us to flip on any Spanish dude whatsoever."

I stood there in this "all-black" huddle nodding my head in agreement. I also stood there puzzled as I thought how respected I was in the dorm because there I stood holding in my hands the decision to start a race war or not. It took me by surprise; I never knew I had such power.

I noticed Pedro and a couple of his people looking over at us, and their eyes told me they knew what that congregation was all about. I looked over at Pedro, and he waved for me to come over to holla at him. Instead of me going to him, I motioned for him to come over to me. He walked over and asked if he could speak to me alone.

"No, whatever you gotta say, say it."

He then looked over our faces and got right to it. "Listen, we didn't mean any disrespect toward any of you guys. What happened is, this guy is a Blood and he was well-known for busting his gun on our brothers on Rikers at will. We told him last week, that he had a week to leave, and every day he ran around like he was the shit. We didn't think he would try us and not leave on the date assigned. Today made a week and I thought he was getting hit in the yard, but we were told to get him in the dorm tonight."

Then this light-skinned brother interrupted, "Yeah, he was repping that Blood on the Island and was definitely tearing those Puerto Ricans' asses up."

Pedro looked at me like I told you. "Maybe we should have said something. I was wrong not coming to you first."

I felt comfortable with his explanation, and so did the rest of the brothers, so nothing popped off. What gave the story a whole new twist was when my bunky came back from the box. The story he had to tell left me with my mouth wide open. He informed me that, when they had their hearing about the incident, all the Blood dude was saying was how they were all just playing, how they knew each other from NY, and how they would never really be fighting. My bunky then looked me in the eyes.

"That dude proved to truly be Blood."

I remember thinking *Hell yeah*. I mean the average cat wouldn't want to return to population, knowing there are over one hundred Nietas on the compound, yet this dude still wanted to come back to population, to do battle, knowing he's on his own.

> In this very moment
> I'm king
> In this very moment
> I slayed Goliath with a sling.

-Nicki Manaj

Lesson 21

"When one door closes, another opens."
Alexander Graham Bell

I loved and went to school to cook, so after seven months in I-block, I signed up to work with Reg in the mess hall. I was transferred to C-block where the great majority of the convicts worked in the mess hall. I was sent to cell 21 on gallery 7. Now, I knew Reg was also in C-block, and if we didn't work the same meals, we would for sure see each other in the Field House and yard. Now let me show you G.O.D's genius. My good buddy Reg, whom I'd fought with and laughed with, was on 7 gallery 20 cell; my next cell neighbor. Go figure. I walked to his cell, and there he was, lying on his bed fully clothed to the boots, so I stood in front of his cell.

"Reg, G.O.D is great."

He looked up at me and smiled. "I knew it Smallz, I knew it!"

Once again, it was me and Reg against the world. The mess hall was a good hustle 'cause you could take food and sell it to convicts who didn't work in the mess hall. Hot commodities were things like rice because the rice sold at commissary was that minute tice nonsense. If you got your hands on some cooking oil and flour, you could flip that like hot cakes. I would sell a few items, but you could basically catch me in the cell putting those ingredients to some flavorful use. Reg was doing his thing in that mess hall. He was getting plenty packs of cigarettes. Plus he had dudes buying him everything he needed from the commissary, so he never had to touch the money he received from the so-called "free world."

After working in the mess hall for a couple of months, I ended up fracturing my ankle jumping off a truck unpacking food, which had me on crutches. It sure was a crazy feeling walking the Coliseum disabled 'cause shit was damn near always popping off there. I done witnessed gang fights where everyone had weapons of some sort, as well as many face slashings and stabbings. I once saw a guy get slapped in the face with a 10lb weight and a Correctional Officer knocked out by a prisoner. Still, I walked through the valley of death, unharmed.

Once healed, I was transferred back to I-block. This time I was caged on the 8th gallery. If memory serves me correctly, 6 and 4 galleries were restricted to the brothers who were on "Keep Lock." Man! These brothers would be up all night, screaming back and forth to each other. This reminded me of a lyric from our late, great brother Tupac Shakur, when speaking about his stay at NY's Clinton Danamora: "Hearing brothers screaming all night, wishing they stop!" Yeah, it was hard to get any shut eye with all the ruckus during the night. Yet during the day, you wouldn't even know them brothers existed because that was when they shut their eyes.

Every year, on the anniversary of the Attica riots in the 70s, we convicts would usually go on a food strike, for a couple of days. For those who are not familiar with the riots in Attica, well, the convicts took over the prison and held correctional officers hostage. Long story short, police were sent inside, killing convicts and COs alike.

So the word passed around that we were going to recognize the food strike, which I was happy to do. Shit, I always participated in this demonstration ever since I'd been incarcerated. The day of the strike, they cracked gallery 8 out for breakfast. I slammed my gate back shut and looked down the gallery with my mirror and noticed more than half of the gallery going to chow. I lay in that bed listening to all the gates opening in the entire I–block and to the many feet that pitter-pattered their way to the mess hall.

You see, the only way it worked was if the majority of the convicts participated. The strike was set up to hit the prison system in the pockets in consequence of us not eating, they would have to throw out plenty of food. Since there was a state wide menu and the prisoners worked in the mess hall, they could never try to feed those same meals to us on later date. I don't think I need to tell you how many bodies they had housed in these state facilities, which added up to big money wasted on food. I found it a bit disturbing to see and to hear how many guys went to chow, because prior facilities where I'd done time, more of us adhered to the strike. I mean, if someone didn't have any food, there were plenty of brothers who would feed them, especially within the Islamic community.

So I knew that those who didn't go to chow would have to answer to the authorities, who I knew would be coming around soon, to administer their punishment. I soon heard footsteps and keys jingling down the catwalk. I stuck my mirror out of the gate to obtain a clear view. As I figured, there was this pig walking through. He stopped at my brother's Faruque's cell. With pen in hand, he scribbled something on the pad he was carrying. He continued his walk to my cell.

"Why didn't you lock out for chow this morning?"

I had what I thought was a great excuse, so I tried it on for size. "I start dialysis today, so I'm told I'll be getting transferred to G-block some time this morning."

He looked up at me from his pad. "Oh, okay."

He then scribbled in his pad and went on to ask his question to the next soldier. The reason I wasn't sure my excuse would work is because I was told by my doctor that I would be getting transferred at 11 a.m. to start dialysis at noon. It was only 6:30 a.m. but I just didn't know if the administration knew the true schedule.

It was around 11:30 a.m. when they packed me and sent me to G-block's Flats. All I really had time for was to drop my bags and go straight to that Dialysis Unit known to me as the "Haunted House."

As soon as I walked in, I was led to this olive green recliner chair, which was draped in a dark green blanket. The CO who was assigned to the center was pretty cool. I figured he may be that way because he's in there all by his lonesome. It would be damn near impossible for him to get help in there soon enough to avoid the pain; if something ever happened. Then again, who knows, he may have been a truly nice guy. He schooled me about making sure my seat was clean. He showed me where the spray bottles of bleach were. You see, what I was about to start was called hemo-dialysis. The word "Hemo" means blood, and sometimes blood spilled, and the chairs could be contaminated at any given minute. That there was food for thought.

When I sat, this nurse named Rebecca sat down in a chair with wheels next to me. She got my arm all cleaned up in order to stick two big, fat, long-ass needles into the vein, which was connected to an artery in my arm. Before sticking me, she asked if I would like to be stuck first with Novocain to numb the area, and I accepted. I accepted for two reasons: first, those big ass needles. Second, the dude next to me made two of the most painful faces I had seen in a while, as I watched when he got stuck.

She stuck me with the novocain, which stung like nobody's business. Then, she stuck the first needle. I felt a little pressure, but no pain and it was the same with the next needle. The nurse then taped up my arm in order to keep the needle fastened. She then got up and started to press some buttons on the machine in order to program it. I sat there and watched blood leave my arm through a tube and enter the machine and return back into my arm from the second tube. I remember saying to myself, *Damn Smallz!*

That was my first treatment and there would be plenty others. In fact, after that first time, I began to feel much better. Not that I felt bad. But after treatment I felt a change for the better. Eventually I lost the urge to urinate. And then, eventually, I couldn't release a drop. This would leave me feeling very bloated and a bit sluggish which would become a problem sometimes between treatments. The machine didn't only clean my blood. It also took off the extra weight I may have gained between treatments due to overdoing my fluid intake and not being able to take a leak.

I had to sit tied to that machine three times a week, three-and-a-half hours a treatment. I utilized that time by engaging in plenty of studying. For the first two and a half hours, I would have my face in the books and then for the last hour, I would turn on my own personal TV which had cable and watched BET or Colombo.

If memory serves me correctly, I was on dialysis for about two months, when, one day in the mosque, after Jumah services, some of the brothers were having a bit of a heated conversation with the outside Imam. I swear I can't remember what the beef was about, yet I do remember the Imam running out of the mosque to return with the police.

It is forbidden to wear your shoes in the mosque although the Imam allowed them COs to run up in their boots and all. He pointed out brothers who were arguing with him and who I guess he thought would harm him. And these cops were just throwing them down, cuffing them up, and taking them away. I honestly didn't think the Imam was in any danger at all, yet, on the other hand, I guess he wasn't taking any chances. He was in the midst of killers, you know.

The rest of the brothers didn't appreciate him letting those police in the mosque, to step all over the prayer rug and handcuff brothers in the one place they could come to be in peace. I didn't like it either; however, I didn't take it as hard as the others. You see, they took it so hard, that there was a hit put on the Imam. Mind you, the heads of security were the brothers that I hung with. Hakim was given the honors of terminating the Imam. The whole thing was planned in a way that the Imam had no chance once he stepped in G-block. There were about five different brothers who held certain posts to assure Hakim's getaway, and his plan was to slit his throat from ear-to-ear.

Now I thought they were all out of their fucking minds with this killing the Imam talk. And you should've seen Hakim: he was cool as a fan, in his every day, happy-go-lucky self, waiting for his cue, to kill again.

I told Hakim, "When you get your cue, let me know, so I can get my ass as far away from you as possible." Man, I had 'bout thirteen more months on my bid to do. I didn't need that shit to come back to haunt me.

G.O.D was on the Imam's side because he became ill and didn't come in the days following the incident and eventually resigned from his position as Imam all together. Or maybe he knew brothers weren't letting him slide with his actions and didn't want to see what was awaiting him.

Meanwhile, back at the ranch, Helen, still hadn't made any moves to visit me, so I just stopped asking her. Then, one day, while on the phone with my dude Gee, Helen's name came up. I then brought up the topic of this dude Terry who lived in the new building that she had moved into, and how she said he reminded her so much of me, so she had a crush on him. Knowing that I didn't want her to mess around with another man, I prayed she wouldn't cheat with someone who stayed in the same building that she would have me to stay once I touched down.

So as I said this dude's name came up, Gee said in a very surprised voice, "She told you about him?"

In an even more surprised voice I answered him. "Yeah, she told me 'bout him. Why what's up?"

His voice was like a detective's. "What did she tell you about him?"

By now, I was a little uneasy but I went along with him. "Well, she told me he lived in the building and he reminded her of me so she had a crush on him. Why! Did she fuck him?"

"Yeah, she fucked him."

"How do you know?"

"She told me herself."

"How long has this been going on?"

"She told me this like last year sometime, but I don't think she's still dealing with him."

I thought to myself, she told you this last year. So I asked, "Dog, why didn't you tell me this sooner?"

In a slightly apologetic voice, he replied, "I didn't know how to tell you."

"You just tell me Gee."

"I was worried about your health. I don't know anything about that dialysis shit."

I guess I could understand him not informing me because of him being worried about my health. I mean, I didn't know anything about dialysis in the beginning neither. I put that behind me due to the fact that Gee really had nothing to do with this. She was the one I needed to speak with. I told Gee I was gonna holla back at him, and we ended our call. I picked the phone back up and dialed the numbers to make Helen's phone say "ring, ring."

The phone was picked up and it was her.

"Hello."

"What's up Helen? Did you ever holla at my counselor about visiting your Baby?"

She had no idea that I was being sarcastic, yet I knew since it had been so long without her calling my counselor. She would more than likely tell me something she hadn't been saying. Using her little voice she used when she wanted to tell me something I may not approve of, she started off in the same way she did every time.

"Howard???" Her famous pause followed.

"What?"

"I went to see a divorce lawyer today."

"Did you ask about an annulment?"

She paused like she was surprised that we were on the same page. You see, as time went by, I started to realize that prison wasn't a place to be having a wife, especially one who couldn't find the strength to hold on. I could only imagine how hard it had to be on her. It's been said that "You cut off the head and the body will fall." I, being the head, of my family, that was cut off and the body being my family that will fall soon after. She didn't think they would go for an annulment. I thought that, since we never consummated the marriage, we had a chance.

"So are you seeing someone?"

"This is not about another man."

"Then what?"

"It's about me."

"Listen love, you ain't got to hide anything from me. I can't be with ya, I know you lonely. So who's the guy, what is he like?" I hoped my choice of words would make her want to get all that shit off of her chest.

After a moment she spoke.

"Howard ... I met a guy; his name is Jody. I really like him, the girls really like him. They get along great." She then ended by saying, "Sorry, I never meant to hurt you, and once you get home, I hope you won't treat other women you meet foul because I hurt you."

Once she was finished, I calmly said, "Thank you."

She sounded a little confused as she asked, "Unh, what did you say?"

"Helen, I've been waiting damn near fifteen months for you to tell me something, so I could tell you Gee told me how you were fucking that nigga in the building, Terry."

I just wanted her to believe that I was strong enough to carry that information so long without ever revealing her secret; meaning that there was never any secret, just a game. Now, she believed I won.

"I don't know what you are talking about."

After a while, she finally admitted to the accusation. I'm sure it was a great load taken off of her shoulders, and trust me it was indeed a great load taken off mine. The way I saw it was, "Okay, my wife is gone; I no longer have to stress anymore. If she's still waiting for me or not, because she's not, she has moved on. I just need to get over it."

It may be hard to believe, but I wasn't mad at her. Let's be real: if I had to wait for her to do five years in prison, I probably would have left also. However, I know I would have never taken the girls out of her life. So as long as she and the children kept in touch, it was all good. I had watched so many other guys' wives leave them, how could I think I was special? Shit happens.

One thing that I was kind of disappointed about was the fact that she never once asked how I was coping now that I was on dialysis. She didn't ask that night or any other night after, knowing that had been a great concern of mine for years. One day, when I was on the phone with her, I briefly mentioned the word dialysis. Her voice suggested she really didn't want to talk about it.

"Oh yeah, how's that going?"

"You know me, I roll with the punches."

Not long after, she and the girls moved with this dude Jody somewhere outta New York. She wrote me a letter with no return address, only a Post Office Box number. That was the only way I could correspond with my children. She also gave me a phone number that I was to only use in the event of an emergency. And that was the last I heard from them during my stay in prison.

I had told Reg my situation, and he seemed to have taken it just as hard as I did. He was passing me a plate of waffles in the mess hall, when I brought it to his attention. With this shocked look on his face and pain in his voice, he asked

"Word, Smallz?"

When I sat to eat, he came and sat with me; we both sat there in silence. I remember when I first came to prison; dudes would talk freely on how their wives left them. I think it was a form of therapy because I found myself talking to anyone who had an ear to hear how my wife left me here for dead.

It's funny how the universe works, though. Would you believe that, not too long after, New York's Governor Pataki passed a bill that would allow non-violent inmates to go home early. It was called the Merit Bill. I forget how much time it knocked off, but I do know that the time that I had in surpassed it. So I was one of the first convicts to go to the board with that new bill. I guess it's true when it's said "when one door closes another door opens."

So, one evening, while coming back from rec, I stepped into my cell and noticed a small piece of paper on the ground. I picked it up and it said that I would be going to the next Parole Board coming up that month. That small piece of paper which I held in my hand was the equivalent of a crystal ball because I suddenly began to receive visions of me back home with my loved ones.

It was like two weeks later when I went to see those people on the Parole Board. My bid was a five-to-ten, meaning my earliest release would be in five years, the max ten years. There was also a conditional release between in which they basically had to let you go if you didn't catch any new charges. So, my conditional release was seven-and-a-half years.

I knew I had a good chance at going home because I had what they were looking for: a non-violent crime. Plus, knowing that the system viewed all drug dealers as users, I volunteered in AA meetings, NA meetings, parenting classes, an 18-month drug group, plus five months of that other drug group called Casat. I felt ready.

I walked in the room and sat before four people: three men and one woman. They asked me questions like, "Did I learn my lesson? What am I going to do if they decide to let me go home?" Blaa Blaa Blaa.

I answered the first question, "Yes, I most certainly have learned my lesson. I had enough time to do a lot of soul searching and feel like I have really found the True and Living G.O.D and this is not a place for such an individual."

The next question I answered, "I pray that you find it in your hearts to let me return home, and if so, I hope to pursue a career in the culinary arts. I attended culinary school and was arrested before I could get my certificate. Plus, I've done a lot of cooking while in prison and worked the mess hall, so yes, that is what I will be doing if or when I am released."

And as far as the Blaa, Blaa, Blaa, believe me, I had an answer for each of them as well.

I walked out the Board Room feeling good because there wasn't anything that they were able to dispute with me on. I was told that I would receive the result of their decision that next day during mail call. I don't think I got much sleep that night. All I could think of was going home and staying out of these types of settings.

Later that next day after lunch, while looking outside of my cell with a mirror, I spotted the police walking down the gallery giving out mail. He stopped at my cell and threw an envelope inside. I ripped it open, and in short, it said I was going home, with a release date for two weeks later. I stood there with that paper in my hand feeling like a free man. My nightmare was indeed over, though I stood in a locked cage.

Those two weeks went by, way too slowly, and the day before I was to return home, I received some bad news from my doctor. He told me that the dialysis unit that was to assist me wouldn't be able to receive me as a patient until the following week. Their reason was because they had a patient who was coming in from out of state to visit his family for the Thanksgiving holiday. The bad news hit me like a sledgehammer. How do I get news like this, the day before I leave to return home? You see, if I couldn't receive treatment on the street, I would have to stay incarcerated until I could.

To make matters worse, that next morning my cell cracked open, and a police came to the gate and asked me if I was ready. It hurt me so bad to tell him that I couldn't go because of my medical issues. He looked at me like I lost my mind and walked off to call for more info on the subject. I thought to myself, Maybe I should have kept my mouth shut and just gone home. I then dismissed the thought because I would need to have a set place for me to receive my treatments.

As I traveled the prison that day, all I heard was, "What happened, I thought you were going home today?" It was crazy, but I managed to make it to the day in question, December 4, 1997, when the same police, who I told I couldn't leave, came back to my cage and with a smile on his face.

"Hey McAdams, if I crack this cell, are you going to go home, or are you going to give me another story about how you want to stay here with us wonderful people?"

I thought that was pretty funny, so with a smile also on my face and my hands wrapped around those cold prison bars, I replied, "Maaan, stop playing, let me out of here, for real!"

Still smiling, he said, "Alrighty then, I was just making sure, you know." He then screamed down the gallery to the officer at the controls.

"Crack four."

With bags in hand, I stepped out of "that" cell, and next I heard that cage gate slam. You may have heard many people speak of their emotions once they heard that gate slam from behind, with them inside for the first time. Some may say that's when they knew it was real. For me, I knew it was real when I felt them cold handcuffs tighten behind me. Hearing that gate slam, with me on the other side of it; sent chills up my spine.

I was free to start anew.

I'll Smile Tomorrow

> There been times that I thought
> I couldn't last for long
> But now I think I'm able to carry on
> It's been a long, a long time coming
> But I know a change is gonna come,
> oh yes it will.

-Sam Cooke

Lesson 22

"G.O.D sometimes puts us in situations that seem too much for us, so that we will learn that no situation is too much for Him/her. Just when you think G.O.D is all you have, you will find she/he is all you need."

Author Unknown

I was told to wait at the Officer's Station because there was another lucky fellow who would also be heading home to his family. He came downstairs, and to my surprise, it was this Latin King dude, whom you could say I was slightly intimidated by. I say that because, if we ever had war with the Kings, I told myself, he'd be the first one that I'd hit with something sharp. He just looked like he could be trouble.

His name was Hawk, and all truth be told, I learned that he was a pretty cool guy. Once we got to talking we left all that jailhouse drama in the prison. One of the COs drove us to the bus station, where we found out that we had about an hour until the next bus to the city arrived. From afar, we noticed the symbol for McDonald's in the sky, so we walked to it and enjoyed us some breakfast, as we sat their laughing and talking about whatever.

On the bus ride, I sat by myself and read some scripture from out of the Holy Qur'an and Bible. When I got tired of that, I just gazed out of the window, anticipating my return to the city. The bus had TVs, and some comedy was showing because Hawk was in the back dying laughing. Then Hawk called me and, with one hand, motioned for me to come to him and, with the other hand, offered me one of the ears to his earphones. So I accepted his invitation, sat by him, put the earpiece in my, ear and, soon thereafter, we both were just laughing out loud and giving each other daps. Yeah, Hawk was cool, so when our bus reached the city and we got off at the Port Authority, I introduced him to my pops who was waiting right there for his boy to arrive.

My mom was there as well, but she was upstairs. We all hugged and kissed and then took the # 2 train to the Bronx. The trains were a lot different from the last time I rode them, a lot cleaner and they were actually different trains from back then. Yet, some things never change, like you still had the underprivileged asking for change; I always tried to give because I believed, regardless of if they were on drugs or not, they had to eat to sustain life.

Speaking about eating, I used to dream about stuffing my greedy face with pizza. As soon as I got home, I went right next door to my house and ordered two slices to go. Then my family took me out to eat at City Island (an island full of seafood restaurants) in the Bronx. It was me, my parents, my sister, and her family. This would be the first time I lay eyes on her new baby girl D'airah, and during our dinner conversation, my sister asked my parents, "Did you tell him?"

Pops answered with a sharp, "No!"

It was like saying, "shut the hell up." Immediately, I figured out the riddle. So, after dinner, as we all were walking out the door, I pulled Pops to the side.

"Helen's pregnant, isn't she?"

He gave me this sorry look. "Yeah, she is."

I put my hand on his shoulder and said, "I'm good, Pops. She and I weren't meant to be." Then I thought within, so be it.

That evening, I decided to give her a call, and when she picked up, she was surprised when she heard my voice.

"What's up Helen, how the hell are you?"

She then asked in her funny little voice, "Where are you?"

"I'm home girl."

"Are you home or on a furlough?"

"Nah, I'm home. It's all over."

She then congratulated me, sounding so happy for me. I won't say she wasn't happy for my release, yet I can say, from where I stood, it was hard to tell. Since the divorce hadn't gone through the last time I checked, we were still married.

"So what's up with this divorce? Did it go through yet or what?"

Where the conversation went next struck me as a bit shocking. "It's not final yet."

"Not yet. So what's the hold up?"

She then says, "But…"

She hesitated, so I asked, "What?"

"But, you're home now."

Confused, yet knowing where she was going, I told her, "Helen, continue on with that procedure." I then congratulated her on her pregnancy.

She paused for a second; then, in a very nervous tone, she said, "Thank you. How did you know?"

I told her some shit like "You know me, my ear never left them streets." The truth is, one day she had popped up at my parents' home with the girls and her girlfriend China, and Kiyanah told my moms that "My mommy is having a baby."

That next morning, I had my first appointment with a dialysis unit down in the city. This was the only unit that would accept me with no medical insurance yet they pointed me in the right direction in order to obtain insurance. My parents came down with me, but they weren't allowed in the back where the treatment would actually go down, so they took in a movie. I was extremely happy to be home for obvious reasons, but one that was close to my heart was the fact that I would now get my name on the list for a kidney transplant.

Initially, my sister was going to donate one of her kidneys to me. When I was still in Elmira, speaking to her on the phone, she brought it to my attention.

"Howard when you get out of that place, I plan on giving you one of my kidneys"

"Really Nel? You don't have to worry about that something's going to give for your little bruh. Trust."

"I know, but why do you think I'm having this baby; to get it out of the way now because I hear that after surgery, it may be difficult." Wow my big sis ready to make it happen. Feeling a bit uneasy I tell her.

"Ok big sis, okay. If we are indeed a match, hey, let's do it. Thanks a lot."

After my return home, we learned that she and I was indeed a match, but, soon after, she had a change of heart. I wasn't mad, though, because I was worried about her going through such a serious operation, especially one she didn't need to do.

I was home two weeks before any of my old running partners knew I was back on the bricks. In the meantime, I would just be going back and forth between dialysis and home, playing with my little brother.

I'll Smile Tomorrow 315

Yeah, getting to play with Slugger again was like the good old days. However, on the day of my return, I noticed he was very confused as to who I was. It seemed like he didn't know if he should attack or play with me. I could only imagine how my stay in prison must have affected him; every time someone came to the house, him wondering if it could be me. I never told anyone but I would sometime wonder if Slugger had passed away without anyone informing me. Looking down at my lil bruh, I see that he was sporting a bit of a grey mustache however, he still looked strong. That night I figured I'd give him some space. However, that next morning we were back to being best friends.

I called my partner Mobes' house, and his moms picked up. I told her I was home, and she went crazy with happiness.

"I love you as well, Ms. Bunce."

She told me Mobes was at work and that she was going to call him and have him call me back. So like three minutes later, my phone rang and it was my brother Mobes. We got to talking, and in the conversation, I relayed to him that I'd been home for two weeks. The conversation then changed; he wasn't feeling the fact that I'd been home so long, and he didn't know. Seriously, if you bring it up today, he still gets a bit agitated with me.

We didn't stay on the phone long because he was at work. However, he told me he got off at 10 p.m. and would shoot up to my house to scoop me up, once he got off. It was roughly ten fifteen when I heard an air horn honking outside of my house. I stepped out, and there stood my brother Mobes. He had what I thought was a very nice car. It was a 1998 Dodge Stratus Christmas Tree Green, brand new because here we were in '97 and here he was in a '98 whip.

Pointing at the car, I asked, "That's you Fam? (Is that your car?) Mobes replied in a nonchalant way, "Yeah, that's my car."

I jumped in and off we sped. He beefed at me again briefly for not telling him sooner of my return home, so then I revealed to him why it took so long.

"Dog, when Reg and I were in Elmira, we would be on the phone with a friend of his family, and she would tell us that you and Bill were outside her building hustling that very moment. So, I just wanted to chill for a minute, before I got up with you Fam."

He told me, "Smallz, that's bullshit. You see where I just came from? Work nigga. She was just talking to be talking."

It's not that I was judging him if he was slinging. Shit, I knew how it was out there. I mean I had been on the street longer than I was in prison. I just didn't want to be around it any more. We then spoke about everything we could think of, mostly Mobes catching me up with all the happenings in the hood. So that's how it was for a good while, Mobes behind the wheel and me riding shotgun.

I utilized this time to attempt to enlighten my dog on the mysteries of life which were bestowed on me. Mobes would be all ears and asking questions. He would also tell me how that was what I was supposed to be doing. He informed me that he remembered how, back in our most troubling years, he would notice me reading books on the subject. The thing was, by then, I had come to glance spiritually at what I was actually reading, through meditation and conversing with learned men. It's like Prodigy from the hip hop group Mobb Deep said:

"I conversate with many men. It's time to begin again.
Forgot what I already knew. You hear me friend?"

A friend of mine once said that he didn't understand that

particular lyric. But the way I understood it is as so: through conversing with many learned men and women, he learned that he would have to spiritually begin again, in order to re-learn the Ancient Soul Teachings of his Supreme Ancestors. By him asking "you hear me friend?" seems to allude to the fact that some may not even know what he is actually speaking about.

As fate would have it, one day while walking down White Plains Road in the Bronx, I bumped into the big homie Seth, who used to be one of the producers for us at Fortress Entertainment. He gave me the number to the new studio over on Allerton Avenue. Once I got back to the house, I called and asked to speak to Vidal. He got on the phone and was very happy I was home. He then gave me the address to the studio, and I promised him I would stop by some time that evening.

It was approximately 8 p.m. when I knocked on the door, and a very attractive young lady opened it. I asked for Vidal, and she gave me this real nervous look, like I might have come to start some type of trouble. She asked my name.

"Please, tell him it's Smallz."

She closed the door and I thought to myself, Maybe I startled her by wearing a black hooded sweat shirt, black army jacket, black jeans, and black boots.

Moments later, she re-opened the door with a smile on her face, as she invited me in. Once inside, I followed the sounds of the music to the back where my two homies stood, Vidal behind the computer and Charlemagne behind the mixing board. They looked at me and just smiled, and then we exchanged hugs. That night I noticed that Vidal showed me mad love, yet Char was a bit distant. I figured he may have said to himself. Okay, Smallz is home. Let me just fall back and see where his head is these days. If he's ready to handle business or not.

Weeks later, Vidal told me they were moving the studio to another location on Nereid Avenue, right down the block from where I lived and asked me if I would be the General Manager. I was honored. My job responsibilities would be to book all studio sessions and find out if anyone needed tracks. And if no one else was available, I would have to come in and let them pick tracks from Char's very large collection of music. Many times, I would give my advice and help guide them with their projects. When the session was over and before the client received a copy of their work, they would have to pay me. At that time, the charge was fifty dollars an hour. I'd then write them a receipt, give them their CD, and send them on their way.

I really looked forward to going to the studio every day. I got to hear music, lyrics, and what I loved the most, the great conversations and debates that would go on. Like when Jay and Nas were beefing, that would be like an hour debate as to whom we at the studio, felt was the best out of the two. I thought they both were great artists, although I leaned more towards Nas for the simple fact I felt he was more conscious in the majority of his lyrics. I was happy that those brothers could put aside their differences and contribute to the healing of the culture. (Yes the culture of Hip-Hop. It's the way we dress the way we talk the way we walk the way we dance the way we draw the way we spin records etc.) Yeah, on any given night, you could walk in and hear us debating about something pertaining to this wonderful hip-hop culture.

That New Year's was my first one on the street in five years, so my homies Joe and Mobes took me to celebrate at this club in downtown Manhattan. I had on some mean brown suede shoes, beige slacks, brown suede blazer, a bad-ass beige Kango hat, and a pair of tough Versace frames. I felt real good. Believe you me, it beat them state greens I was sporting less than a month ago.

We had a great time that night. My only complaint would be that there were entirely too many people inside of the club. It seemed like the whole world was celebrating in that joint. The suede shoes I had on were garbage by the end of the night. There were so many shoe scuffs on them, I couldn't believe it. Just coming home from prison I wasn't really that fond of crowds. Really, I still feel a little uneasy within them.

When the clock struck twelve, I grabbed the young lady I was two-stepping with and planted one on her. And then, Mobes, Joe and I joined in a three-man hug wishing each other a Happy New Year. Damn, it felt good to be out of that cage!

Not long after New Year's, I had started a relationship with one of the nurses where I received dialysis. Let's just call her Missy. I used to see Missy all the time up there working and would think to myself, Damn, she's sexy.

I hadn't really gotten to meet her because when I came in, she was basically wrapping up her shift. However, there was this one day when one of her patients just so happened to be seated on my left. I noticed that she kept looking at me, and I believe the only way I could know that, is because that I kept looking at her as well.

She looked at me again, and at that moment smiled. I returned the smile, and she told me that I had pretty eyes. I thanked her, and we just started conversing back and forth while she was attending to her patient. She shared with me that she was from Brazil, and that she was also studying to be a doctor. We hit it off, 'cause, just before she left, she passed me her math (phone number), which she had written down on a pack of gauze bandages. Not long after, her apartment was my new hangout.

My first day over I pushed right up on her; sitting real close to her on the couch, rubbing on her knee, playing with her hair, and gazing into her eyes. Though she would play hard to get, I knew she loved it.

Listen! I had just gotten home five weeks ago from the penal system after damn near five years. She had knowledge of the sexual build up, yet she wouldn't sex me. What she would do was touch me, caress me, and kiss on me in the most erotic and sexy way that you could imagine. Man, that shit drove me crazy. I mean she would have me completely nude and send me home with blue balls.

You see, she liked to be in control and wanted to choose when we would actually do it. Then, one night, while kissing all over my naked body, she pulled out a condom, took it out of its wrapper, and rolled the condom down my full erection, all the while looking me in my eyes in her sexy way.

She then grabbed me by the hand, pulled me off the bed, led me over to her dresser and climbed up on top of it. Damn, she looked good with that candlelight reflecting off of her petite body, with her hair all long and curly, smelling like exotic fruits. She then faced me sitting on top of the dresser with legs wide open. She pulled me closer to her by my rock hard manhood. Caressing her fully erect nipples, I then gave the left one a nice couple of licks and kisses. That caused her to throw her head back and make this sexy purring sound. I continued to kiss her neck, ears, and breast. Looking up into her eyes, I could see she was completely horny.

That's when she said, "I need you inside of me, Poppy," as she put me inside of her.

Damn, it felt good, like I was a virgin again. For the first few thrusts or so, I would just watch myself going in and out of her thinking, *damn I'm happy to be home.*

Missy and I would meet like this for almost a year, and we are still good friends to this day.

I'd been home for about six weeks, and eventually, I was blessed to receive a weekend visit from my children. Once they arrived, I hurried out of the door to see my little girls again. When they got out of the car, Allahia who was eight years old gave me a great big hug and kiss. Kiyanah, who was five just stood there looking up at me like "So you my daddy, huh?" You see, Keyz was an infant when I first went down and even though she did visit, she still didn't know who the hell I was, except through stories her mom may have told her.

Finally, I got the opportunity to meet Helen's new man Jody. Although he gave a decent attempt to appear friendly, I noticed the dislike in his eyes. Running those streets for so many years and being in prison for quite a few, I had learned to see at a glance how people really felt about me. Helen would tell me how jealous he was of me and how he didn't want the children to see me again. In fact, she allowed my babies to begin calling him daddy, something that she swore she would never do. I didn't like it a bit. I swear, it hurt me in the core of my soul, but I tried not to sweat it too much because now I was home and able to show my little girls who daddy really was.

It wasn't long after we got in the house that we all were just laughing and having a good old' time. Yes, even Kiyanah. Yet, that next day, when we were sitting at the dining room table having lunch, Kiyanah got mad at me about something and blurted out:

"I hate you, you're not my daddy. I want my real daddy."

Now that would have completely crushed me if she had said this when I was still in prison; on the other hand, I wasn't still in prison. I knew I would probably have to go through something like that sooner or later. I looked over at Allahia, and she was looking at me shrugging her shoulders as if to say I'm sorry Daddy. I don't know why she's acting like that.

I excused myself from the table, went in my room, and came back with a box full of pictures. I started going through pictures with them, and when I came across pictures of Kiyanah and me while she was just a baby, I would point at her in the picture and ask:

"Who's that?"

She then would say, "That's me."

Then I would point to myself holding her in the picture and ask her, "And who's this?"

She would look at me and say, "That's you."

So I went through that routine for a few more pictures with the same results. I then looked at Kiyanah, smiled, and said to her, "I am your daddy. You go and ask Jody if he can show you one picture with him holding you, when you were a little baby." She then looked up at me, in her eyes I could tell she over-stood what I was trying to get across to her.

Still smiling, I said, "Now give your daddy a hug."

She did so without hesitation. Never did she have an outburst like that again. Man, it felt good to be home. That weekend went by so fast, Helen came back to pick the girls up. I felt so sad that I had to let them go with no idea when I would get to see them again. Me needing dialysis every other day and being on parole, made it damn near impossible for me to see the girls. However, being on dialysis made me able to collect social security for my disability, so I received a check each month and so did each of my children.

A few weeks later, Mobes received another job with this Muslim brother who had also hooked me up with employment. Medicaid got wind of it and explained to me that I could no longer work full-time and would have to start working part-time if I wished to continue receiving medical benefits. I was kind of upset at this decision because I was working like sixty hours a week as security on the graveyard shift. It was a good job since it was safe because in order for anyone to come in they would have to bang on the gate, and I would look to see who it was. If you didn't belong, you didn't get in, and I could go right back to sleep, which was all there was to do, after studying and watching TV.

One day, Mobes let our boss borrow his car and that changed everything. When boss man returned the car, it appeared that everything was okay. However, when Mobes gave the car a quick walk-around inspection, he found damage to his car door on the passenger side and confronted him about it. At first, he denied anything happened to the car while it was in his possession. Then, after some feedback from Mobes, he admitted that he let his son hold the car, and that it was his son that had the accident. Mobes explained to him that he wanted him to pay for the car to be fixed, which he did, though from that day, he set out to fire the both of us and got me first because I made a collect call one day. The puzzling thing about that is that he said it was ok as long as I paid for it.

Now out of work, it wasn't a good feeling not being able

to get that extra cash. As for the general manager at the studio, business was slow motion in terms of money yet I still saw it as a place to relax. Mobes was able to get half price shoe and clothing hook-ups from some people he knew; so I could send my children back-to-school and summer clothes. Jody, who they were living with, would start beefing to Helen about why I didn't send his son anything when I sent things to my children. I understood what he was saying. I guess I just wasn't thinking. I could imagine how little Jody must have felt when a big box came into their home, followed by his big sisters getting all excited and there's nothing in the box for him. Taking that into consideration, in my next package, I had a little something in it for him as well, but would you believe that Jody got mad and never let him wear it.

He would always just be talking, trying to paint a horrible picture of me. He even went as far as telling my children that I was once addicted to drugs and that their mom was once a stripper. I would hear how he would just drag my name through the mud, yet, whenever he spoke to me, he did so with the kindest of words. I prayed for him, in hopes that he would recognize who the true and the living G.O.D actually is and to allow the divine force to dwell in his company. Amen!

One day, I received word that he gave Allahia a whipping for opening up one of the social security envelopes which had her name on it. Helen found out and ran to his authorities on base where Jody was a sergeant and filed a complaint. It's on his record to this day. When I got the news that he laid his hands on my daughter, I was vexed, but the only way I knew how to handle it was to take it to the guns or to hurt him somehow. To do so I would need to sneak on Andrews Air Force Base and it's in Maryland, and that wasn't happening. However, that was the first and last time, I heard of him putting his hands on either of my children; although, from what I heard, he was fighting with Helen on the regular.

If he only had known how many of my peoples were actually thirsting to bury him, he may have changed his ways. I never entertained the thought on account of I bear witness to karma. Trust, I'm living proof of this Universal Law. Additionally, I knew that he was an obstacle placed in my path in order to detour me from my personal salvation. He would succeed only if I allowed him to. The way I viewed it was that he was one of those ignorant, insecure brothers who looked to establish his power by assassinating the characters of others and whipping on his wife. As I said earlier, I too put my hands on Helen though that was back when I was twenty years old, and I nipped that in the bud immediately.

There was this one day he and Helen got into it, and Helen went upside his head with a lamp. Would you believe, this cornball had Helen arrested and took the stand in court which helped convict her of a felony. Lucky for her, she only got ninety days, during which she sent the girls to me. That was in 1999, and at that time, I was enrolled in Mercy College majoring in psychology, in hopes of working with troubled adolescents someday. I was only enrolled for one semester, getting A's in every class with a 4.0 GPA when the girls were sent to me.

My parents weren't too thrilled with having children in the house, because they both suffered from high blood pressure. My mom would tell me how sick she was and that she and Pops were gonna have strokes from stressing. Pops would agree and that would be the story whenever there was mention of a visit from my girls. The thing was that they believed Helen would never come back for them, because she had threatened to leave them and not return before.

If it had been up to me, the girls would have stayed with us until I got my kidney transplant and was able to work again without the hassle of dialysis. Lord knows, there was enough room in that house for us all. I must be clear that my parents did love and bonded with the girls. I just felt like we could do more. Though it was hard, I did learn to understand the fact that I was a sickly twenty-nine-year-old man, living with my parents, and I guess, they wanted to live stress free in their golden years. So now I was juggling school, dialysis and raising two children in my parents' home, and it was hard. I would have to come home and throw something together for them to eat most nights, and it was starting to take its toll on me. So I thought long and hard and made the decision to drop out of college.

When it was time for the girls to start school, I enrolled them, in PS 87 right around the corner from the house. My oldest daughter Allahia was starting the fourth grade, and my youngest Kiyanah was starting the first grade. Every morning I would wake up, go upstairs, enter their room and wake them, with the same words every time.

"Rise and shine."

Helen would call me sometimes from jail. One time she called crying to me that Jody hadn't come to see her for over a week. I thought it was sort of ironic that she would be calling me about such a thing, considering she only had ninety days, of which she would only have to do sixty. Jody got her locked up in the first place. The most ironic thing was that she never came to see me in my last two years. In my last year, she disappeared completely from the radar with my babies. Though I thought it was a bit weird, I didn't rub it in her face, since I could empathize with her.

When Helen was released, she went back down to Florida to stay with her sister, Alley, until she got back on her feet. It was during this time that my pops started putting a bit of pressure on her to get her shit together, so she could get her children. That would make me feel terrible, though I did over stand that I brought it all on myself, and knew that I, too, had to get my shit together to really be with my baby girl again. Having two felonies and needing to go to dialysis three times a week made it hard to find an employer to give me that chance I needed. All I could do at such times was pray and remember, "G.O.D may not come when you call but he's always on time."

Since Helen bailed on me when I was in prison, I always told myself and others, "I will be with my girls again." The girls had been staying with us for a whole year, when, eventually, Helen had enough of my pops' talks and made up a lie about how she got an apartment and that we could send the girls to her. I didn't know at the time that she made that story up, until they got down to Florida, and I learned that they all were staying with Alley.

So I questioned Helen on her lie.

"Howard, I was tired of your father always pressuring me about sending for the girls, so I just lied."

I guess I understood her reasons. It was almost a week later, when Helen and her sister got into a heated argument, and Alley kicked her out. Helen and the girls had to take refuge in a women's shelter. When I received the news, I was crushed. I wanted to do something but didn't know what. The only real thing I knew I could do was hit the street and get that paper. However, I knew that street life was designed for us to lose, one way or the other. To lock us up or eventually, leave us lying down in them dead. And let's not forget all those souls that are forced to struggle, to get up money for a high that will eventually leave them with nothing.

In truth, it never crossed my mind to deal drugs again, and the Most High Creator of All knows I had every opportunity and every connection needed to do so. I have learned that through meditation and prayer, I could find peace in the silence. Yes, all the problems of the world were still there, yet it is written, "G.O.D never puts a burden on man that he can't bear." With this in mind, I told myself, I will be with my girls again. I'll Smile Tomorrow.

Just like when I was addicted to cocaine, I never knew how I would beat it, though I knew that I would. When I was thrown in that penal system, I never knew if I would ever make it home again with all the violence going on around me-. Trust me, I could write books on that subject alone. Nonetheless, G.O.D allowed me to walk through the valley of death unharmed; in fact, it was used as a training ground for the discovering of "Knowledge of Self."

Everywhere I went and everyone who really knew me would tell you I would propagate the knowledge that was bestowed on me of the mysteries of the mind, body, and soul. I did explain to you that there where many nights when, in the studio, we would get into different discussions, well, that would be one of them. Remember my team on 241st Street in the Bronx? I, indeed, would go up and build (converse by laying bricks of knowledge) with them all the time.

I know they thought I was out of my fucking mind sometimes because they never thought they would ever hear me talking 'bout G.O.D. See, back when I was out there, only Flip and I would be the ones toting guns; now the whole team had them. And my dog Cujo's house was full of AKs, SKs, shotguns, and a whole buffet of different pistols. Though I wished to travel in peace, I too, had a couple of hammers. Man, it's real out here. And most dudes couldn't care less about your peace talks.

> I don't want to be
> Anything other than
> What I've been
> Trying to be lately.

-Gavin DeGraw

I'll Smile Tomorrow

Lesson 23

I am told, "Only the strong survive." From what I gather, they will outlast the weak. However, the wise will be forever.

H. Keith McAdams
The Author

In March 2001, I had gotten a ten-day pass from my parole officer to go down to Fort Lauderdale, Florida to visit my baby girls. I stayed in the house with them and their mom; however, I slept in the room with the girls. I had such a great time, just like when I visited Florida in 1989. Man, I fell in love with the Sunny State all over again.

One day, Allahia had this class trip to the Miami Sea-aquarium, and she wanted me to go with her. I couldn't wait, yet, on the day of the trip, the teacher looked at me and said, while we were standing right outside of the place, "Okay, since Allahia is a girl, you can take all the girls." She then looked at this little boy's dad and said, "And since Kenny is a boy, you can take all the boys."

Now, I didn't know how the other father felt, but I felt that was a bit unusual. I was just put in charge of ten little girls, including my own, to wander in this great big park and just couldn't help but think, *Aren't you the teacher? Then who are you taking?* But I snapped out of it, and then the girls and I rolled out, and actually had a good time, running around this huge park, getting splashed by Killer Whales and taking flicks. When it was all over I thought, *yeah, today was a good day. Why couldn't Kiyanah be having a class trip somewhere?*

At some point in my visit, this dude Jody got wind from some nosy body that I was in Florida. He called and started arguing with Helen about letting me stay there with her. I tell you their whole relationship was just weird, 'cause, mind you, this dude had Helen put in jail. They were separated by the states between Baltimore, Maryland and Florida, yet he had the nerve to sweat the fact that I was in the presence of Helen and my children.

He told her he was catching a flight down there immediately. Now I didn't think he was that crazy, but if the dude was, it would place me in a fucked up situation. You see, even though I was granted a traveling pass by parole, still I couldn't bust nobody's head wide open. So I was a bit worried about his arrival. However, he never showed up, and when my tenth day came, I went back to New York. Man, I loved NY, although I swore I would move to Florida in a minute if that opportunity ever knocked at my door.

Helen got a job with the Housing Authority in Fort Lauderdale, so I asked her to look into getting me my own place out there. Her superiors explained to her that they could get me a studio apartment, but, on the other hand, they would need me to come down and stay with her for an interview, and in about seven working days, they could move me right into my own place. My parole officer was on board with the whole idea.

"If you do move to Florida, I'll transfer your parole there."

It was around that same time Helen told me that she would look into if she would be a match for a kidney donation. Her gesture took me by surprise, and she went to the dialysis unit that I attended when I was in Florida for the visit, gave her blood, and sent it to my hospital up in New York. It turned out that Helen was indeed a match for donating me a kidney. However, being a match wasn't enough. She would have to come up to New York in order to take a bunch of physical and psychological tests, to see if she was mentally and physically able to go through such an operation.

So she flew into the big city, and together, we went to New York Hospital which was the hospital that I chose to handle my transplant. I couldn't believe Helen was going through with it. I mean she was making all the necessary moves in order to make this happen for me, and mind you, I never asked once for her to do so.

She was back in Florida when we received the news that she had indeed passed all of the necessary tests. We were given a date when the operation would take place, and Helen and I both couldn't wait to get this over with. My operation was scheduled for a Monday, and the Friday before, I had to go down to New York Hospital to speak with the surgeon and the rest of the staff about what medicines to take and what meds not to take and a whole bunch of do's and don'ts.

Listening to the surgeon, I couldn't help but get a bit choked up knowing that, after four years, I would soon be getting a kidney and be free of that dialysis machine once and for all. I was soon asked to leave the room and wait in the waiting area until I was called back in to speak to another doctor. I then pulled a book out of my back pocket and proceeded to study. It was maybe fifteen minutes later when my medical doctor and the social worker came through the front door and went into the room I was previously in with the other doctors and staff. Seconds later, I was called into the room, and once I entered, I felt a very troubling vibe coming from them all.

That's when the main doctor said, "Mr. McAdams, I am so sorry to inform you that something has come up, and we will not be able to proceed with the operation at this time."

I looked over at the social worker, and she was wearing this very sad face. It was like she just wanted to cry. She began telling me how sorry she was, three or so times. I stood there in front of them and smiled.

"It's alright. It's just not meant to be at this point in my life. I'll be okay." I thanked them all for their concern and help and walked out of the door.

As I walked towards the subway, I pulled out my cell phone and gave Helen a call to tell her the horrible news. She was more upset than I was, and I told her I thought it might be because the social worker didn't think Helen was mentally capable to deal with the pressure of donating a kidney.

Still pissed off, Helen told me, "Let me call you right back. I'm gonna call up there and see what in the hell they're talking about."

It was a good two to three months later when Helen came clean during a phone call between the two of us. She told me that she had called the Hospital telling them that she wasn't going through with the operation. She next blurts out, "I'm not going through with it and you're not going to change my mind!"

I thought to myself, *Damn, I never asked you to do this for me and never once did I pressure you to continue with the procedures.*

As far as me moving to Florida, that flame too was doused.

One day I got a call from Helen as my mom and I were actually in Kmart looking for a couple of things I might want to take with me to my new apartment in Florida.

"Helen, me and Moms are in Kmart looking for a couple of

things I could take down there as we speak."

Her reply took me aback. "Stop looking."

I knew where this conversation was going, but I wanted it to be clear, so I asked, "What do you mean?"

In her infamous Helen way, she replied, "Howard . . . you know I'm crazy."

"Helen, what is going on?"

"You not coming here to be with me, you coming to be with the girls and Jody said he wants to be with me and wants me to move back up to Baltimore."

I just chuckled to myself and said, "Okay Helen, I'll talk to you later" and hung up the phone.

All of this happened in 2001, and Allahia turned eleven on September 10th of that year. I had sent her out a gift and called to wish her a Happy Born Day. As on every Born Day that I wasn't with my babies, I spent the night thinking of them and praying also. I would tell myself, "If only I didn't get myself locked up I would be with them." But as crazy as it may sound, I honestly didn't regret my incarceration, because prison may have actually saved my life.

That next morning was September 11, 2001, and I was in the bed half asleep with the radio playing. The radio personality said something that woke me like I had taken a hit of some potent caffeine.

"We have just received information that a commercial air craft has just crashed into the World Trade Center."

I instantly jumped out of the bed, onto my feet, ran into the living room, and turned on the TV. There was a live filming of the plane in one of the towers with smoke and flames shooting out of the building. As I stared at the TV in awe, I saw another aircraft slam right into the next tower. I then screamed up the steps to my parents.

"Turn on the TV; they trying to kill us."

Yes, I was a bit nervous being as how I live in New York and had delivered many packages to the World Trade Center back in my messenger days. As I watched all them people covered in soot, running for their lives, it seemed like I was watching a very well-directed motion picture. Especially, when "those Towers came crumbling to the earth, like they were full of explosives."

That act of terror was to affect me personally because it happened on a Tuesday, and I was due to have dialysis treatment that same day. As the powers that be would have it, Manhattan was locked down, so no vehicles were to go in or out of the city. This was bad news because I had never missed a treatment since I started in '97, plus my last treatment had been on Saturday and I could feel myself needing to be treated. So Pops and I jumped in his caddie to see if there was any way we could get into the city, and the police presence was at an all-time high. So we had to go back home. I couldn't help but think to myself, If things get any worse, I may never be able to receive treatment because who will actually come to work, to give me and others who have medical conditions, the attention we need if there are bombs going off across this city?

That next day, I was able to have treatment, and on the train ride home; I could see and feel the terror in my fellow subway commuters. Everyone was watching everyone, or they were sitting or standing, in deep prayer. For those of you who aren't familiar with New York City's subway system during rush hour, well, the trains were jammed packed; I mean, people are literally on top of each other. The subway system would be a perfect target for any lunatic to strike, with casualties reaching in the tens of thousands. So I would be on the train paranoid as were most of the passengers. That first week after the attacks, I wondered if I should just get off the train and walk that great distance from 110th Street in Manhattan to my home up in the Bronx on 238th. Thank G.O.D nothing else happened, well, at least as of this date.

###

April of 2003, was the next time I was able to see my children again. At this time, Jody was stationed in Virginia with the Air Force, Gee helped me drive from New York to VA to pick them up and bring them back to New York to visit the rest of their family. In order to stay out of my parents' way, my sister allowed us to stay at her co-op for those seven days.

My sister would always tell me, "You shouldn't send those girls back to Helen. It's wrong how she keeps them from you like that. You need to keep them."

I would just say, "Once I get my own place I could think of something, 'because right now, you know how Moms and Pops feel about living in a crowded house."

"Don't worry about them. If you keep them, our parents will get over it."

But I saw it differently. She even suggested that the girls move in with her, while I stayed with my parents. I really didn't like that idea either because I'm sure she and I would eventually bump heads over it.

Time really does fly when you're having fun; our seven-day visit was soon over. Mobes and I took them back to their moms.

It was actually Kiyanah's tenth Born-day, and not too long after that, they moved again, and I wasn't allowed to see the girls any more.

I was still going back and forth to dialysis every other day, and then, one day in 2004, while I was one hour into my treatment, I glanced over at my dialyzer and noticed it wasn't mine. Now this was a big deal because the person whose dialyzer it was had reused his dialyzer, so that meant his blood had run though that dialyzer numerous times. I then called for the technician who had put me on the machine that day and brought it to his attention. He began fixing his mistake, while at the same time speaking to me with a smile on his face, so I could believe it wasn't such a big deal.

"Yeah, thank you for pointing that out to me. I'll have you back rolling in a minute."

Looking up at him, I thought to myself, this dude must really think I 'm some type of an idiot or something."

"Who's the nurse in charge today?"

You should have seen how his nonchalant, everything is okay… it's no big deal attitude suddenly changed, with that simple question. Let me tell you, it was indeed a big deal to him. He completely stopped what he was doing, then looked at me like he was dying of thirst and I had the only pitcher of cold water in the world.

He then blurted out, "No please, everything is okay. I'll just change the dialyzer and get you a new one. Trust me, it's okay."

Not trying to hear that foolishness, I asked him, "Are you telling me that I should keep this accident of yours between the two of us? If you are, I won't. My name is McAdams; the name on that dialyzer says McDonald. I don't know if he has any health issues that I need to know about."

He started begging me not to tell and ensuring me that the dialyzers were cleaned with some type of chemical, so I had no reason to fear. Seeing I wasn't trying to hear that, out of desperation, he said, "If I get on the computer and check the patient's medical history and he's not sick, will you not tell anyone? If you tell, they will surely fire me."

In order to find out the truth, I agreed. However, I had my fingers crossed. Hell yeah, I was gonna speak on this issue. You see, Missy had informed me years back to get a brand new dialyzer every time I got on the machine, so mistakes like this wouldn't happen. What really disturbed me was that this was stated on my sheet. He was supposed to go in the back and get me a new dialyzer, not up front off the rack where all the reused ones were sitting. Plus, at that time, I was a third-shift patient, and McDonald was a fourth-shift patient, so there was no way this was supposed to happen.

When he came back, he didn't tell me about anything he found on the computer. Instead, he pointed at this one nurse across the large room.

"Tina is the head nurse on duty. I told her everything. She will be right over to speak with you momentarily."

I was now thinking to myself, *now, this guy is really getting me angry.* That wasn't an easy thing to do those days, but the nurse he pointed to was his best friend. I was told she got him the job there. So I picked the phone up to call Missy who wasn't working there anymore. She was actually finishing up medical school. Then I noticed Tina come up and stand there, waiting for me to finish the call. I also noticed that she wore a very nervous look on her face, and before I hung the phone up, she just walked away.

Missy never picked up, so, when my treatment was over, Nancy, who was the real nurse in charge for that night, came to me and explained the procedure for cleaning the dialyzers. I wasn't concerned with her foolishness either. All I wanted to know was if McDonald had AIDS, or anything else I should be worried about.

So I interrupted her and asked, "Does McDonald have any disease that I need to be worried about?"

Her face got this real blank look on it, and then she said, "I don't know, and I am not allowed to look nor reveal medical information about any patient."

Not hearing what I wanted to hear, I walked away from her. I then saw Wendell, this African brother from Nigeria and explained the situation to him. Thinking he was a cool dude and would understand my concern, I then asked him about McDonald. He too started talking about how well the dialyzers were cleaned. Then the guilty party made a mistake and spoke.

"I told you, it's okay, they clean them good."

At that point, I had heard enough about all that cleaning nonsense. Still struggling to keep it peaceful, I blurted, "I don't give a shit how good they clean them dialyzers. They are cleaned for the purpose that the same patient can use it again, not for another patient to use it after them. So please, don't bring that silly shit up again."

Now that knucklehead made another attempt to appeal to my humane side. "Please don't tell my boss, they are going to fire me."

His plea didn't work; I just looked him in his eyes and said, "Maybe you should be fired."

I then left the clinic and went to a Chucky Cheese party being held for my youngest niece D'airah, in Co-op City, the Bronx. My next dialysis day, I asked a buddy of mine to point McDonald out to me when he came in, and he did so. Like I said, I was third shift and McDonald was fourth, so he came in when they were taking me off the machine. The next time I went to dialysis, I arrived early so I could get off early, to go downstairs and wait for McDonald to come to the unit.

When I saw him, I immediately approached him and explained, "Excuse me sir, there was a little accident with our dialyzers and they gave me yours by mistake. Now sir, I know, in any other case, this would be none of my business, but, with this being said, I would like to know if I have anything to worry about, like HIV or hepatitis."

He looked at me, and with a sorry look on his face, he said, "You should be worried about HIV and Hepatitis."

He then walked into the building. I was left standing there with what felt like the world on my shoulders. The doctors then explained to me that they were going to take numerous tests to see if I had contracted any of these diseases and that it would be an eight-month process. I called Missy and she confirmed that those tests would be an eight-month process, and if at the end I was found negative, it would mean I hadn't contracted any diseases.

I can't begin to tell you how the days, weeks, and months that followed affected me, but, in short, I was completely stressing. Of course, I didn't want the news to come back positive for anything. Thank G.O.D for my studies in prayer and meditation; without them, I would have surely crumbled.

After about five months, I was told by Diana, the social worker at the unit, about another patient who had gotten on the list in

Philadelphia for a transplant and received a kidney within weeks. See, I'd been waiting for a kidney in New York for over seven years, and thought maybe I should check this Philly spot out. So I gave them a call, and they gave me an appointment to come in. My brother Mobes and I jumped in the car for that two-hour ride to Philadelphia's Albert Einstein Hospital. Our boy Joe met us there because he had moved into a big beautiful home out in Philly a couple of years back. It felt good to have my homies there with me as we sat in a large room at a large table and spoke to a number of doctors.

We talked to each doctor separately, and I remember Joe making an observation about how scary acting some of them were in our presence. On the other hand, there was this one doctor who walked right in the room, he wasn't at all scary acting. He dealt with us like he was one of our buddies. His name was Doctor Zaki, and he would be the surgeon who would actually do the surgery, if and when the time came.

Dr. Zaki had once worked in Harlem's St. Luke Hospital for years and had a very basic understanding of our 'hood. So he, like the other doctors, looked over my records and felt I was a great candidate for a transplant. Zaki then began telling us how he should be able to have me a kidney within weeks. Since I already been on the list in New York for almost seven years and Philly's list was only two, I just shot right up to the top of their list. That was the first sign of light for me receiving a kidney. We all left the hospital feeling really hopeful.

It was two days later when I received a letter from Florida saying that my name had come up for an apartment in Fort Lauderdale. That was the same area I was moving to, when Helen was hooking me up. Maann, my babies aren't even in Florida any more, why go now? I snatched up the phone and called Mobes. When he got on the phone, I told him the deal.

"Mobes, I just got this letter speaking on how they have an apartment for me in Florida. Now they wanna holla, when my children done moved back to B-more. I ain't going down there Fam."

Mobes blurted out, "Nigga, stop playing; you always talking 'bout how you love Florida and wanna get outta New York."

As he was talking, I was thinking, *you're right, that is what I said*. The next words out of his mouth are what really changed my mind.

"Smallz, if you don't want it, let me get it."

I just grinned to myself and from that point on I was all in. "I'm moving to Florida."

So I gave them a call and set a date for an appointment, that next month.

I received a call two weeks later from Albert Einstein Hospital for a kidney transplant, and they needed me to get down there ASAP. Not long after the call, my parents and I were on the highway, headed to Philly.

On the way there, all I could think about was how my life would change after this day, being free from that machine and all. However, I couldn't help but acknowledge that, in order for me to get a kidney; someone had to have passed away, so I uttered a prayer to myself for that person's soul to travel in eternal happiness.

Once we got to the hospital, the nurses took my blood pressure and things of that nature, then, an hour later, a doctor came in the room where my parents and I were waiting. He stated, "Mr.

McAdams, I am sorry to inform you that we will not be able to perform this surgery. We have found that the kidney wasn't any good."

Broken hearted and very disappointed, my parents and I jumped back into my father's Cadillac and headed back to the Big Apple. I tried to look at the situation a little more positively, so I told myself, this experience did show me how close I was to actually receiving this kidney transplant.

I don't think it was more than a week later, when I had the appointment for those apartments down in Florida. Pops and I hopped on a plane towards that Sunny State to see what they were talking about. My appointment was at Fort Lauderdale's Kennedy Homes on Broward Boulevard. That was actually where Helen and the girls lived when I came down in 2001 to visit. They needed me to bring down a police report from New York to even attend this interview. I had already informed them over the phone of my prior felonies before I even bought a ticket to come down because I didn't want to hear anything 'bout how I couldn't get the apartment because of some police foolishness.

The lady over the phone informed me that, as long as it had been at least ten years since the crime, I would be just fine. I went down in 1993, and it was now 2004 plus I had finished parole. At the meeting, the lady looked over my application and saw the police report.

She said, "Ooh wee" with her eyes looking at the sheet with a shocked expression on her face. I jumped right into defense mode and started to explain that ten year thing I was told.

She just smiled at me and said, "Alright, calm down." So I followed her instructions and fell back into chill mode.

She asked if I had the three hundred and fifty dollar deposit. I handed her the money order. She then looked over the papers I bought in about my disability income. She started punching on the calculator and then informed me that my rent would be $105.00 a month. At this, my pops and I looked at each other with amazement because up in New York, rent would be much higher.

She told me that, if I brought her another money order for $105, she could send me to the apartment, where someone would be waiting with the keys. I told her about how I should be getting a kidney in a few weeks or so and that I'd be back for the apartment, right after the procedure. She explained that it would be okay as long as I sent in my rent. So I signed a bunch of papers, and Pops and I hopped back in the car to meet the lady who would give me a walk-through of the apartment and my keys.

Driving into the housing complex, I fell in love with the areas freshly cut grass and pretty palm trees. It looked like a place I could raise my children for sure. Once I walked into the apartment, I knew instantly I had made the right decision to move. I got the keys, went back to New York, and waited for the hospital to call me with the great news of a transplant.

One day, while I was on my way to dialysis treatment, I received a phone call from the hospital in Philly telling me that they had a kidney for me. I informed them that I was on my way to dialysis and they informed that I should receive my treatment and then come down for the transplant.

I called my parents and told them the good news, so they were going to meet me after treatment, and we could head out. When my treatment was over, I called the hospital and they told me I could go home but to stay by the phone for further info. By the time I got home, I received a call that they couldn't give me that kidney, and how sorry they were for getting my hopes high, but not to worry, I was at the top of the list; something would be coming soon.

Though armed with that divine instinct of "rolling with the punches of life," I couldn't help but feel a bit disappointed. About a month later, I received another call from the hospital, and I was told not to eat or drink and to stay by my phone for further instructions. Hours passed, and I never received a return call from the hospital, so I called them, and they claimed someone was supposed to call me hours ago to tell me that it wasn't happening that day.

It was perhaps another month, when I was called again and told not to eat or drink, and to stay by the phone with the same result. No kidney transplant. That was my fourth false alarm, and to make matters worse, Florida was calling and asking me when I was going to move into my apartment. I told them what was happening, and they asked me to send them a letter from my social worker stating that I was, indeed, waiting for a transplant. That was not a problem. I asked the social worker, Diana, to take care of it, and she hooked me up with a great letter to send out to them confirming the entire hold up.

Weeks later, I received another call from one of the ladies in Florida.

"Mr. McAdams, I am calling because we have a lady here, who really needs an apartment and I wanted to know if you will be willing to give up yours. When you are finished with your health issues, we will give you another apartment, if one is available."

Out of all her words, the one that stood out was the little two-letter word if, so I told her, "Listen, I am truly sorry that it's taken me this long to get out there; however, I, too, need that apartment, so, I won't agree to give it up. I am doing what you asked, as far as paying my rent on time. I certainly wouldn't be doing so if I didn't intend on returning."

She replied, "You are right about your rent. I have people who have lived here for years, and they seem to not be able to pay on time. I just called to ask if you were willing to give up the apartment and you're not. Not to worry; that is your apartment."

We hung up, and I opened the Bible back up and started to study. It had been four false alarms, and I was starting to really feel like it was some type of game those doctors were playing with me. I was starting to lose even more weight than before with the stress, plus I had just recently developed stomach issues. I had been given a colonoscopy to determine why I was in such pain and had no appetite. The colonoscopy found that I had a condition called diverticulitis and that my large intestine was beginning to narrow. It was the root of the pain and constipation and was causing the loss of appetite and weight loss.

On top of it all, it had been over a year, and I still hadn't seen my daughters and hadn't heard from them in eight months. In addition, my pops was starting to really want me to just get up and go to Florida. I tried to explain that I was trying to save money to get my car fixed to handle the long trip. Having a car was almost a necessity in Florida, and besides, I could pack all of my belongings in the car and haul it down in one shot. Pops told me all I needed was the blow-up bed I purchased for the move, and how I could take that on the plane with me.

I often felt very sick because of my kidney and stomach issues and didn't feel I had too many people in my corner. I had read that many people who suffer from chronic illnesses will find that their family may seem to be unsupportive; many times it's because they are also hurt since they cannot do anything to help their loved one. My family may not agree with my feelings on this issue; however, this is how I perceived things.

Out of all the homies I had, Mobes and Gee were probably the only ones that I would share my feelings about my kidney issues with. Besides my family, they were also the ones I sought for support. Also, going back and forth to the studio was a great help in keeping my mind from dwelling on the issue. You see, most nights we would be in there having so much fun it would be hard to tell what I was going through. And, for those nights when we weren't clowning, I would just have my face buried in a book.

Since the incident at dialysis, I was seeing a psychologist to help me deal with the issue mentally. So far, all of my blood work was coming back negative for HIV and hepatitis. Though that was indeed good news, I still couldn't help but to understand that the eight months of testing was not yet over. So I wouldn't count my eggs before they hatched, though it did feel good knowing that, so far, so good.

I was called twice more for a transplant, and neither time did I receive a kidney. Such repeated near misses affected me so badly that I decided to just give up on the kidney and go to my apartment in Florida. My pops paid to get my car fixed, and the two of us took that long drive to Fort Lauderdale, which didn't turn out to be such an easy task. The same problem I had with my car was still evident, although my pops had the car looked at and supposedly fixed. When you pressed on the gas, the car started to jerk and hesitate. Considering it was my car, I knew just how to drive it, but my pops couldn't deal. Out of the twenty-six hour drive, Pops did six.

It was a long hard drive, and we couldn't stop at any hotels since I had an appointment for dialysis down in Ft. Lauderdale at 11 a.m. the next day. By the grace of G.O.D, we made it. My pops stayed for a couple of days and caught a flight back to the Big Apple.

On my fifth day in Florida, I was late for dialysis because I was getting my gas turned on and had to be there in the apartment. I told my downstairs neighbor, Mrs. Kate, the situation, and she demanded, "Boy, you go take care of your treatment. I'll see that everything here is taken care of for you."

Yes, she and her husband Mr. Gee, her brother Fredrick X, her daughter Pam, and Pam's husband Nate, were indeed a blessing in helping me when I first came down to Florida. I then thanked her and shot to dialysis. I was a half hour late and soon as I walked through the door the receptionist saw me and jumped out of her seat.

"I am so sorry that I am late."

She cut me off. "I have been trying to get in touch with you since 6:30 a.m."

I was about to tell her that my phone was dead, as I thought 6:30 is kinda early if I have to be there for treatment at 11:30am. While all of that traveled through my mind, she was totally excited.

"They have a kidney for you in Philly!"

Though she was smiling from ear to ear, I was thinking, *they ain't got a fucking kidney for me, in no damn Philly*.

She asked if I had the money to catch a flight and I told her no. She asked, "Do you have any family members who could send you the money?"

Right now I'm thinking, *my pops just gave me money to get my lights put on, and I doubt if he could spare a last minute plane ticket to Philly.* So my answer to her was, "No, I can't think of anyone who could send me the money."

She left to talk to the social worker, and at that point, I was thinking, you guys could just put me on the machine and forget about that kidney they 'claim' they have for me. I then explained to the social worker, the nurse, and the receptionist how I was called for a kidney six different times with no results.

So they called Philly, and Dr. Zaki himself told them that he definitely had a kidney for me. Then, the social worker went into her purse and handed her credit card to the receptionist to book me a flight. Even though Dr. Zaki offered to pay back the cost of the flight, I couldn't help but think how nice it was of her to pay for me. Thanks to her, off I went to the Fort Lauderdale airport to catch a plane to Philadelphia.

Once I got off the plane, I jumped into an ambulance that was awaiting my arrival. It was a pretty long drive to the hospital, and we drove through an area in Philly that I recall the driver calling West Philadelphia. It was a long strip of pure ghetto. I mean it looked like everyone was on the same level of struggle. I thought I was from the ghetto until that drive through West Philly. It may sound bad, but if a person had come through there wearing jewelry or something of great value, they might deserve to get their shit taken. Looking out of that window, I could tell that times were definitely hard. Yet I could also see how the people were still able to smile. I noticed a little old couple smiling, crossing the street, and holding hands.

Once I got to the hospital, it wasn't hard to tell that this time was indeed the real deal because I was the center of attention. After I was prepped, I spoke to a number of doctors including Dr. Zaki. Then, around 9:45 p.m., I was given anesthesia to put me to sleep.

When I came thru, I was strapped into a stretcher, with tubes coming out of my chest and a respirator down my throat in ICU. I don't care what anyone says, a respirator is not intended for anyone who is awake. It felt like I was going to die right there: I couldn't breathe, and I'm pretty sure that, when I was still unconscious, I slept like a baby. I was so scared because I started gagging, but when I noticed that I had one of those hospital bells attached to my hand, I pressed it like a wild man.

To my rescue came a caramel-complexioned sister. When she got close enough for me to grab her that is what I did. I couldn't speak, but I grunted and pleaded with my intense facial expressions for her to help me.

"Do you want me to give you something to write with?"

I nodded my head up and down like a thirsty man being offered drink. Yes.

She left the room and came back with pencil and pad. She had to hold the pad near my bound hand in order for me to write.

The first thing I wrote down was, "Please! Take this thing out of my mouth."

"I can't remove the respirator. A doctor has to make that decision."

"But I can't breathe."

"You will have to relax. If you calm down, you will find it a lot easier to breathe."

"My chest hurts bad."

You don't know what happened, do you?"

As I looked up at her, I noticed her shake her head and roll her eyes at herself as if to say, "That was stupid, how could he know?"

She explained. "I bet your chest is hurting, because I'm sure they were pressing, pushing and probably banging on it when you had complications and flat lined up in the operating room. So just calm down; you will be just fine."

Flat lined up in the operating room? I continued to gag and still found it hard to breathe. The nurse left the room to check on another patient. Believe me, I tried to calm down, but, after a while, I just had to ring that bell again, and she spent the last few minutes of her shift reading and answering my questions.

When her shift was over, a couple of other nurses came in her place, and they could really care less if I couldn't breathe or was gagging. In fact, after I had rung the bell a couple of times, the lady nurse came in and got up close to my face.

"You are not going to be acting like a baby with me tonight."

In my hand, I had a note telling her that I couldn't breathe, and the guy nurse said, "You better lie there and shut up because we are not going to be catering to you tonight."

I was thinking, *damn, these two white people are gonna let me die in here today*. I then noticed in the back, a tall Indian-looking man dressed like a doctor listening on. It looked like he was paying a great deal of attention to me.

He threw his hand up and said, "Take it out."

I started writing on the pad and showed him what it read: "Thank you!"

A little later, Dr. Zaki came to see me, and the first thing out of his mouth was, "You really had me scared last night Howie, we thought we lost you for a minute buddy."

I started thinking back to what the first nurse had said to me in the I.C.U that morning, about me flat lining. Zaki went on to say, "I don't know what happen or how you came back, but I am truly excited to be speaking with you right now."

Later, my pops had spent that night with me and my mom stayed at the hotel because she couldn't sleep in a chair overnight. Another doctor came and really poured it on thick the next day when my father was with me.

"I've never seen anything like it in my life. I mean the way it all happened; it is a miracle that you are here today."

My pops and I looked at each other. The doctor went on to say, "You are here for a reason. I promise you; you have work to do. I don't know what, but you have some serious work to do."

Shortly after a couple of nurses entered my room, he would ask me while pointing at the nurses, "Can I tell them your story?"

I looked at him, still amazed that this doctor was so intrigued with my, what I like to call, "Resurrection," so I told him, "Sure."

He looked at his audience and said as he pointed at me, "His birthday is July 15, 2004." The nurses looked at him and then at me with a look of confusion, since that would mean that I was only a couple of days old. He then told them the story.

When I was well enough to be sent upstairs to my room in a ward, it seemed like every nurse up there had heard that I had flat-lined in the O.R., and a lot of them would tell me how lucky I was. I was supposed to leave three days after the operation, but I still had holes in my chest from the tubes that were placed inside in order to drain the blood out of my lungs. My lungs collapsed from them pushing down on my chest to save my life. I had to wait for my lungs to get strong and for the holes to heal before I was discharged from the hospital. It took me twelve days to get out of there and back to my parents' house to recuperate.

I couldn't go straight back to Fort Lauderdale since I had to stay closer to Philly so I could see the doctors three times a week in order for them to keep an eye on my kidney's condition. After about five months, I was able to head back to my apartment in Florida. I wasn't working, so I used that time to get more into myself. The apartment complex in which I stayed was sitting on the water, so, if one was to look for me, if I wasn't in the apartment, I would be found sitting by the water under a palm tree studying or in meditation. Some mornings I would sit there and watch the sun rise in its complete glory.

I had moved to Florida alone, although I did have family there who lived in Boca Raton who helped me out a lot. Like my cousin Jeanie and her husband Bob who picked me up from the airport and bought me a bunch of groceries to take back to the apartment. I also had some very nice neighbors who had also given me some guidance. Like the time when I needed a car mechanic, they recommend a good one, at a steal of a price. If I needed to be somewhere they were always available to give me the best directions. It is the little things that matter most.

I was down there a little over a year when Kiyanah and Jody got into it, and he put her out of his house. When Helen returned home, she saw Kiyanah standing outside of the door and found out what happened. That is when she finally packed hers and the girls' bags and left him. They ended up staying with a friend and her family, which I didn't like, since that couple had two teenage boys. So I asked her to send the girls to me until she could get on her feet, which she declined. What she did agree to letting the girls come and visit me Christmas of that year, 2005, and I was to send them back to her in Virginia the day before New Year's.

The girls and I had a lot of fun. They got to see their aunt and cousins who they loved dearly, plus all the friends that they hadn't seen since they lived down here in 2001. Just before the girls came down to visit, they and Helen had moved out of that one family's house to move in with Helen's boss from work. I didn't like all the moving around, but I preferred them there than where they were. What I wanted most was for her to just let me have them, but, for that to happen, The Most High would have to touch her heart.

It was December 30th, so that next day I would have to send my girls back to their mom. It pained me, although it was a blessing to be able to have them for a little while. The girls and I were just getting back in the car from eating lunch at IHOP when I got a call from Helen. She was talking about being a truck driver; something she had been talking about for the past few months. I knew Helen always liked to drive, but I didn't think she would like driving in and out of state on a regular basis. The subject changed, and I was telling her that we had so much fun that I wished I didn't have to send them back the following day. That's when she said something I was waiting to hear since the day I first stepped out of that prison.

"Howard, you can keep the girls."

Not believing my ears, I asked, "Helen, did I hear you right?"

She replied, "Howard, I have given this truck driver thing some real thought, and I am going to go for it. So yes, I am going to let you have the girls. Besides, if I am going to drive trucks in and out of state I can't keep them, now can I? In addition, I know they are in good hands with you."

I would be lying if I told you I remember just what I said at that time, without making up something that sounds good. What I can say is I was extremely joyful. It almost matched the emotions I had on the days that those little girls were born. I remember coming out of prison saying that I was gonna be with my girls again. Not knowing how, but just knowing.

When Helen and I hung up the phone, I told the girls the good news. I remember Kiyanah looking at me smiling.

"Why are you smiling?"

"You're happy, aren't you, Daddy?"

I smiled back and said, "Yes baby girl, I am happy."

You hear that word "Daddy"? I used to hear children call that out to their fathers which would make me smile. However, I noticed that moments later, it left me feeling a bit empty inside. Maybe because I was denied access to my daughters. To make it worse, they were forced to call some other man daddy for years. So when I hear them call me Daddy these days, I cherish the moment. I never take it for granted.

I know the girls are in good hands and love me very much. I also know that their mom raised them to the ages of fifteen and twelve. That being said, I do inner-stand that they may rather stay with their mom because of the time they spent together. Yet, I over stand that, "G.O.D is the best of planners."

That being said, I often think back to the days of my drug addiction, and I believe, and though it may sound unwise, that situation saved mine and my buddies' lives. I say this because we were definitely on our way to some heavy drug dealing activities. Shit, we had every connection possible to do so. Just think, what would have happened if Richie Blacker had gotten mad at us and schooled us on the effects of using that drug shit and ordered us not to ever use it again. I believe we would all probably be dead today trying to chase those Federal Reserve notes (Money). However, Richie didn't do so since he, himself knew no better.

Through the grace of G.O.D, I overcame that hurdle, and not too long after, I looked to get all the money I spent using by going back to them streets to sell that poison. Then again, through G.O.D's love and grace, instead of being killed on the streets, I was thrown in a prison. Then in a system created to incarcerate and destroy the Mind, Body and Spirit, I came in contact with those who were to pass me the tools to build and free my Mind, Body and Soul—my personal trinity.

During all my troubled times, I did a lot of praying and calling on the Most High, and as the saying goes, "G.O.D may not come when you call, but He's always on time." Yeah, that reminds me back eleven years ago when I was thrown in that cage after that riot in Governor Correctional Facility, and it was written on the wall that "GODISNOWHERE." Back then I interpreted that as meaning, "God is No Where." Today, though, I look at it a little differently. Maybe the writer meant, "God is Now Here" Again, G.O.D may not come when you call, but He's always on time.

Today, my partner Mobes is also staying out of trouble and dabbling in a little real estate with his sister Lynnel. My boy Gee went to college and has directed a few music videos and commercials. My homie Cee went back to school and will soon have a degree in engineering. My dude Mike (Hart-boy) has like 3 jobs, one being a head cook in a juvenile delinquent facility, my boy Flip is still throwing down in the kitchen, only now, in a big prestigious member's only restaurant. I just got finished reading a twelve-page letter from my partner Reg; sorry to say, he's still in prison. He will have done sixteen years hard time when he comes home in January 2009, and he, too, has written some books. Remain strong Reg; it's all downhill from here.

I would often check up on some of my brothers via the web to see if they made their board, or if the parole board hit them with more time. One day, I jumped out of my seat and hollered out "Billy Scott"! Now, armed with his government name, I ran to the computer. With a big smile on my face, I was now able to research the whereabouts of my big homie, my big brother, yes, my teacher Nur.

Today, I bear witness to the True and Living G.O.D, who goes by many names: I received a successful kidney transplant; I have positioned myself to be sitting on a couple of dollars; I went and found a job doing what I went to school for in the Culinary Arts; and my baby girls and I are finally together. I have no dealings with negative activity whatsoever, and I am striving to soon publish books that I pray will help others.

In my life, I have received so many blessings, some that I am aware of and others that I am not. Nonetheless, I am dearly appreciative. Speaking of blessings—after my scare in the dialysis unit, I'm blessed to say that I'm negative for H.I.V. and hepatitis.

I am blessed to inform you that I have met a very special lady whom I've grown to love and adore. We were married in front of a small audience on a beautiful spring day in the park. I can still hear the beautiful symphony of birds singing during the ceremony.

I am also blessed to share that from this union was born a beautiful baby boy. We call him Atum Ray (he who shines light in the dark.).

I know there will be those who know me from back in the day, who may say to themselves and to others, "Your Boy Smallz turned out to be a true square." All I can humbly say to those who feel this way is: of my own free will and accord "I AM"!

> I know you're in a better place
> Even though I can't see your face
> I know you're smiling down on me
> Saying everything's okay.

-R-Kelly

Lesson 24

"For life and death are one,
even as the river and the sea are one."

Kahlil Gibran

The girls and I had been together seven months and five days when I received a call from Helen's sister Alley. She was crying hysterically as she informed me that Helen had been in a car accident in which she had lost her life. Her words caused me to throw my cell phone in complete shock. It just seemed unbelievable since the girls and I had just seen her less than twenty-four hours earlier. In fact, she had just quit her job to move to Florida to stay with her sister, and she was on her way back to North or South Carolina to return the pickup truck that she had rented. It was said that she lost control of the vehicle somewhere in Georgia, where she was ejected fifty feet from the vehicle and died instantly.

Allahia and Kiyanah were at the movies when I received the news. After the movie, I picked them up, brought them home, sat them down, and with tears in my eyes, informed them of their mom's passing. This was no easy task, as I expected; it hit them hard. The days that followed were hard for us all. I tried to explain to them to use this to go hard at school and to succeed in life, because that is what their mom always wanted from them, and she is indeed watching.

"Make her proud!"

It's good that their Aunt Alley doesn't live far from us because they get to hang with her a lot. Plus, Alley reminds us a lot of Helen, so they get to see their mom through her. I sit in silence, praying that Helen's soul travels in eternal peace and that all of her spiritual questions are finally answered.

Helen and I had a very rough and rugged relationship. Still, she and I managed to be friends through it all. We also have two beautiful daughters together who bear witness that, no matter what obstacles were placed in our paths, their mother and father still maintained a strong bond.

So Helen, from the bottom of the heart of your old high school sweetheart, the father of your daughters, your first husband and best friend; you are truly loved and will indeed be missed. A-men!

MAY YOUR DAYS BE BLESSED

Your Brother,

Keith

I'll Smile Tomorrow

AUTHOR'S NOTE

Life in these bodies are nothing more than one divine experience and death is nothing more than the spirit leaving the body in order to continue its experience outside of its former vehicle. So in essence, the spirit never dies. That's why you may hear death referred to as "passed on." That is just what happened. His or her spirit has passed on to another form of life. There is an ancient saying that reads "The body is of earth, the soul is of heaven." Remember – "God blew His spirit into man's nostrils and man became "A Living Soul"".

REFERENCES

African Proverb. (n.d.).; Ancient Egyptian Proverb. (n.d.).; Bill Withers (1980). Lean On Me. Elektra/Sony Music Entertainment Inc.; Brown, H. J. (1991). Life's Little Instruction Book (1st ed.). Thomas Nelson.; Brownsville Ka (2001). Therapy.; Carroll, L. (1865). Alice's Adventures in Wonderland. England: Macmillan.; Chapman, Tracy (1995). At This Point in My Life. Elektra.; Christopher "Biggie Smalls" Wallace (1994). Everyday Struggle. Bad Boy Records.; Cosby, B. (1993, June). Ebony, 48(8), p. 25.; Dehuti/Hermes. (n.d.).; Drake (2010). Light Up. Cash Money Records/Young Money Ent./Universal Rec.; Eric B. & Rakim (1995). Follow the Leader. MCA Records.; Gavin DeGraw (2003). I Don't Want to Be. J Records.; Gibran, K. (1923). The Prophet.; Grand Master Flash and the Furious Five (1982). The Message. Sugar Hill Records/Electra.; Gregory "Gee Ali" Martin (1999). The Realism Part 2000.; Lauryn Hill (1998). That Thing. On The Miseducation of Lauryn Hill. Columbia Records.; Leighton, R. (n.d.).; Leroy Robert "Satchel" Paige. (n.d.).; LL Cool J (1987). I Need Love. Island Def Jam.; Lupe Fiasco (2007). The Cool.; Luther Vandross (1999). House Is Not a Home. Epic/Legacy.; Lyfe Jennings (2006). Down Here, Up There. Sony.; Mills, S. (1992). Ebony Magazine.; Nasir Jones (1999). New York State of Mind Part II. On I Am. Sony Music Entertainment Inc.; Niki Manaj (2010). Moment 4 Life. Cash Money Records/Motown Records.; Pete Rock & C.L. Smooth (1992). They Reminisce Over You.; Pitch Black (2003). It's All Real. Motown Records.; R. Kelly (2000). I Wish. On Tp-2.Com. Jive.; Sam Cooke (1963). A Change Is Gonna Come. RCA Records.; Shakespeare, W. (n.d.). Twelfth Night.; Shizzie Raw . (1992). Ghetto Stylin.; Sir Isaac Newton. (n.d.).; Talib Kweli (1994). The Beautiful Struggle. Rawkus.; Tupac Shakur (1996). Hail Mary. Death Row Records/Interscope Records.; Ueshiba, M. (2007). The Art of Peace. Shambhala.; Wu-Tang Clan (1993). C.R.E.A.M. On Enter the Wu-Tang (36 Chambers). RCA.; York, R. D. (1996). Your Potential.

www.ingramcontent.com/pod-product-compliance
Lightning Source LLC
Chambersburg PA
CBHW051417290426
44109CB00016B/1331